LINOCUT PRINTMAKING

A GUIDE TO CREATING BEAUTIFUL PRINTS

3dtotal Publishing

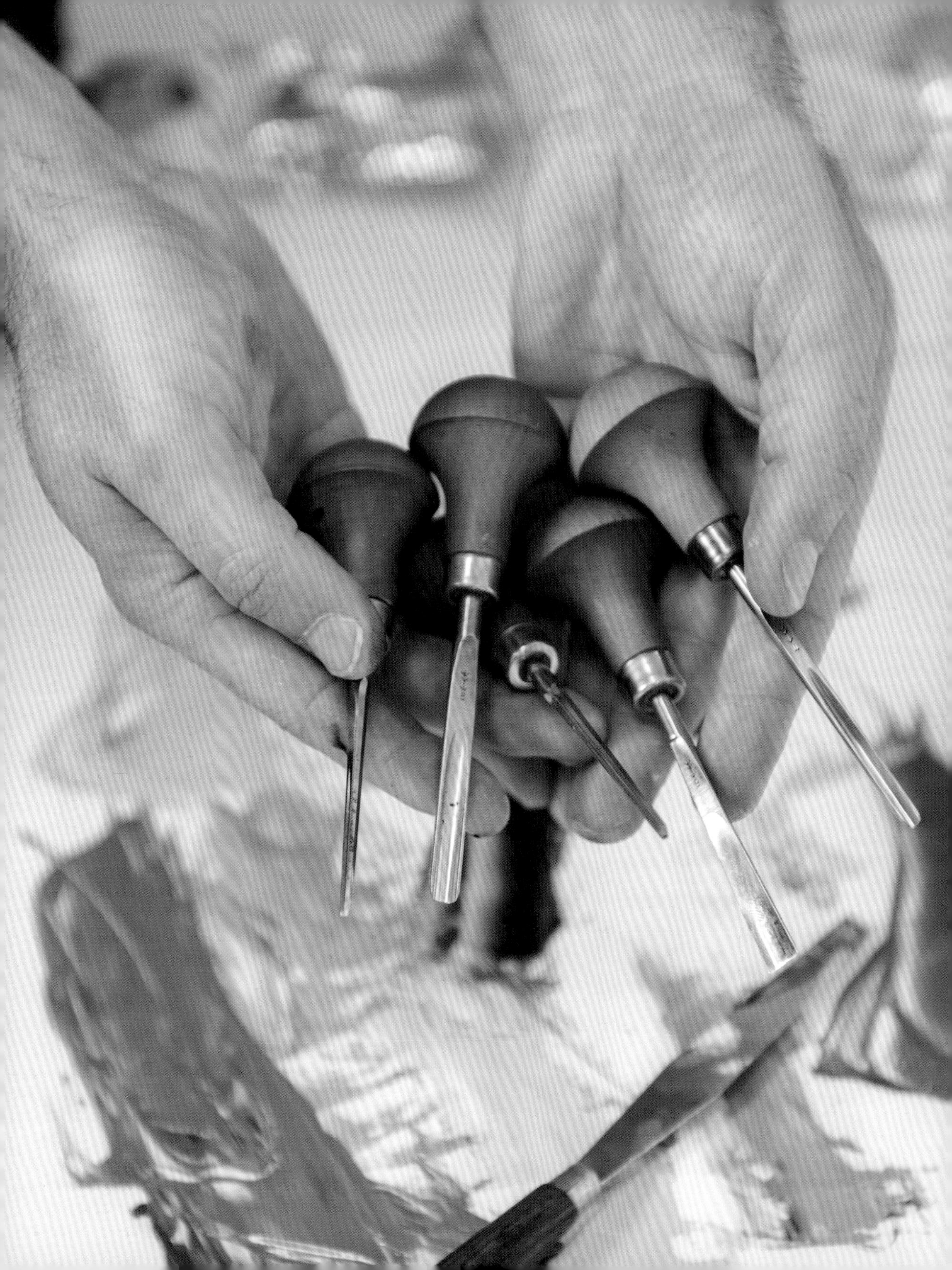

LINOCUT PRINTMAKING

A GUIDE TO CREATING BEAUTIFUL PRINTS

3dtotal Publishing

3dtotal Publishing

Correspondence: **publishing@3dtotal.com**
Website: **store.3dtotal.com**

Every effort has been made to ensure the credits and contact information
listed are present and correct. In the case of any errors that have occurred,
the publisher respectfully directs readers to **store.3dtotal.com/pages/
information** for any updated information and corrections.

First published in the United Kingdom, 2025,
by 3dtotal Publishing.

Address: 3dtotal.com Ltd,
29 Foregate Street, Worcester,
WR1 1DS, United Kingdom.

Soft cover ISBN: 978-1-915992-20-8

Printed and Bound in Shanghai, China, by KS Printing.

Visit **store.3dtotal.com** for a complete list of available book titles.

Editor: Philippa Barker
Designer: Fiona Tarbet
Lead Editor: Samantha Rigby
Lead Designer: Joseph Cartwright
Studio Manager: Simon Morse
Managing Director: Tom Greenway

Front cover artwork © Gareth Barnes (Spindle Printer).

Back cover artwork by individual artists as credited throughout the book.

Always follow good safety practice when using
sharp tools. Children should not use the cutting
or carving tools mentioned in this book.

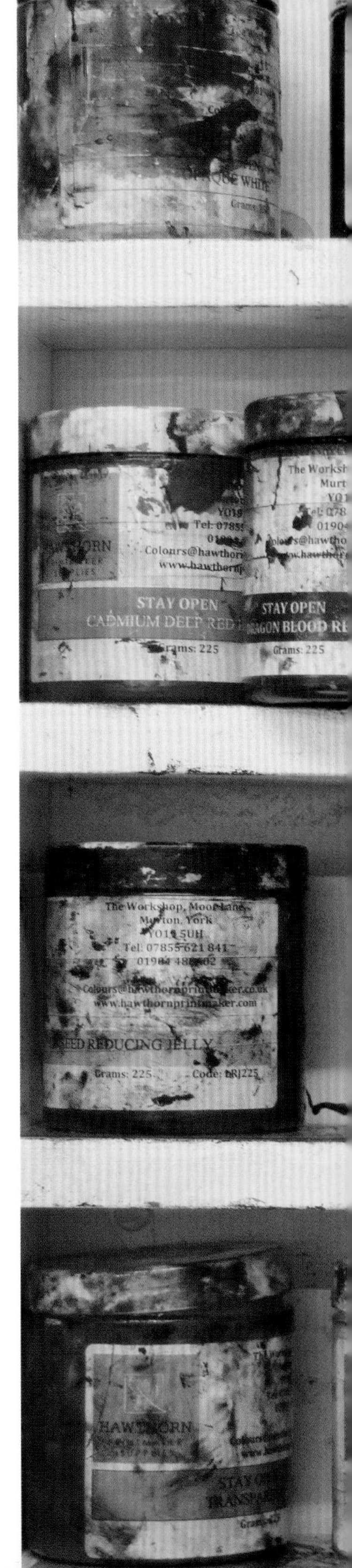

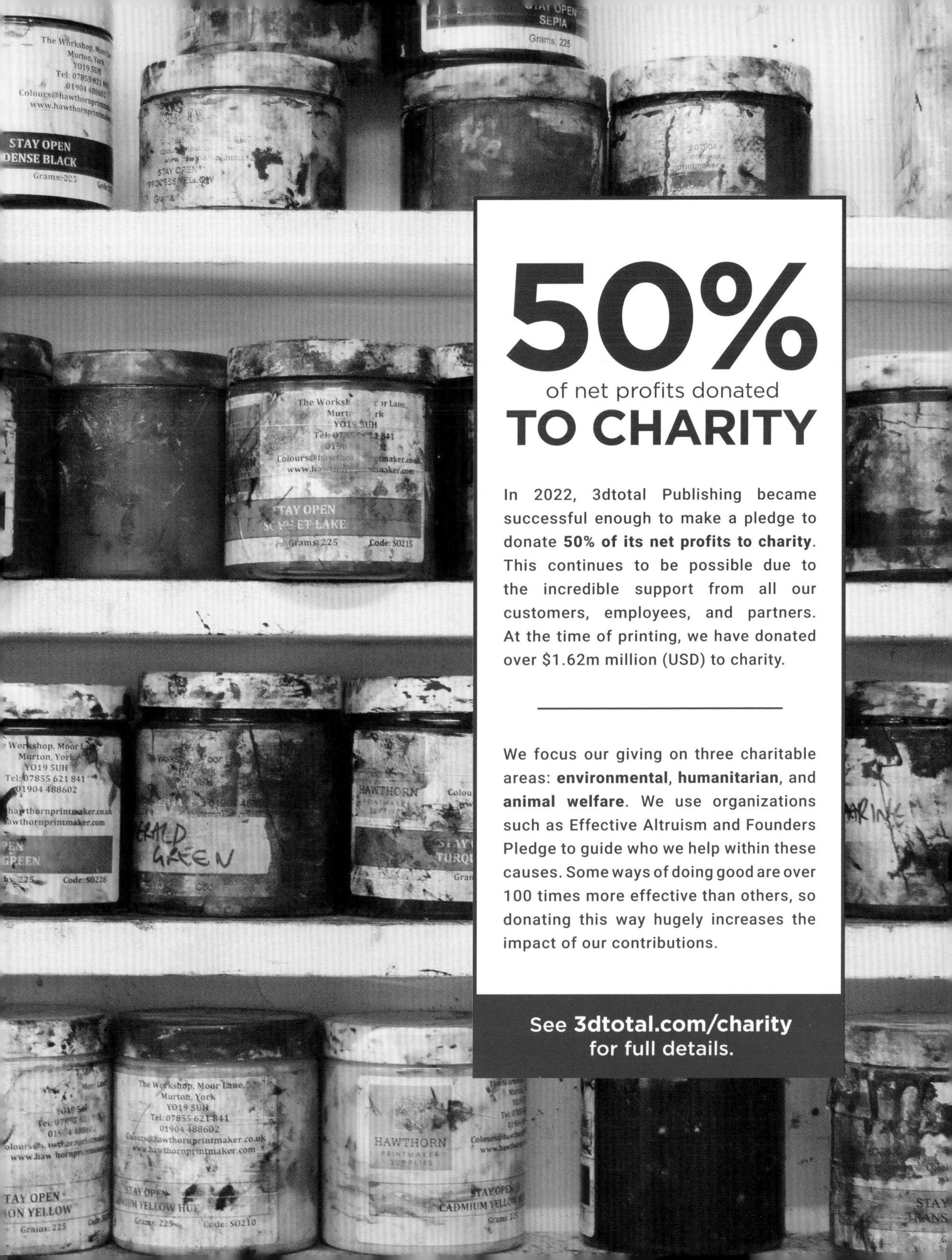

50%
of net profits donated
TO CHARITY

In 2022, 3dtotal Publishing became successful enough to make a pledge to donate 50% of its net profits to charity. This continues to be possible due to the incredible support from all our customers, employees, and partners. At the time of printing, we have donated over $1.62m million (USD) to charity.

We focus our giving on three charitable areas: environmental, humanitarian, and animal welfare. We use organizations such as Effective Altruism and Founders Pledge to guide who we help within these causes. Some ways of doing good are over 100 times more effective than others, so donating this way hugely increases the impact of our contributions.

See 3dtotal.com/charity for full details.

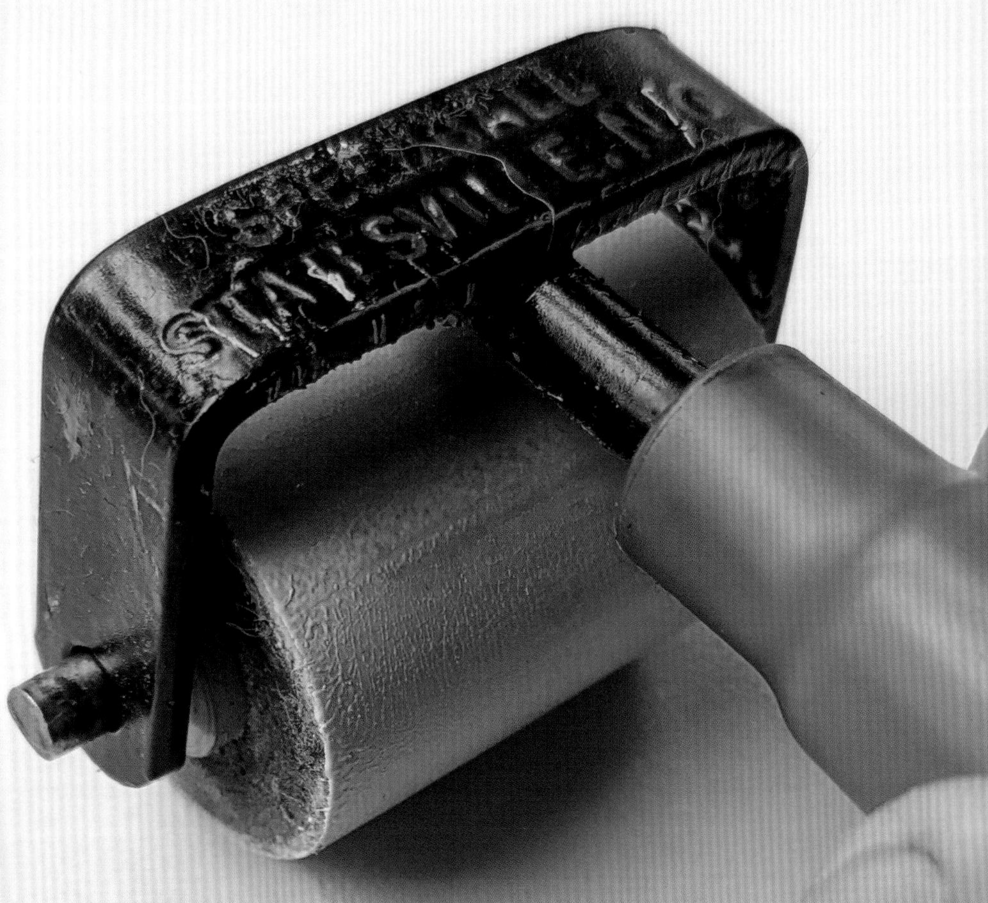

DOWNLOADABLE RESOURCES

Drawing can be challenging and it's not unusual to need a little extra help. The tutorials marked with a download symbol have line work that can be downloaded to help you complete the project. Once you have completed the eight tutorials in the book, there is also an exclusive bonus tutorial that will take you a step further in terms of complexity and skill. These resources are all available at the link below:

store.3dtotal.com/tools/downloadables/resources

CONTENTS

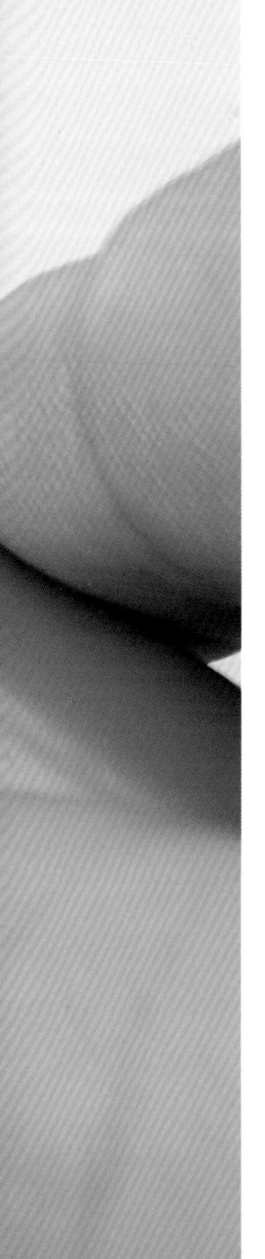

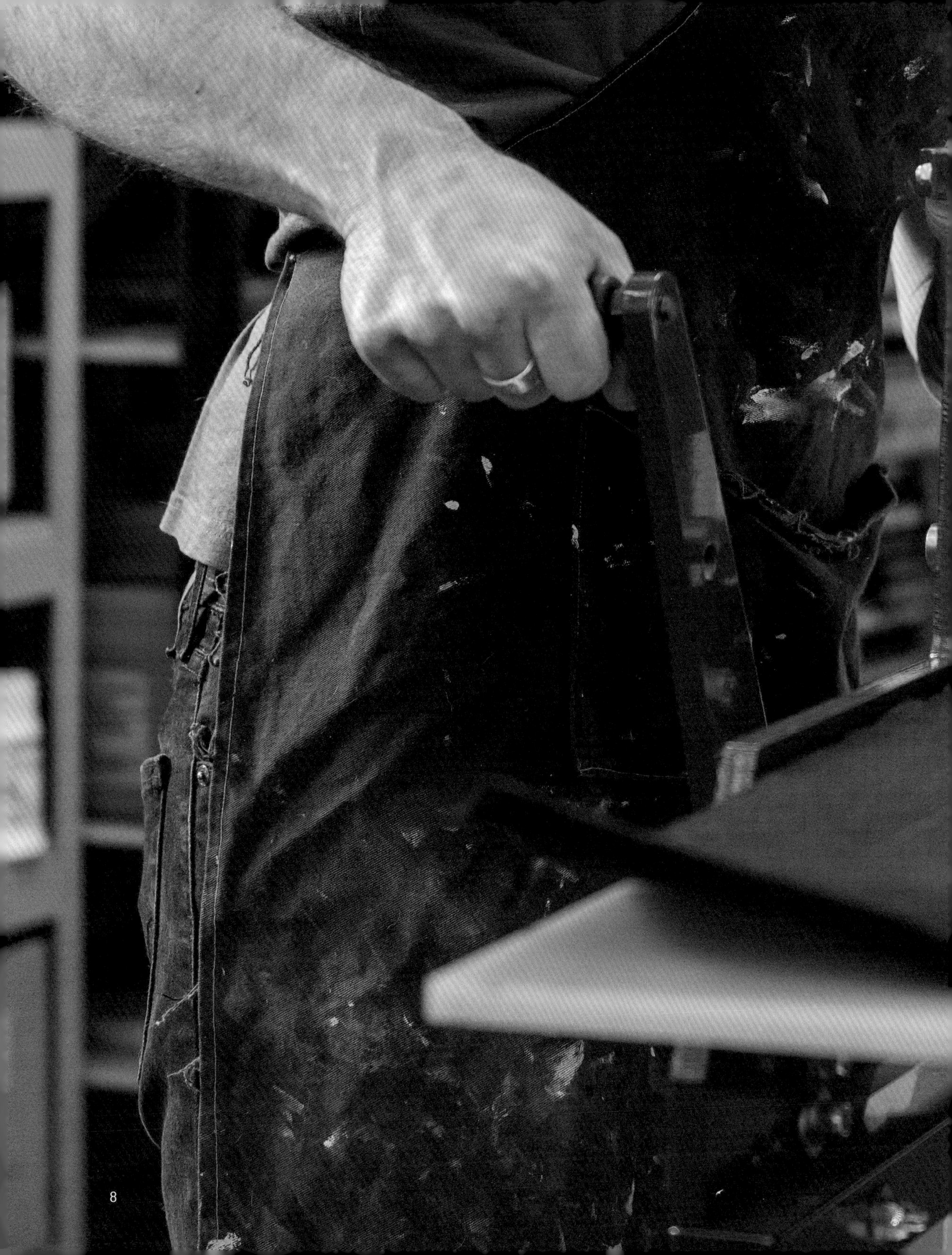

INTRODUCTION

BY GARETH BARNES (SPINDLE PRINTER)

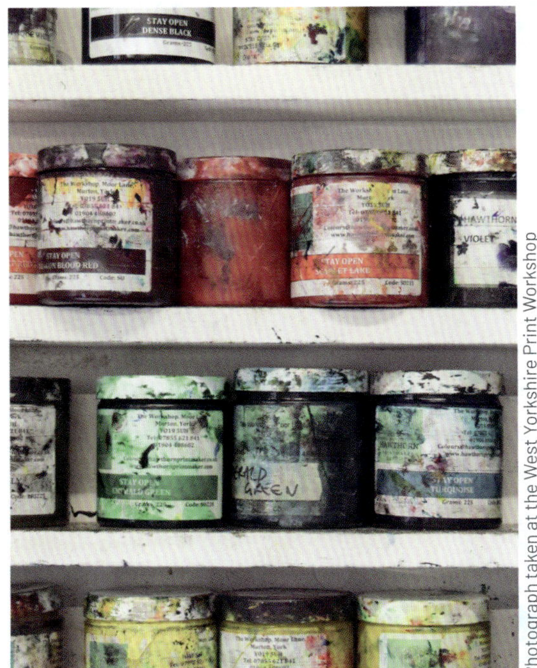

Photograph taken at the West Yorkshire Print Workshop

LINOCUT PRINTMAKING

Linocutting is a type of relief printmaking that involves carving away parts of an image from a linoleum block, leaving behind a flat design that is then inked. A piece of paper or fabric is then placed on top, and pressure is applied – either with a spoon, a flat tool called a baren, or a press – to transfer the image.

When cutting into the lino block, you are removing the areas you don't want to see in the final artwork, rather than creating the exact image, as you would if drawing a picture. You are working on a design that is a reverse of the final image. This might sound a little confusing, but after making a print or two, it will become much clearer.

Like many printmaking methods, the beauty of linocut printing is the ability to reproduce the same image multiple times. Though the lino will eventually wear out, you will be able to create numerous copies of an image you have spent hours carving. This is of particular benefit if you plan to sell them, but also means you can create lovely gifts, or even print handmade Christmas cards. Unlike screen-printing, which tends to reproduce designs more uniformly, each linocut print you make will be a little different. There will be subtle differences in the inking from one print to another, giving every print a one-of-a-kind, handmade feel.

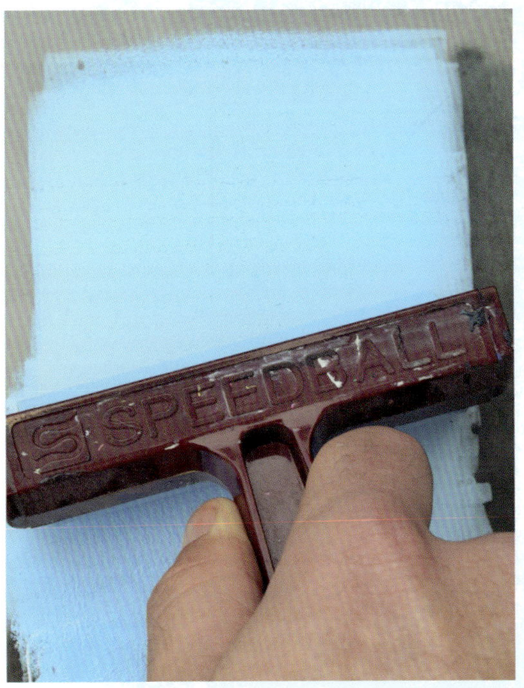

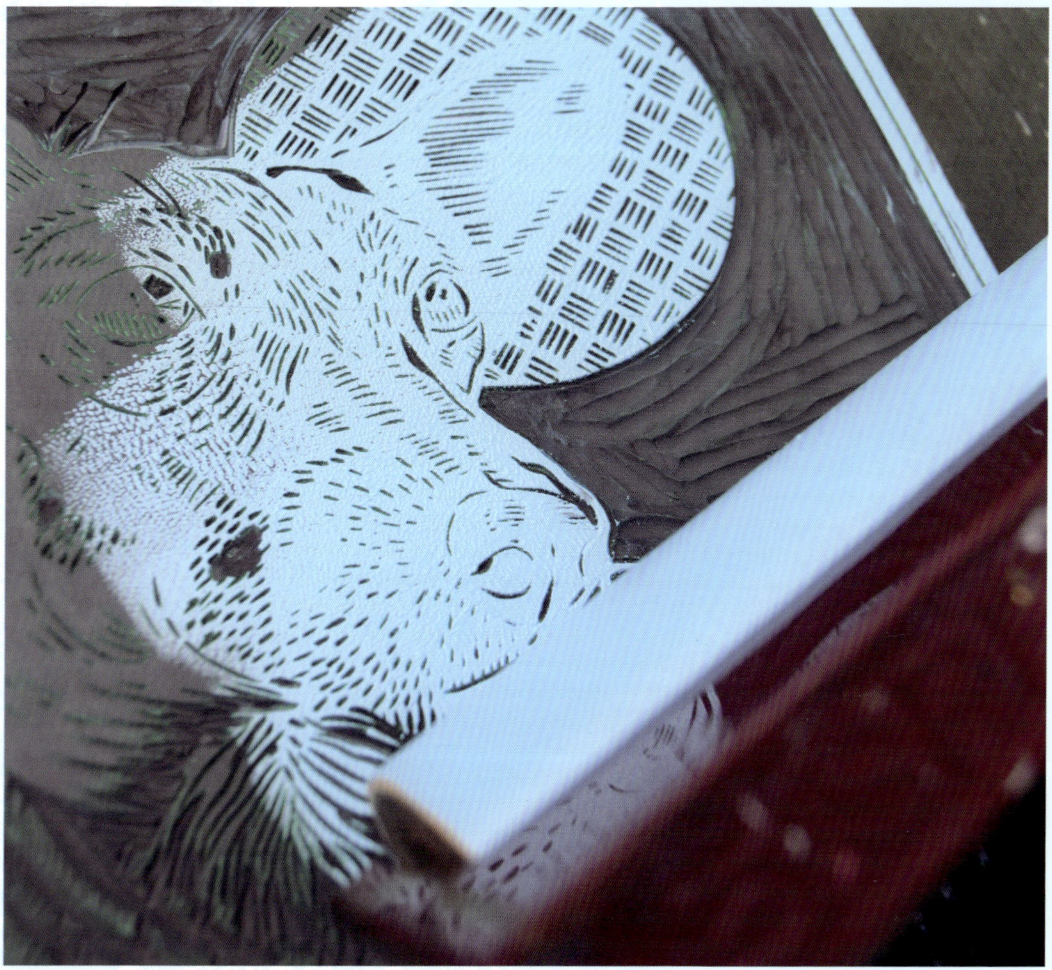

HISTORY

Lino (short for linoleum) was originally invented as a flooring material in the 19th century and can still be found in many kitchens. Known for its durability, it was made from a mix of natural materials – such as cork dust, linseed oil, and sawdust – with canvas on the underside to hold it all together. But it wasn't destined to remain on the floor...

In the early 20th century, artists such as Pablo Picasso, Henri Matisse, and Kathleen Bagot saw the potential of using lino as an art material. It remained a popular printmaking option throughout the 20th century. While for a time it was seen as more suitable for student and 'amateur' artists, a recent boom in popularity has seen linocut printmaking embraced by artists of all ages, styles, and levels of experience. Today it is a respected and well-loved printmaking method.

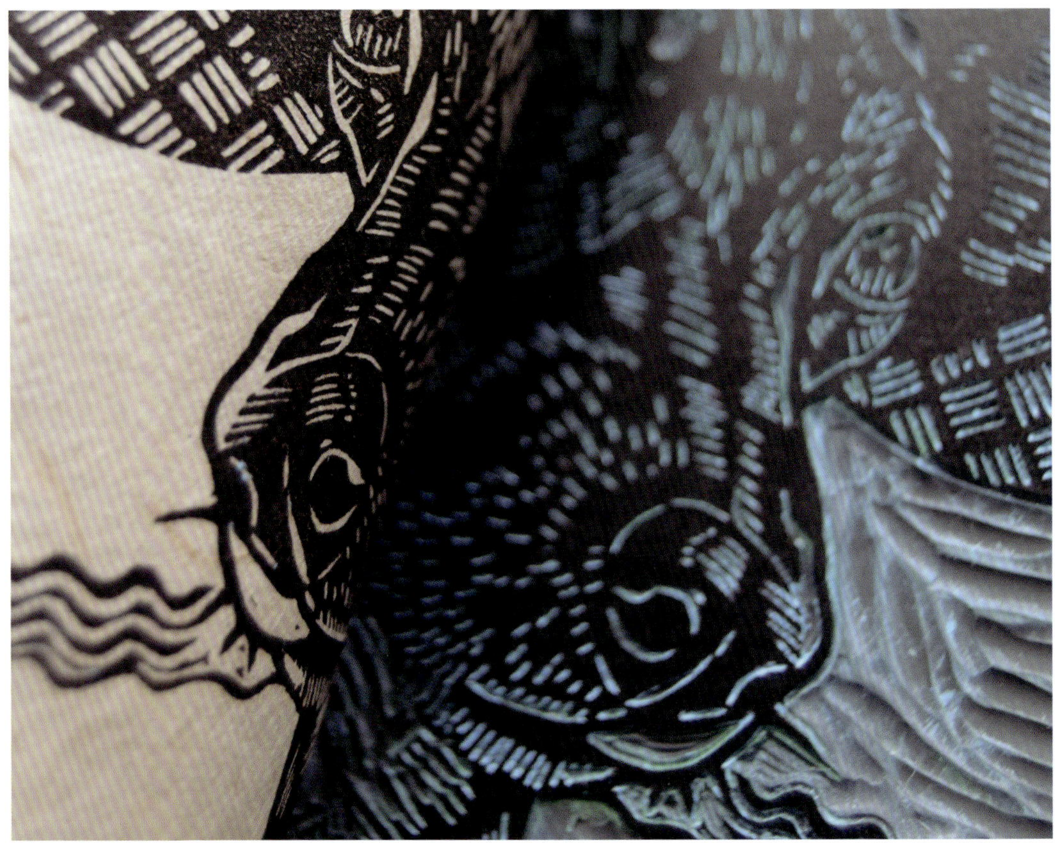

RELIEF PRINTMAKING

There are a few different types of relief printmaking, the most similar to linocut being wood engraving and woodcut printing. Though woodcut uses similar tools to linocut, enabling you to create similar types of prints, there are a few key differences. Notably, woodcut printing requires you to consider the wood grain as you carve. Carving too deeply, or against the grain, especially with tools that are not sharp enough, can result in unwanted pieces of wood flaking off. With wood engraving, you carve into the end grain, or cross-section, of the wood, and on a much smaller scale. While a wider range of tools can be used in wood engraving to achieve incredible levels of detail, linocut lets you carve cleanly in any direction with any tool, without fear of taking out chunks by mistake. Lino also allows you to create beautifully crisp and detailed work.

KEEP GOING

Linocut printmaking can be a therapeutic and rewarding process, but, like any skill, it requires practice, and this book can help. Read through *Materials* (page 14) and *Processes* (page 42) to learn the basics, then work through the *Technique Tutorials* (page 70), learning from each printmaker in turn. Go easy on yourself if it doesn't work exactly how you imagined. Keep going, experiment, and most importantly, have fun!

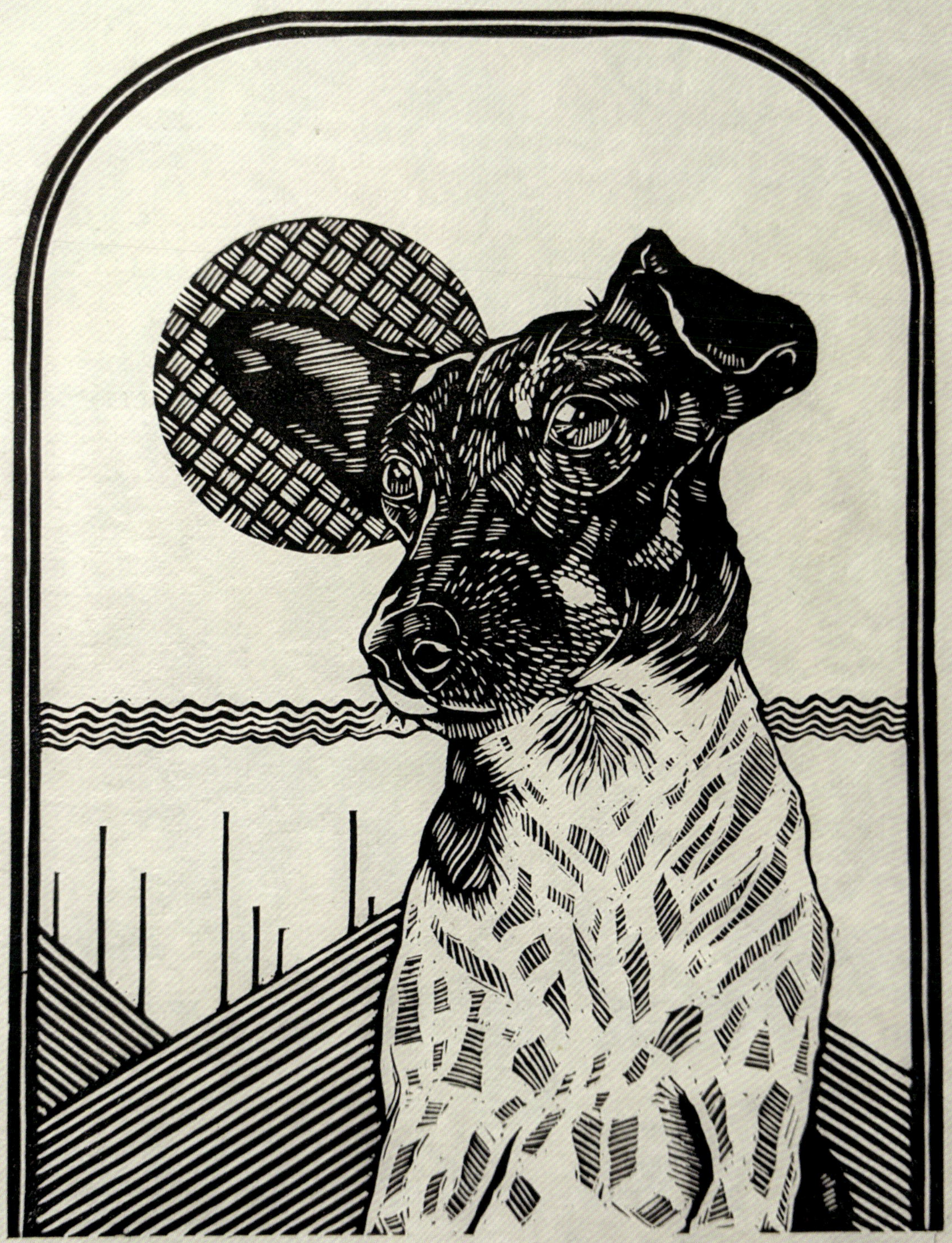

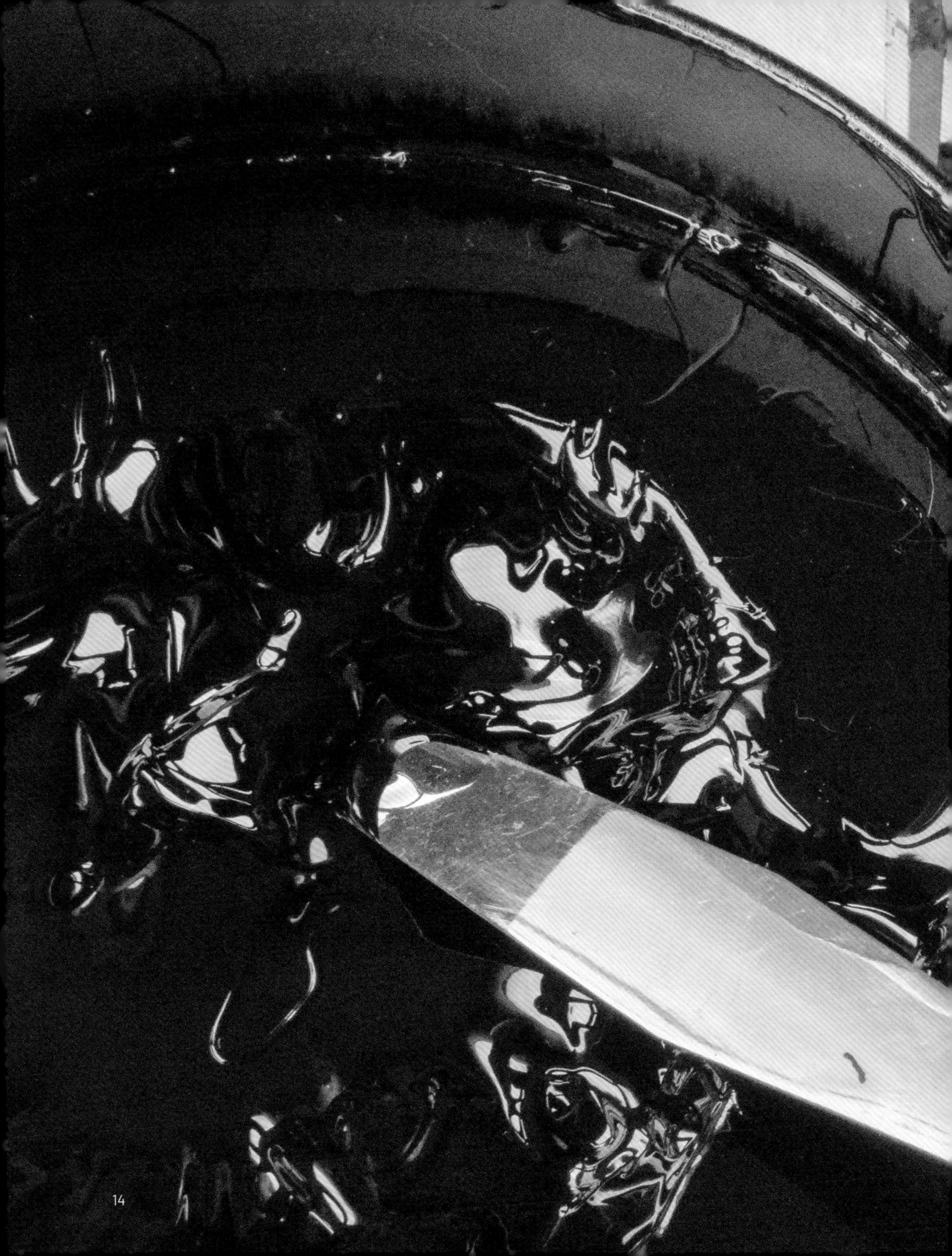

MATERIALS

BY GARETH BARNES (SPINDLE PRINTER)

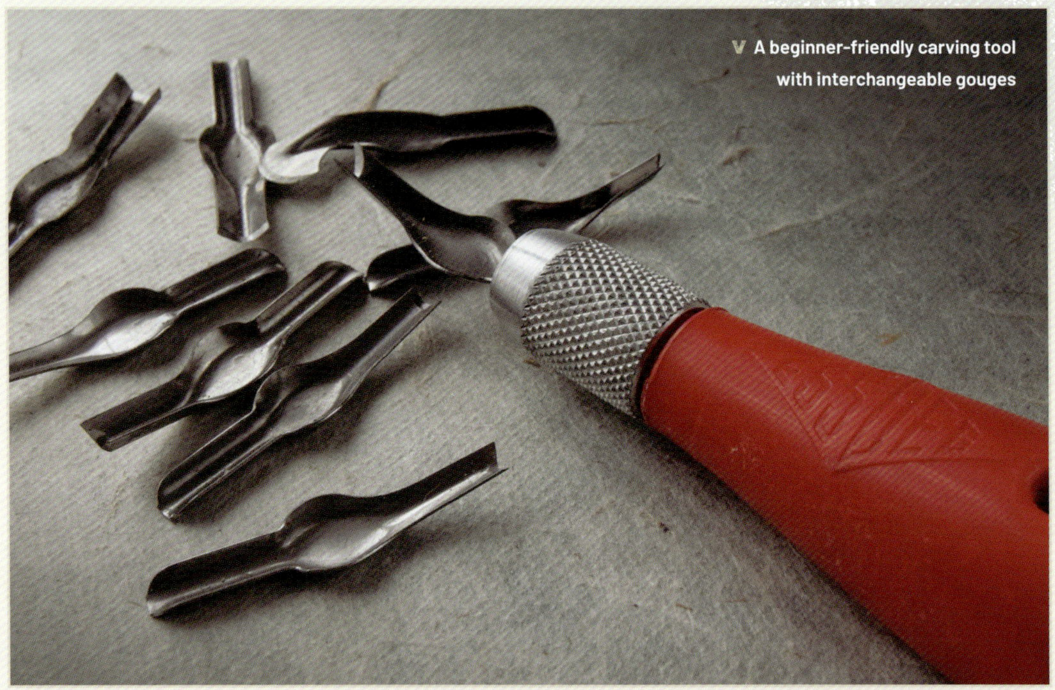
A beginner-friendly carving tool with interchangeable gouges

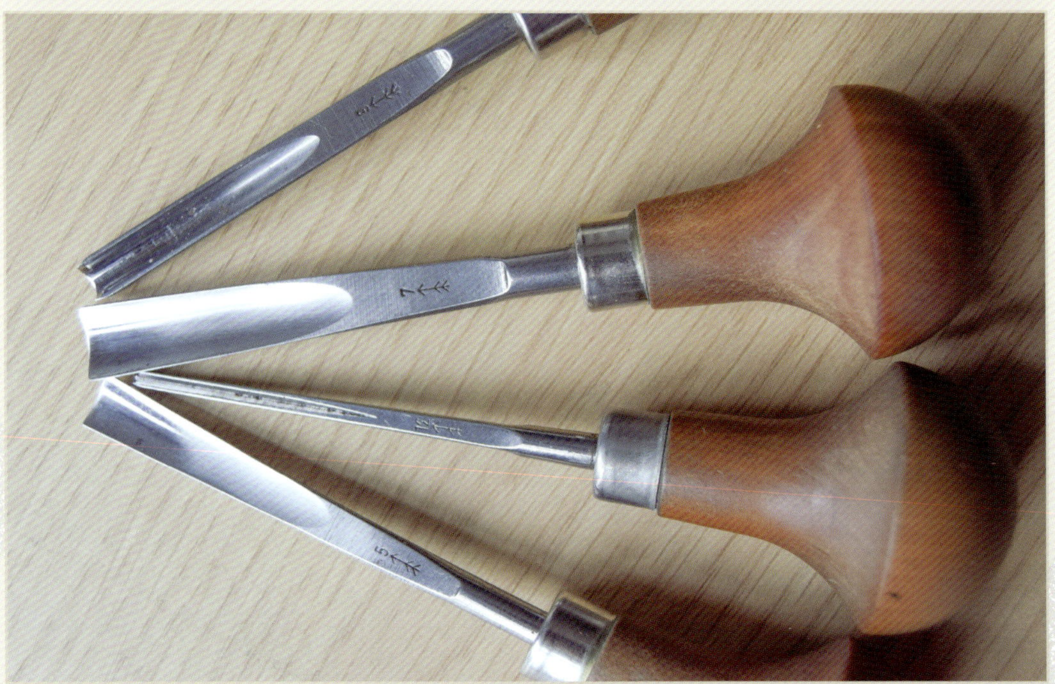

CARVING TOOLS

Carving tools are essential pieces of equipment for linocut printmaking. Like most art materials, there are a range of different brands, designs, and levels of quality. It's important to find tools that you are comfortable using, while also factoring in cost. For beginners, a cheap carving tool with interchangeable tips is a popular choice. This allows you to switch the tips, which are secured in the handle, when you want to carve with a different line thickness or shape.

Many printmakers decide to buy separate tools for different kinds of mark-making as they grow in experience and skill. Carving tools made from wood and steel are well designed, fit nicely in the hand, and are built to last (as long as you sharpen them regularly). They can be bought individually or in a set, and although they are a little more expensive, they are worth the investment.

Owning a variety of different tool shapes will enable you to create an interesting range of marks in your work. There are two common types, U-shaped and V-shaped, both of which come in a range of sizes. The very smallest V-shaped tool is perfect for carving outlines and finer detailed work, whereas the broadest U-shaped tool is useful for quickly clearing large areas. How you use the tools is up to you, depending on the look or style you're trying to create in the design.

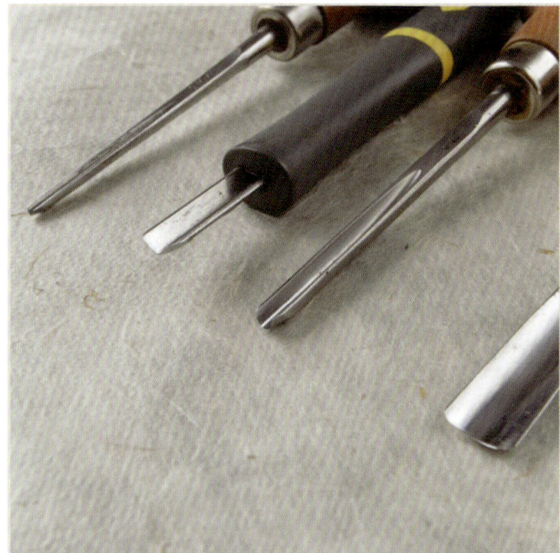

∧ Tiny tools are useful for carving details, while larger tools are good for clearing bigger areas

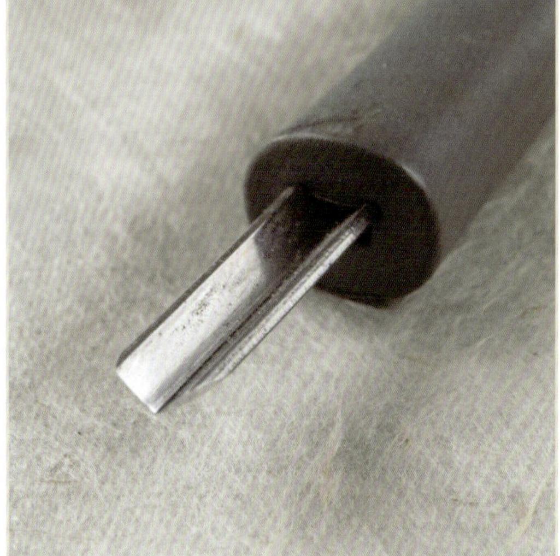

∨ A V-shaped tool

ROLLERS

Rollers, also known as brayers, are another piece of essential kit. They are used to transfer ink to the lino block before it is pressed onto paper. There are a wide range of different rollers available, made from different materials and of varying size, hardness, and cost.

The main thing to consider when buying a roller is size. A 10 cm roller will suffice if you plan to work on a small scale, giving you the option to ink a range of different block sizes. For larger prints, there are rollers that range from 30 cm up to 50 cm, or bigger. As you progress on your lino-printing journey, it can be useful to have a variety of roller sizes in your kit, including skinny rollers for inking small, fiddly areas. Owning multiple rollers is also useful when using different inks at the same time.

Rollers are available in a range of hardness levels, from soft and spongy to firm. Softer rollers will create a slightly softer edge to the lines you print, while harder rollers will produce a crisper finish. If carving detailed designs, opt for a roller of medium to firm hardness to ensure any little details remain nice and clear. If creating bolder, more graphic designs, any type of roller will work.

▼ Smaller rollers, such as these 5 cm and 1 cm options, are ideal for inking fiddly areas

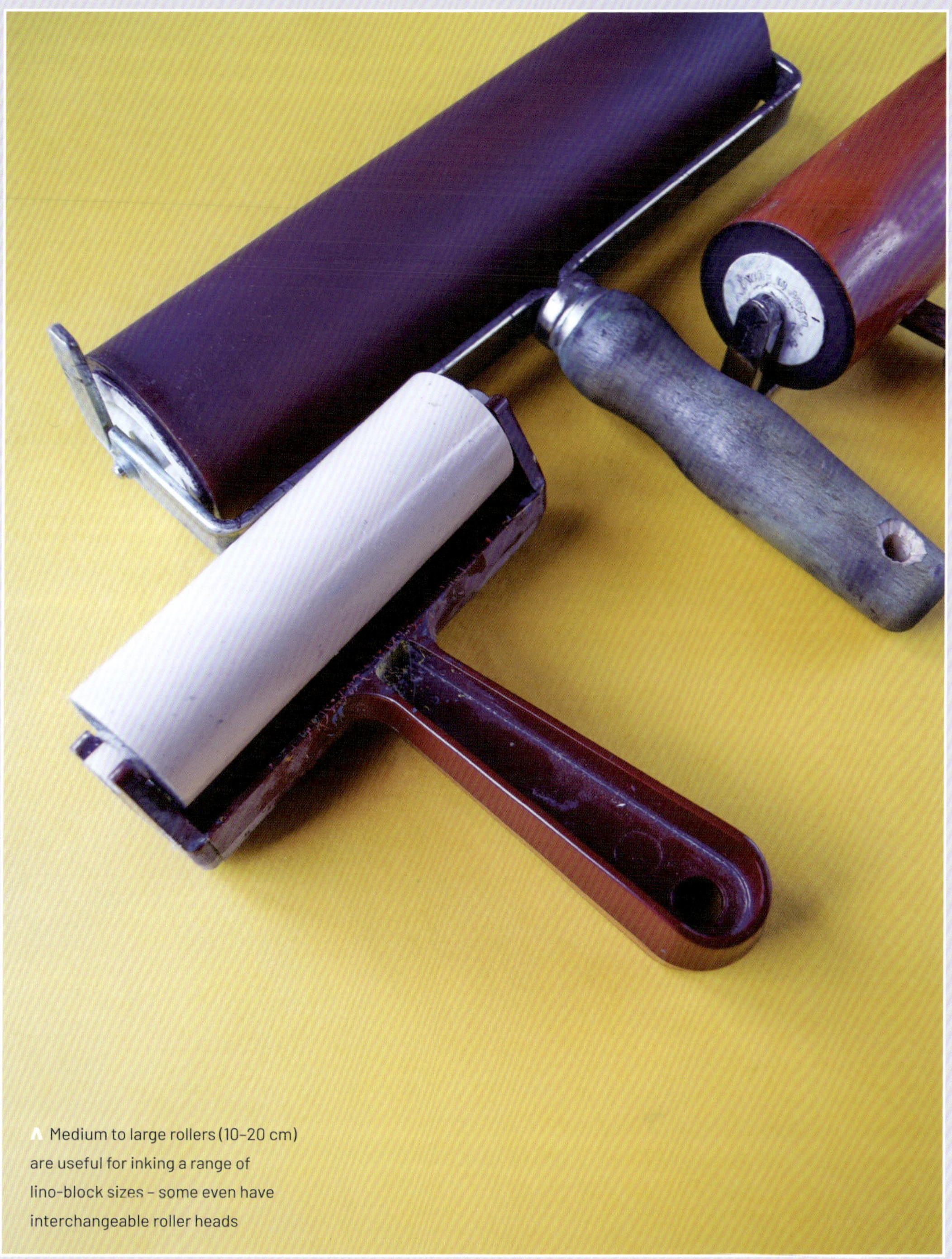

A Medium to large rollers (10–20 cm) are useful for inking a range of lino-block sizes – some even have interchangeable roller heads

INKS

There are two choices of ink – water-based or oil-based – both of which have their benefits and limitations. Experiment to see which you like best.

WATER-BASED INKS

Available from most art stores, water-based inks are generally more affordable. As they are water-soluble, you can easily clean your inky rollers and equipment with just water. This, along with their cheaper price, makes them a popular choice for beginners.

Water-based ink dries very quickly, which can be a positive when the finished print dries in good time. On the flip-side, the ink can often dry as you're using it, which can be problematic if you're printing multiple copies. It's a more fluid, runny ink compared to oil-based, so not ideal for fine work, as it can 'flood' those little spaces you've taken hours carving out, losing the detail. When dry it has a chalky, slightly uneven finish, which can suit certain projects really well.

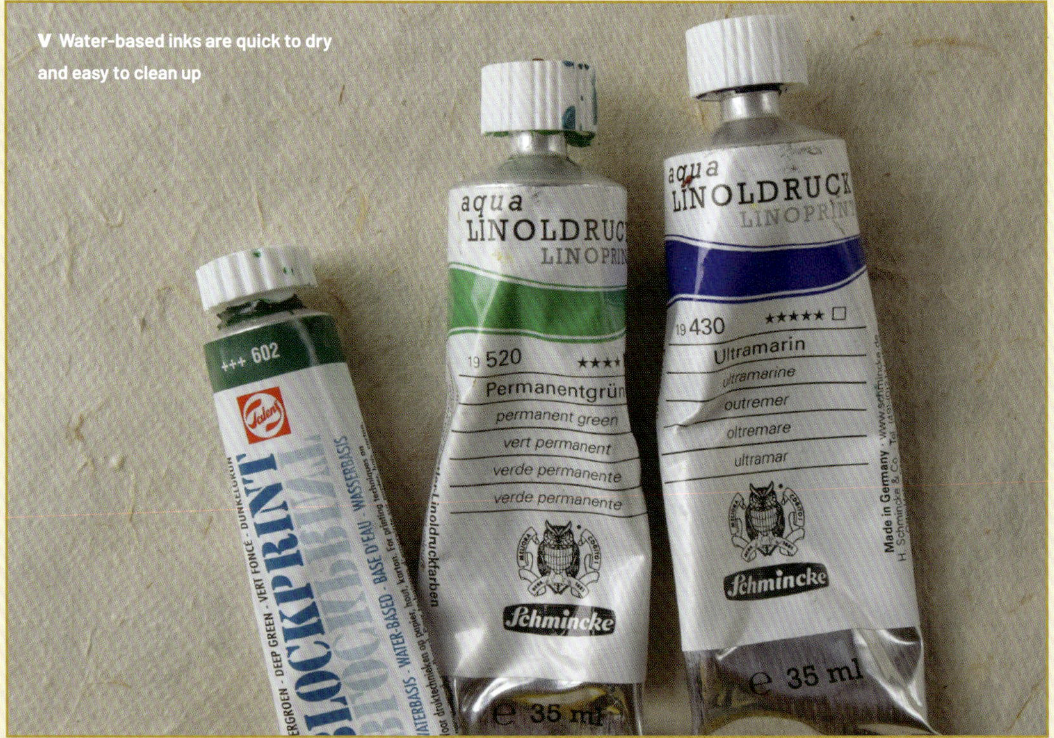

∨ Water-based inks are quick to dry and easy to clean up

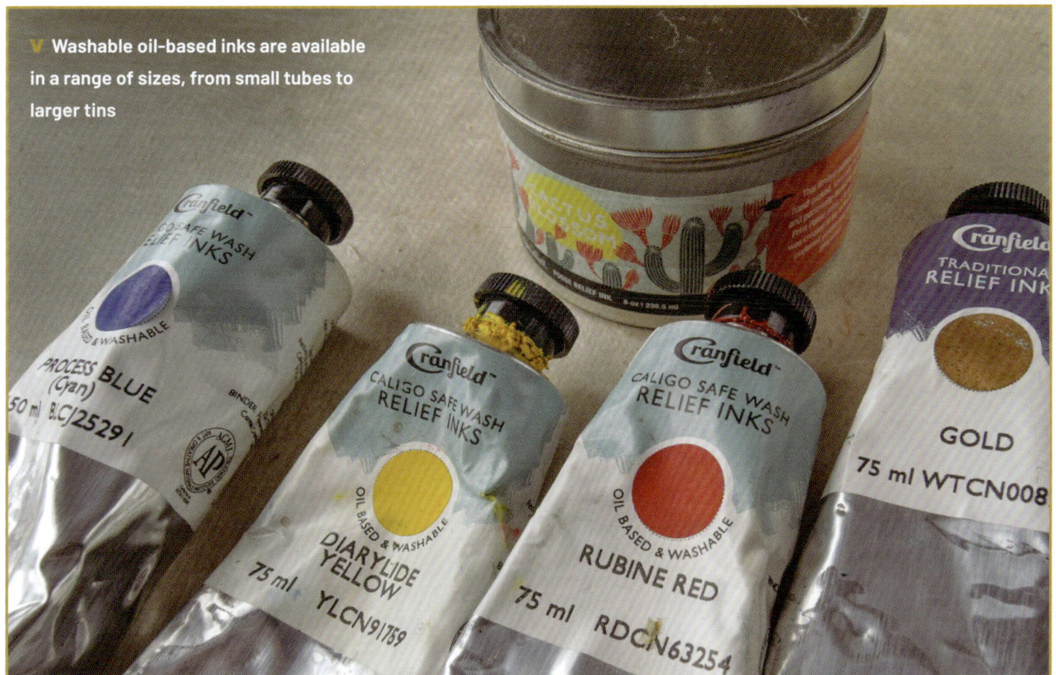

OIL-BASED INKS

There are two types of oil-based ink: the traditional kind that needs to be cleaned using stronger solvents, and another kind that can be cleaned with soapy water or vegetable oil. There isn't a huge difference between the two in terms of finish, though some printmakers will prefer one over the other. Being able to avoid stronger solvents and clean tools with water has made washable oil-based inks a popular choice.

Compared with water-based inks, oil-based inks have a flatter, more even finish. The printed colours stay brighter when dried and the ink doesn't dry on the roller midway through printing. They have a thicker consistency than water-based, which works better for detailed designs and makes for more consistently inked prints. Although slightly more expensive, oil-based inks are worth investing in when you feel ready.

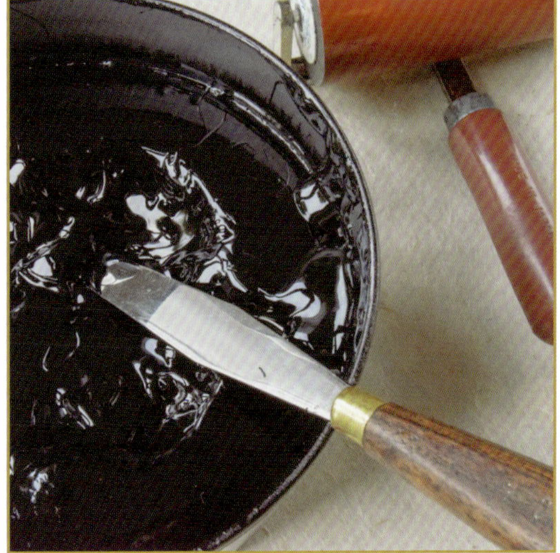

It can be more cost-effective to buy ink that you use regularly in a tin rather than a tube – and to avoid a thin skin forming on the top of the ink inside the tin, tape over the tin seal and store it upside down

PAPER

Although technically you could transfer a print onto almost any flat surface or material, there are certain kinds of paper that printmakers typically favour. A beautiful paper can really enhance a print, so it's worth using the best you can.

Paper can be bought in pads, individual sheets, or on a roll. Some papers will have straight-cut edges, while others (usually handmade papers) will have rougher, deckled (uneven and feathered) edges, which can be a lovely feature. When choosing what type of paper to use, it's worth considering weight, surface, and colour.

WEIGHT

Paper weight is measured in gsm (grams per square metre). A sheet of 30 gsm paper is regarded as lightweight, while 140 gsm is considered heavy. While the paper thickness you choose to use is largely down to personal preference, it also depends on how you plan to press the print. If transferring the print by hand – using the back of a spoon, for example (as you'll learn about on page 28) – then a lightweight paper will be much easier than heavy paper, which might need multiple pressings to transfer the image cleanly. Prints on heavy papers are better transferred using table-top or book presses, or a heavier-duty etching press.

< Japanese papers – such as Kitakata, Hosho, and Mitsumata washi – are great for relief printmaking, as is medium-weight textured handmade paper and Nepalese lokta paper

SURFACE

Paper with a deep texture, like most watercolour papers, won't pick up ink as consistently as smooth paper. You can still use textured paper if you have access to a heavy press, or if you soak the paper first. However, it may be wiser to opt for a paper that is smooth or only lightly textured. Many handmade papers have soft fibrous textures, which can add a lovely look to a print.

Λ The subtle textures and fibres of handmade papers, such as lokta, can enhance a print and give it warmth

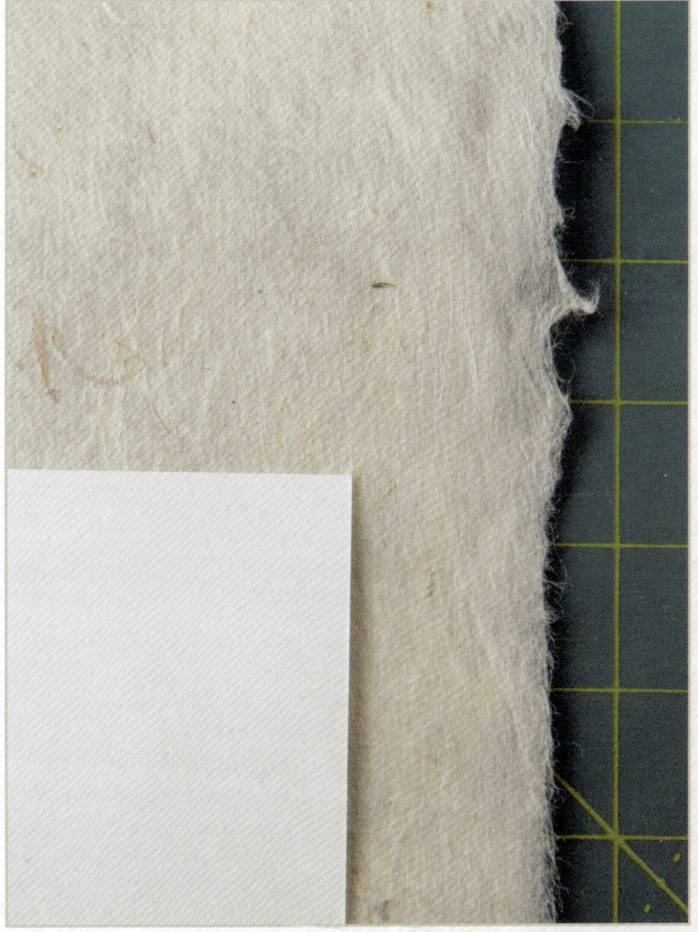

> Hard, sharp edged paper shown next to soft, deckled-edge paper

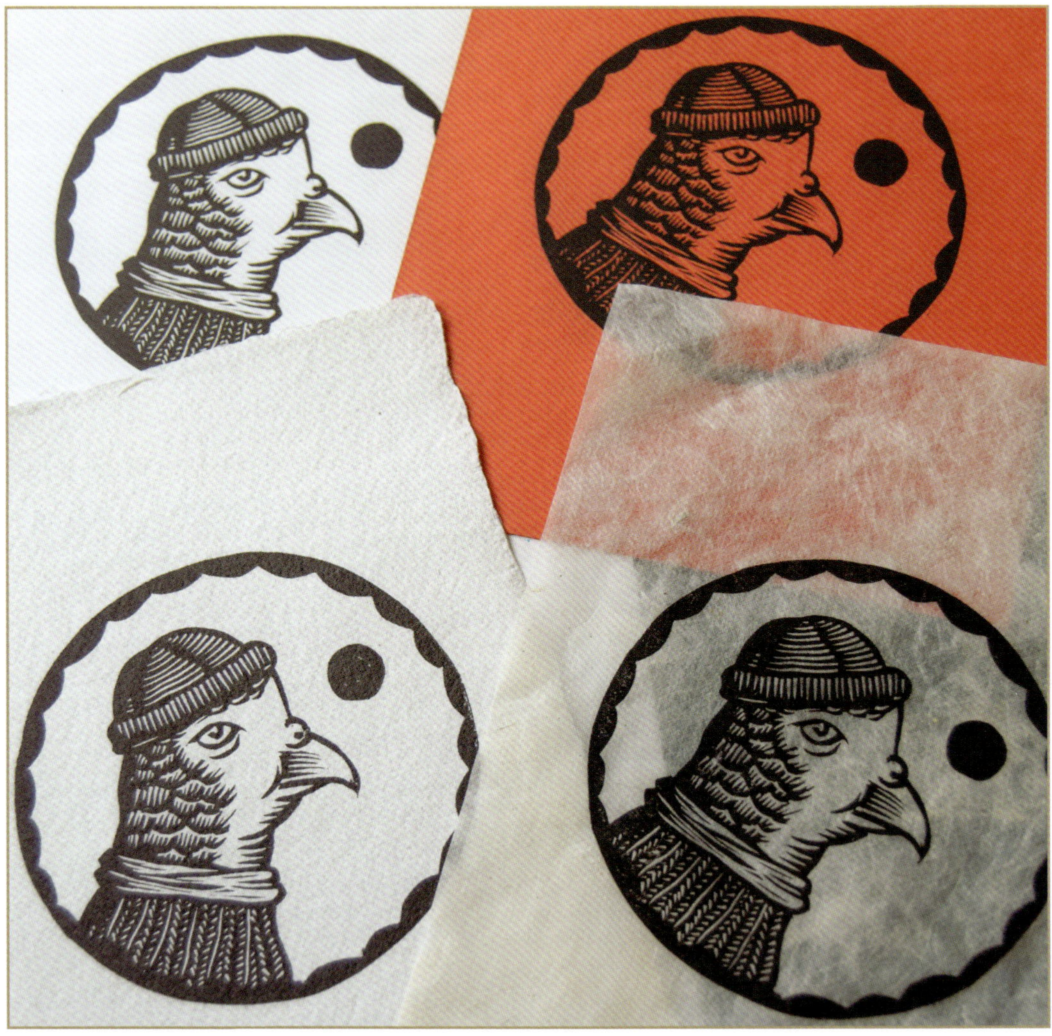

∧ Same print, different look. Clockwise from top left: Hosho paper, coloured cartridge paper, very lightweight lokta paper, and textured handmade Khadi paper

COLOUR

Though white paper is most frequently used, don't overlook coloured papers. Many Japanese and Nepalese papers have beautiful warm tones, while other handmade papers are available in a variety of colours that can really bring a print to life.

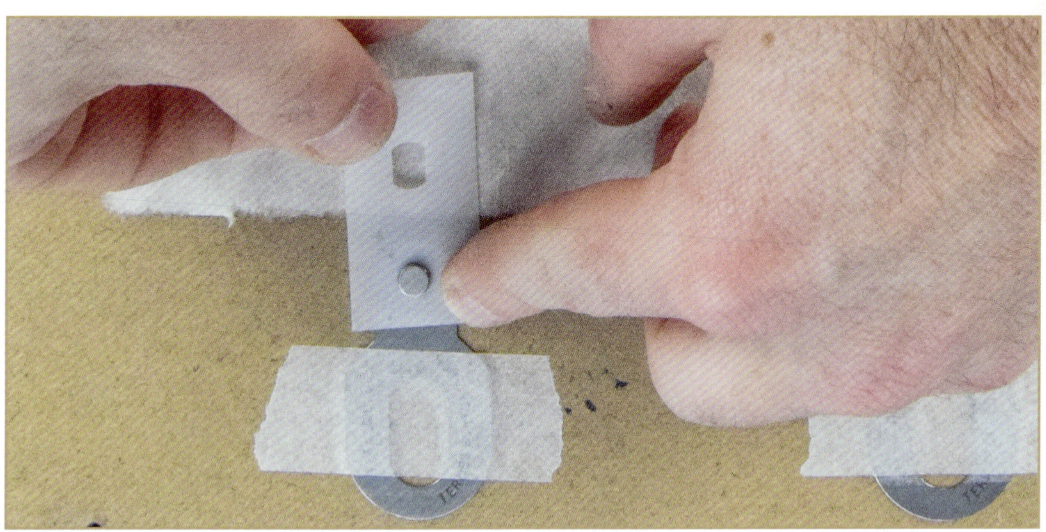

REGISTRATION

Registration materials – tools that help align your print correctly – are essential when lining up the paper over the lino block. They are especially important for multi-layered prints, such as multi-block and reduction, where alignment is key.

- Registration pins are used to clip the tabbed paper to ensure it sits on top of the inked lino block in exactly the same position each time.

- Registration tabs are little plastic tabs that are taped onto the reverse side of the paper. They snap onto the pins you've placed, ensuring your paper is in the correct spot.

Some printmakers opt to use print paper and lino blocks of the exact same size, and use the edges to align their prints. Some simply use tape to mark the position.

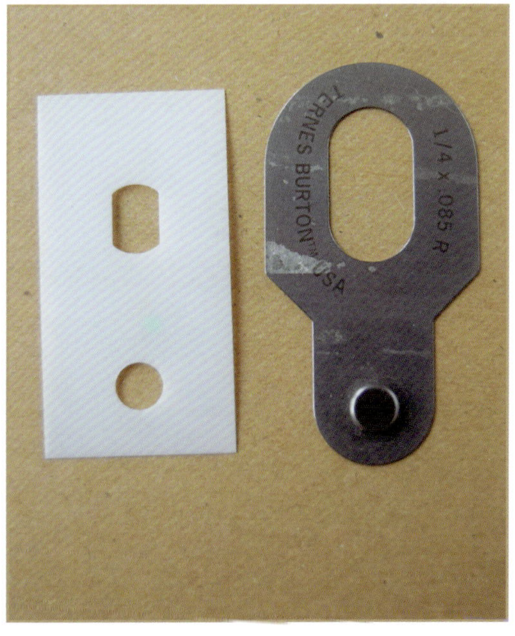

LINO

Lino allows you to carve a variety of different marks, lines, and shapes into its surface to create an image. Like most art materials, there are different types available to suit every style and budget.

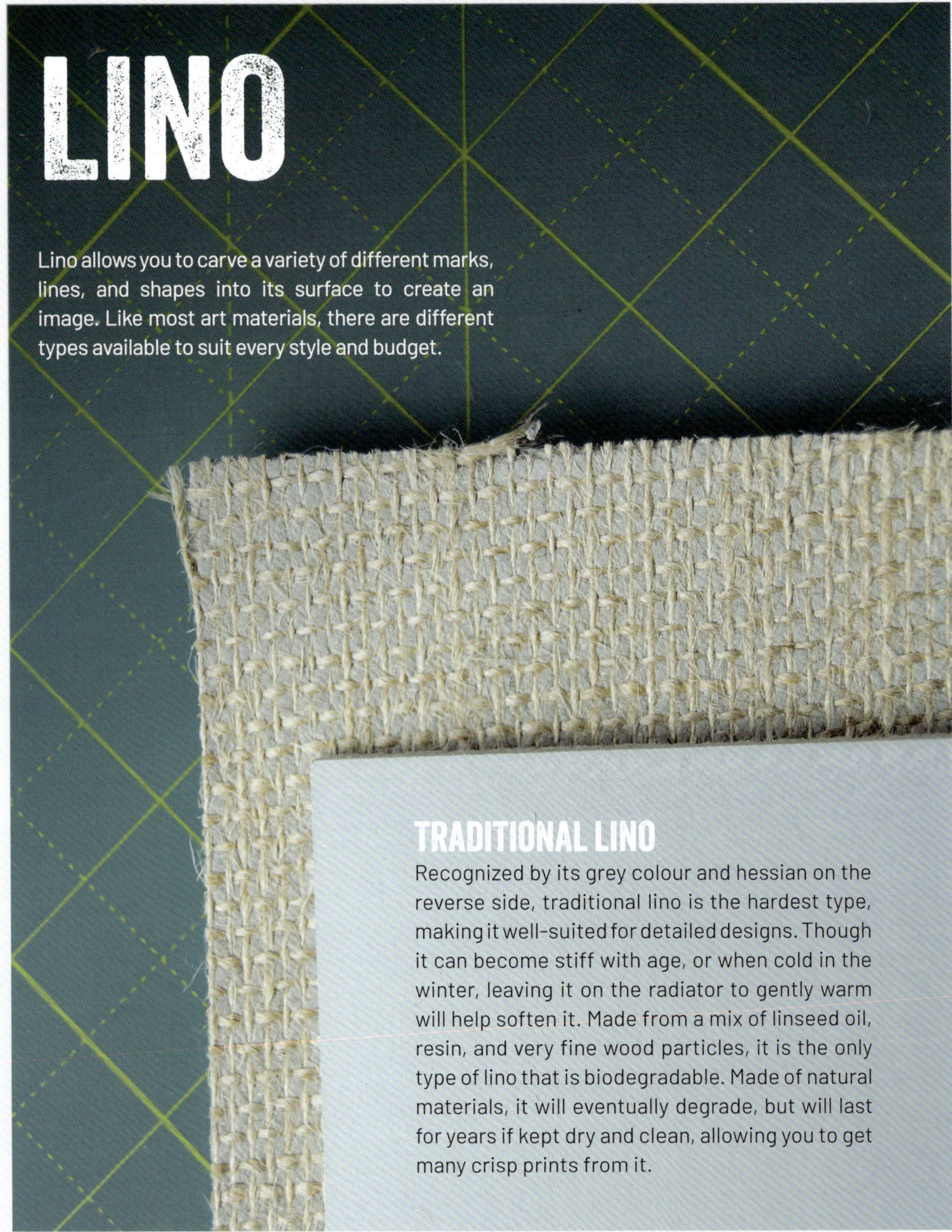

TRADITIONAL LINO

Recognized by its grey colour and hessian on the reverse side, traditional lino is the hardest type, making it well-suited for detailed designs. Though it can become stiff with age, or when cold in the winter, leaving it on the radiator to gently warm will help soften it. Made from a mix of linseed oil, resin, and very fine wood particles, it is the only type of lino that is biodegradable. Made of natural materials, it will eventually degrade, but will last for years if kept dry and clean, allowing you to get many crisp prints from it.

∧ Traditional hessian-backed lino is the most environmentally friendly option and is brilliant for detailed work

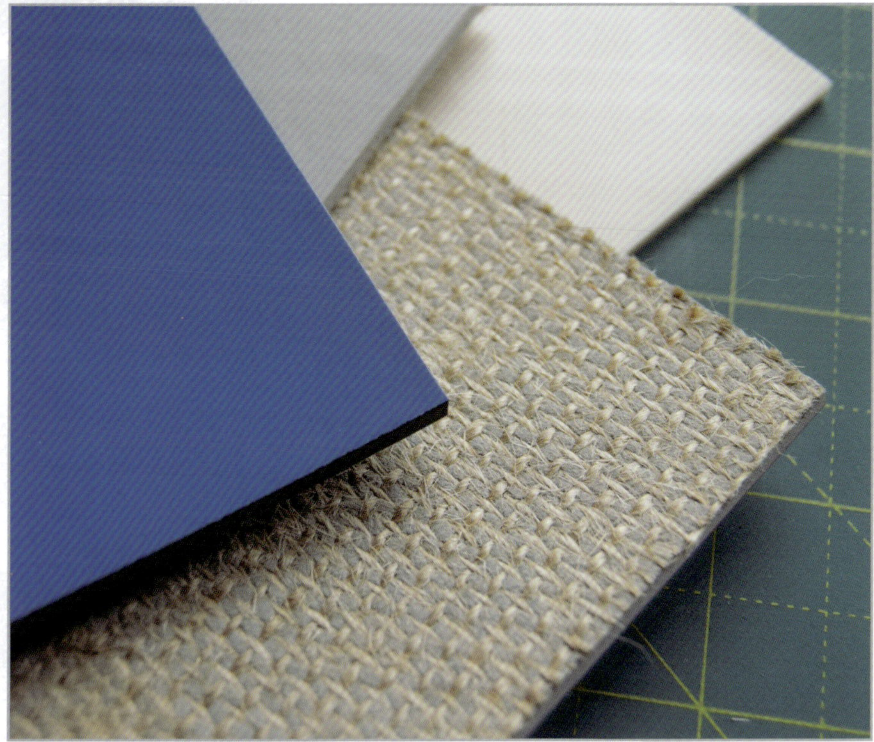

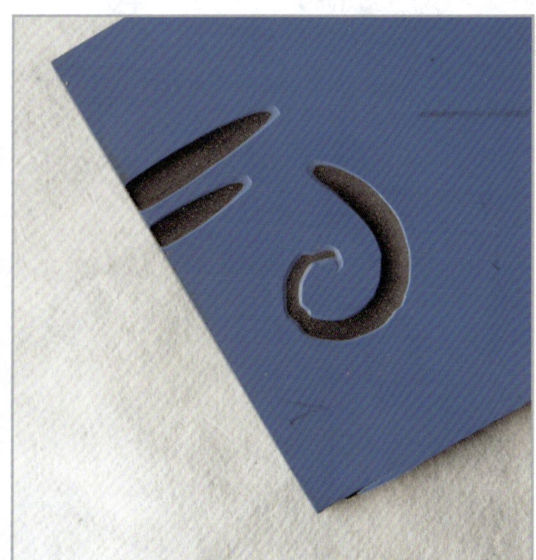

⋀ Japanese vinyl has a black core beneath the coloured
coating, making it easier to see what has been carved

VINYL

There are three main kinds of vinyl lino: SoftCut,
Speedy-Carve, and Japanese.

SOFTCUT

With its smooth surface, softcut lino is firm
enough to print fairly detailed designs. It is also
particularly useful for large, flat areas.

SPEEDY-CARVE

Though similar to SoftCut, Speedy-Carve lino is
usually pink in colour. It has a slightly spongier feel
and is better suited to stamps than larger prints.

JAPANESE

With a coloured coating on both sides, Japanese
lino allows you to easily track where you have
carved. Much firmer than SoftCut, it is perfect
for more detailed carving.

TRANSFERRING THE IMAGE

There are many different methods that can be used to press the print (transfer the image from lino to paper). The method you choose will depend on your budget, choice of paper, and the size of your workspace. Also, if trying out other printmaking methods, such as etching, you may want to invest in equipment that can press all types of print.

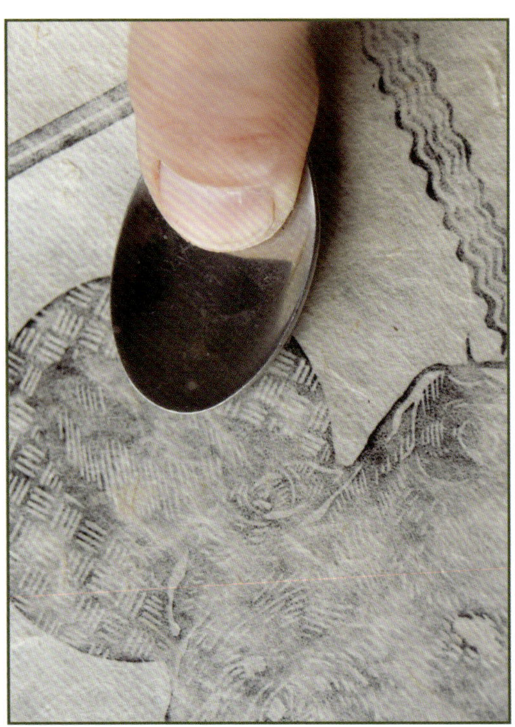

∧ The back of a spoon works well on lightweight paper

SPOONS

This might sound odd, but spoons can be surprisingly effective for transferring an image to paper. Whether metal or wooden, the curved underside of the spoon concentrates pressure on a small area. This is a great option for lightweight to medium-weight papers, but if using heavy paper or attempting a really large print, they can prove hard work.

BARENS

A staple in any relief-printmaker's kit, barens are available in various shapes, sizes, and materials, from lightweight bamboo to heavier glass. There are also heavy steel barens with ball bearings that are suited to a range of paper thicknesses.

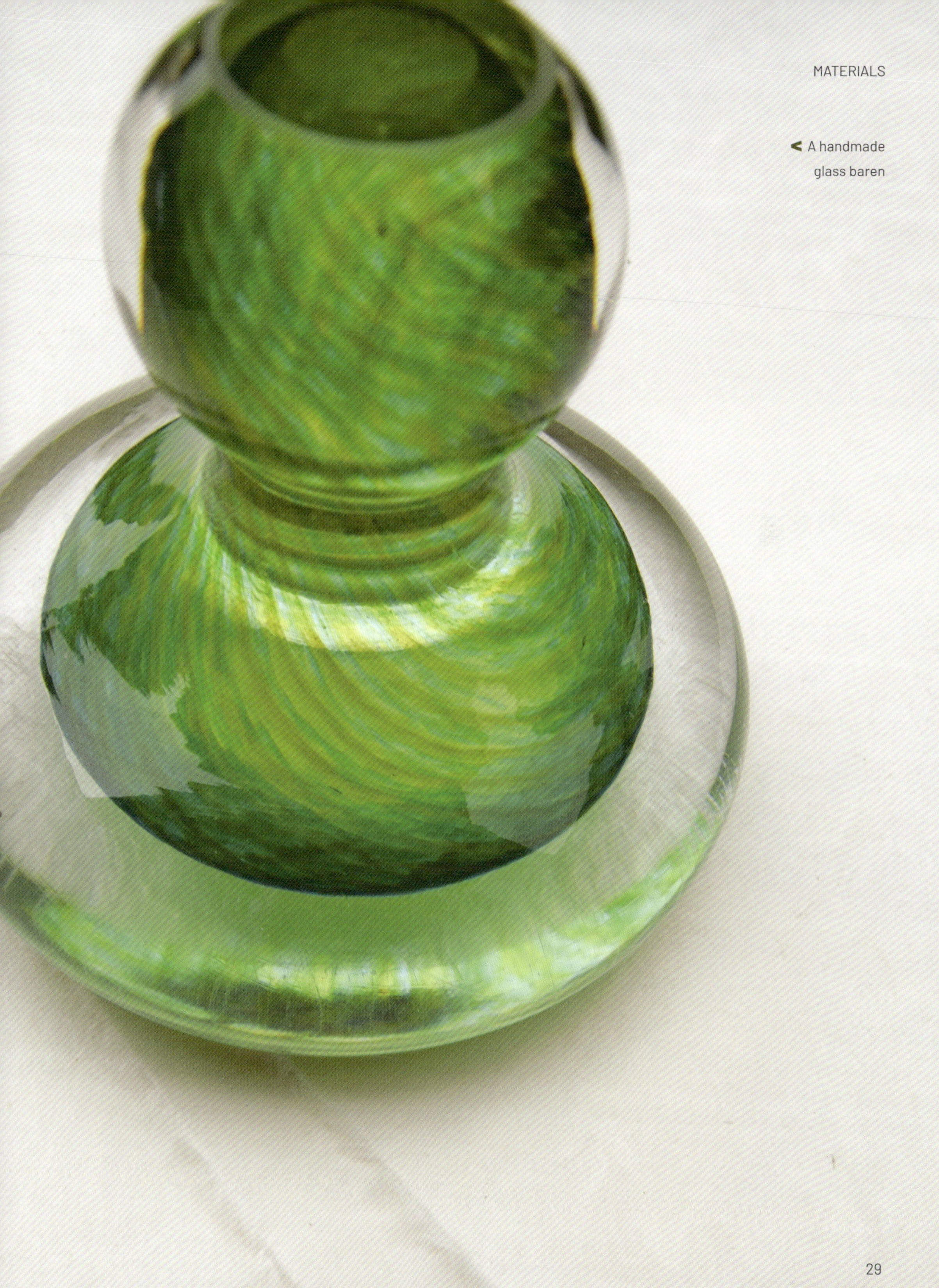

< A handmade
glass baren

TABLE-TOP PRESSES

Whether hinged or hand-levered, table-top presses are usually portable and more affordable than heavy-duty presses, making them popular with home-based printmakers. They enable you to print onto a range of different paper types, with less effort than required when using a spoon or baren. Allowing you to print up to around 42 × 59.4 cm (16.5 × 23.4 in), they also work well with heavy paper.

BOOK PRESSES

Typically made from wood or cast iron, book presses enable you to print up to approximately 29.7 × 42 cm (11.7 × 16.5 in). While they are ideal for heavy papers, they are not well-suited for lightweight papers.

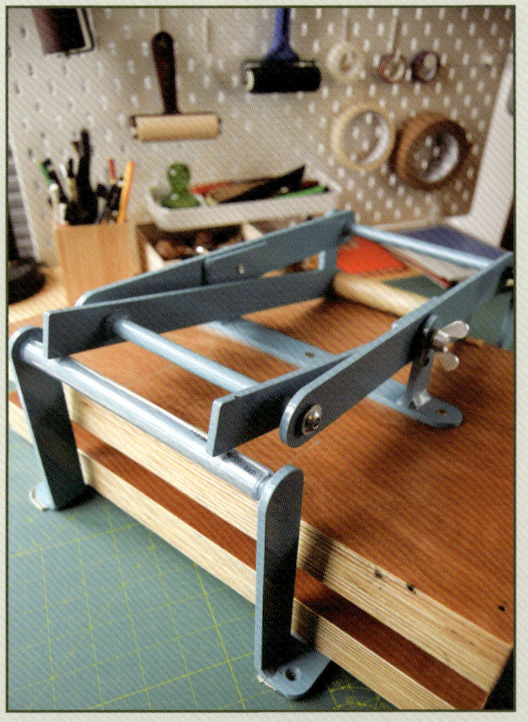

V A popular hinged table-top press with a sturdy frame and heavy wooden plates

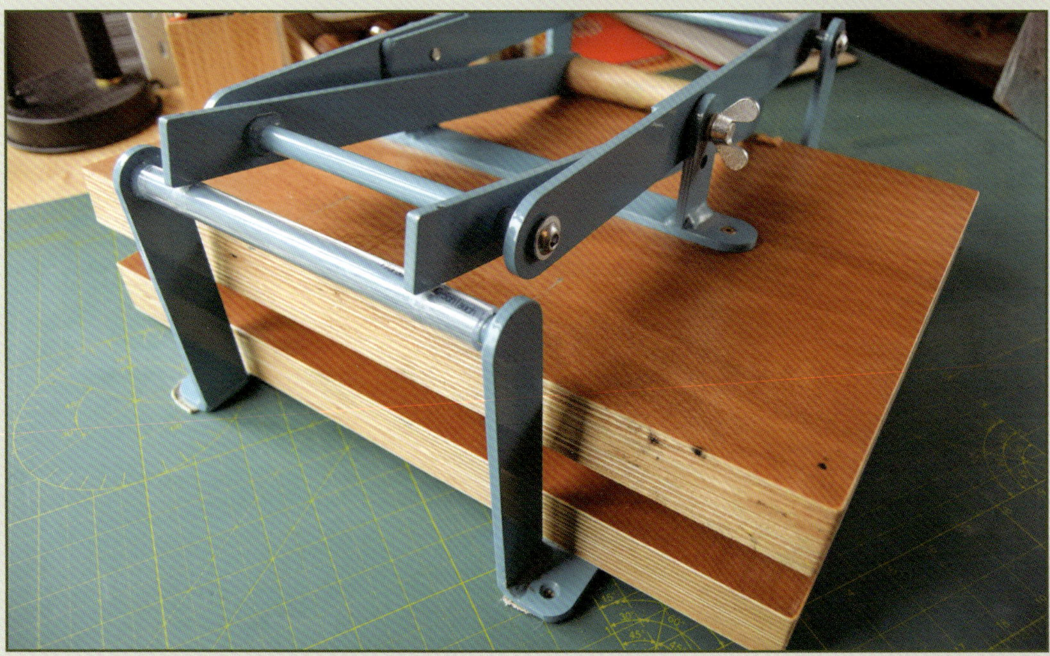

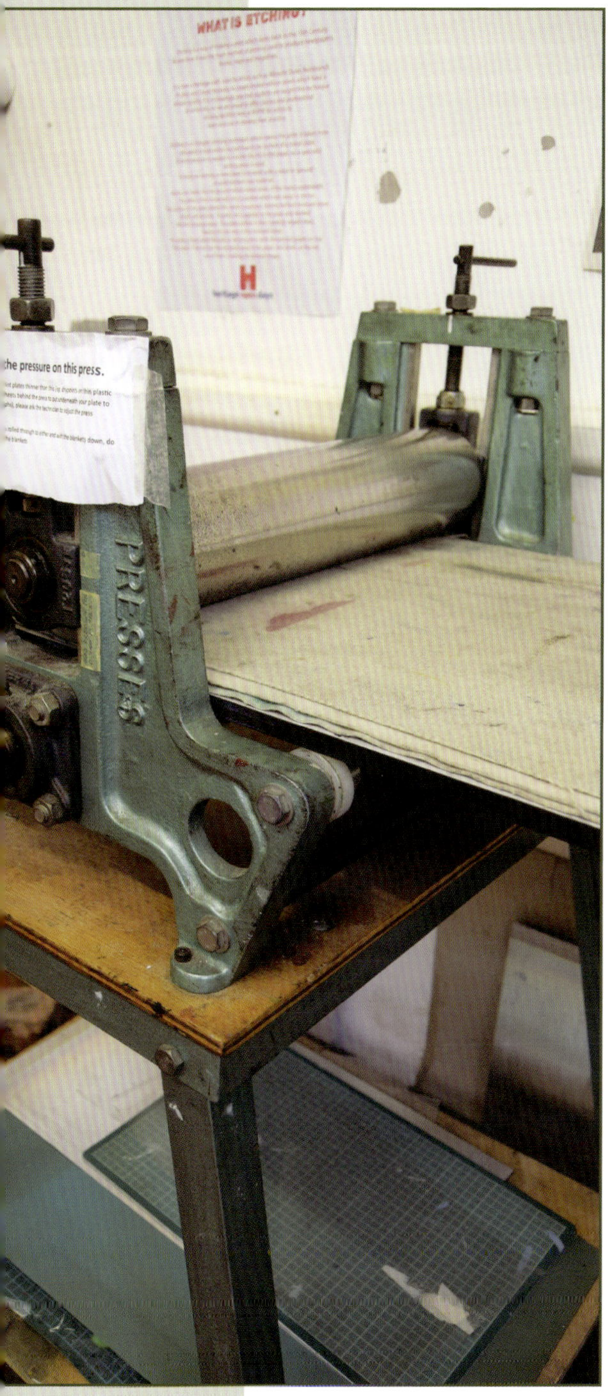

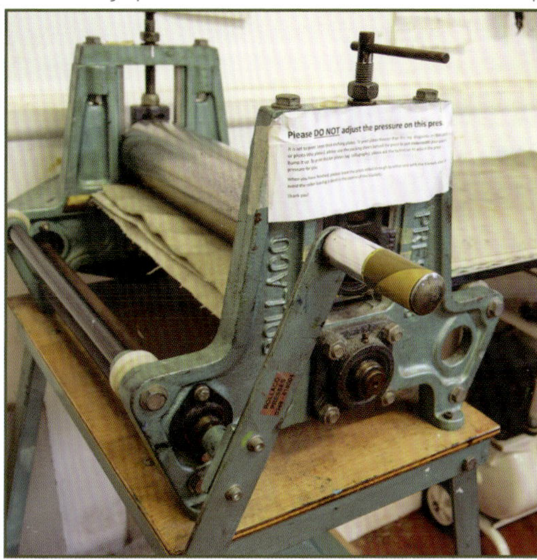

Λ A classic etching press where the lino block and paper sit on the flat 'bed' and are passed under and pressed beneath a heavy-duty roller; this is great for larger prints and when using thick paper

ETCHING PRESSES

These come in a range of sizes and prices, from smaller table-top options that can print up to 42 × 59.4 cm (16.5 × 23.4 in), through to heavy floor-mounted kinds that press prints up to 84.1 × 118.9 cm (33.1 × 46.8 in). Their main advantage is their ability to press numerous types of print, including etchings and drypoints.

START SIMPLE

When starting out, begin by using lightweight paper and experimenting with the back of a spoon or a baren. Once you feel confident with these, you could consider investing in a table-top press. See if there are any local printmaking workshops that offer the option to use their facilities, as they will often have larger-scale presses.

SHARPENING

Keeping your tools sharp will not only make it easier to carve with them, and carve more accurately, but will also make you less likely to injure yourself. Blunt tools require more pressure and can quickly skim the surface rather than cut into the lino as you push. There are two pieces of equipment required for sharpening.

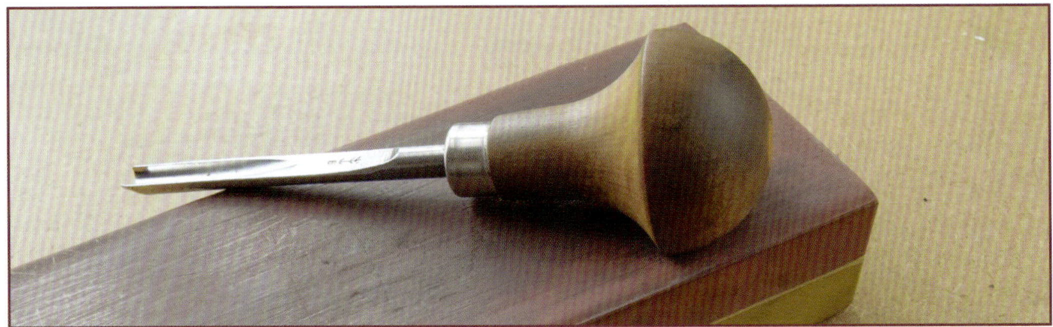

∧ A Japanese whetstone with two grit options; a little dab of water or oil should be added to the stone before sharpening to help the tools glide smoothly across the surface

SHARPENING STONE

It's good practice to regularly sharpen your tools on a sharpening stone, or even before every new lino project. There are various types, including Japanese whetstones and Arkansas stones, both of which are available in different grades of smoothness.

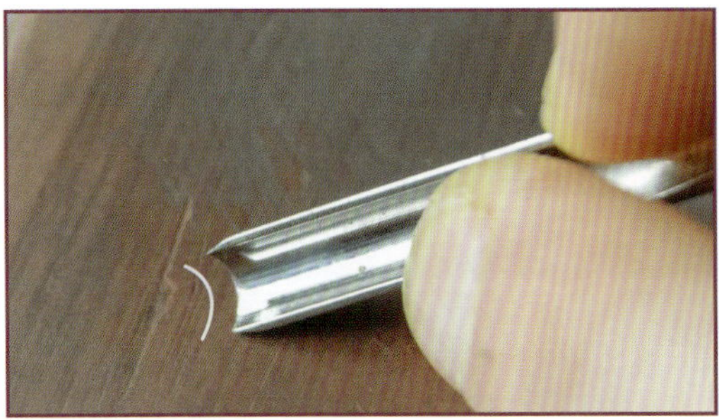

∧ A U-shaped tool is sharpened and honed by twisting it from side to side and corner to corner

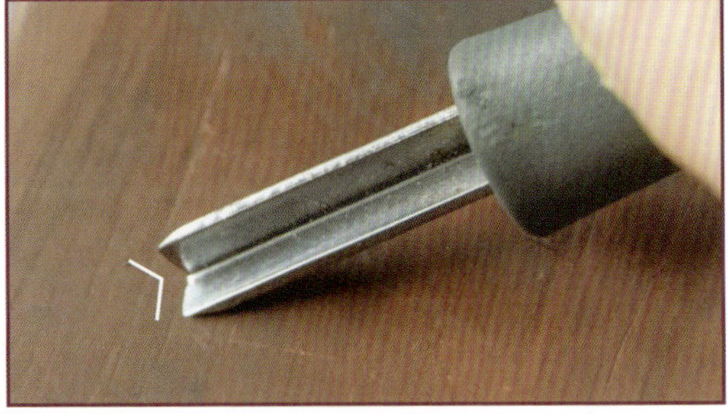

∧ A V-shaped tool is sharpened and honed by drawing each flat exterior side towards you

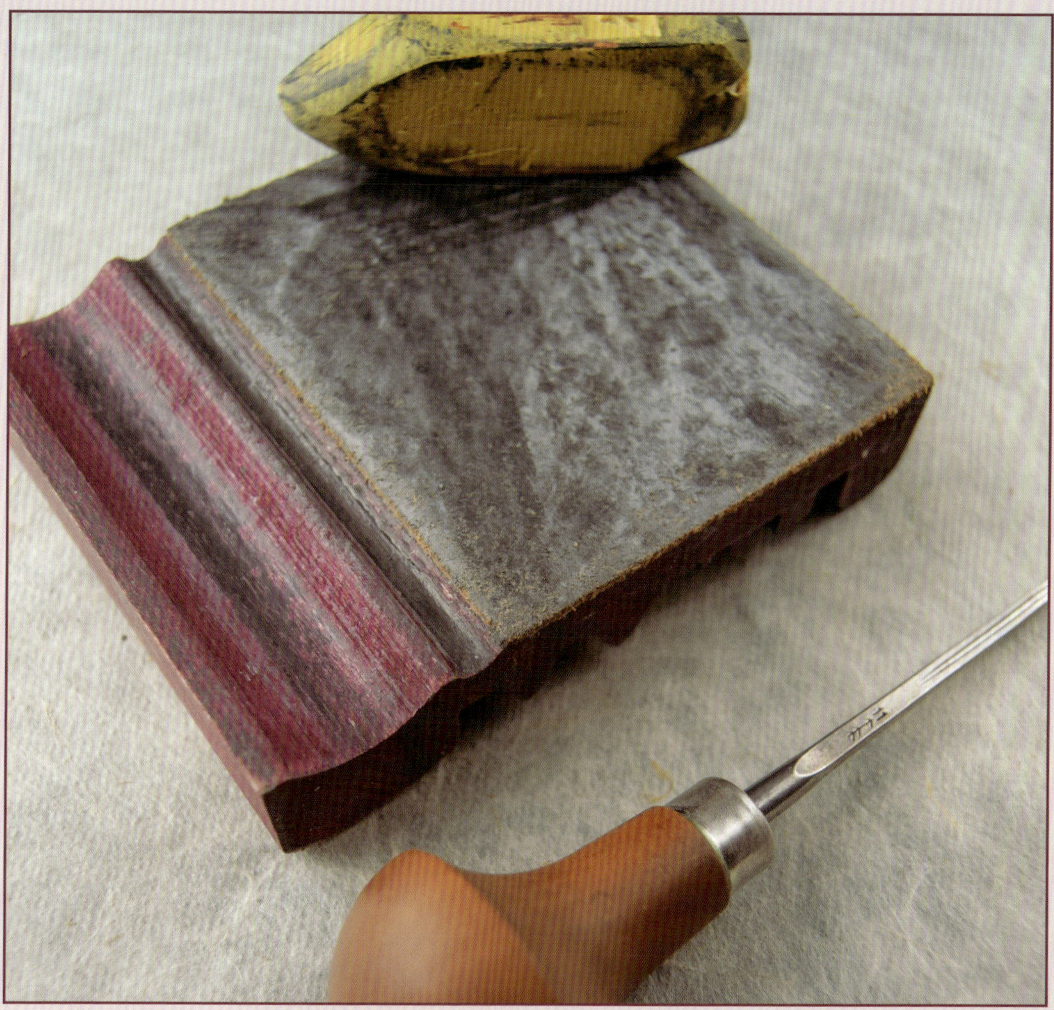

Λ The classic strop, with leather surface and polishing medium, also has a pointed edging on the reverse for smoothing the inside of the V- and U-shaped tools

STROP

A strop is a honing tool that can be used to keep the edges of carving tools sharp. It is made of leather, onto which a buffing polish must be rubbed before honing. As a general rule, you should aim to hone your carving tools on a strop for one to two minutes for every thirty to sixty minutes of carving.

Some strops and stones have curved or pointed features that allow you to smooth the insides of the carving tools, too. Ideally your tools should be sharpened at a very shallow angle, around 20°, and then also at a slightly raised angle, about 30°.

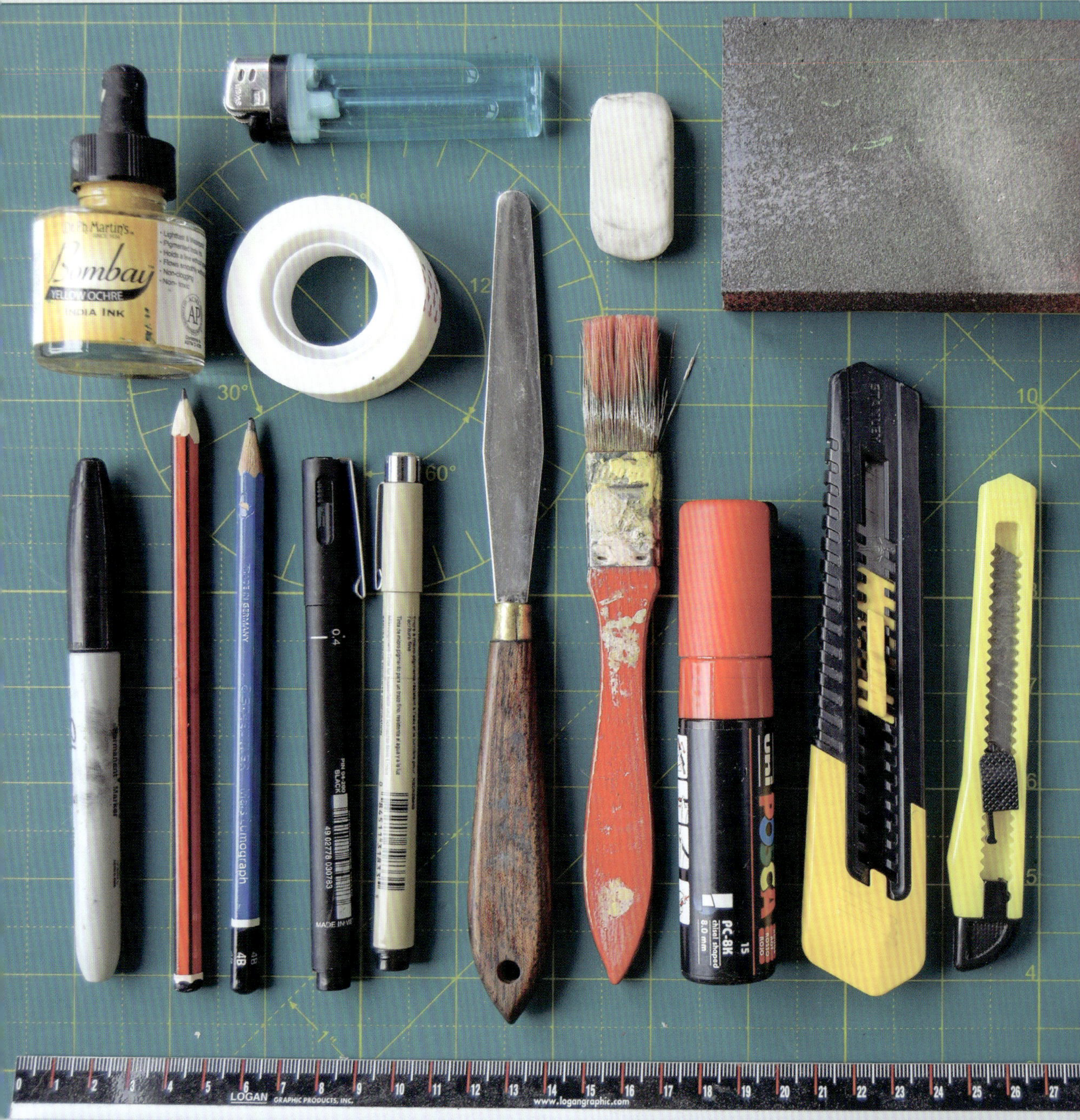

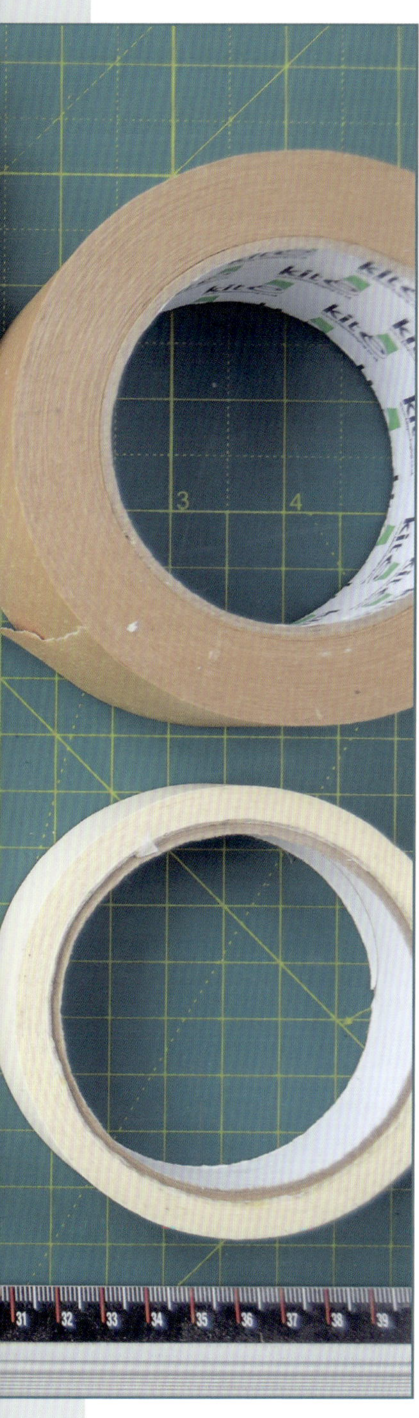

EXTRA GEAR

There are various other tools and materials you may need as a linocut printmaker, including:

KEEPING CLEAN & TIDY
Brushes
Apron
Gloves

DRAWING
Pencils
Eraser
Fine pens
Marker pen

LINO PREPARATION
Fine sandpaper or block
Posca marker or ink

CUTTING
Cutting mat
Scalpel
Craft knives
Steel ruler

MIXING INK
Palette knife
Surface to mix on (*ideally a sheet of thick glass, as it's hard, smooth, and easy to clean*)

TAPE
High- and low-tack masking tape

◄ Other useful bits of kit you will need, all of which are available at most art or DIY shops, or online

CLEANING MATERIALS

Printmaking can be a messy business. A few tools and materials you'll require for clearing up include:

- Paper towels and old rags for cleaning lino, surfaces, and rollers.

- Solvents for cleaning oil-based ink, of which there are different kinds available, including artist's white spirit or vegetable oil. Citrus-based solvents are better for the environment and don't give off harmful fumes.

- A paint scraper for scraping any excess ink off the mixing plate before the final wipe down.

REUSE LEFTOVER INK

If you end up with unused ink on the plate, there's no need to waste it. If it's unmixed and from a tin, simply scrape it up and put it back. If it's a mixed colour, transfer it to an airtight jar. This will reduce waste and save you both time and money.

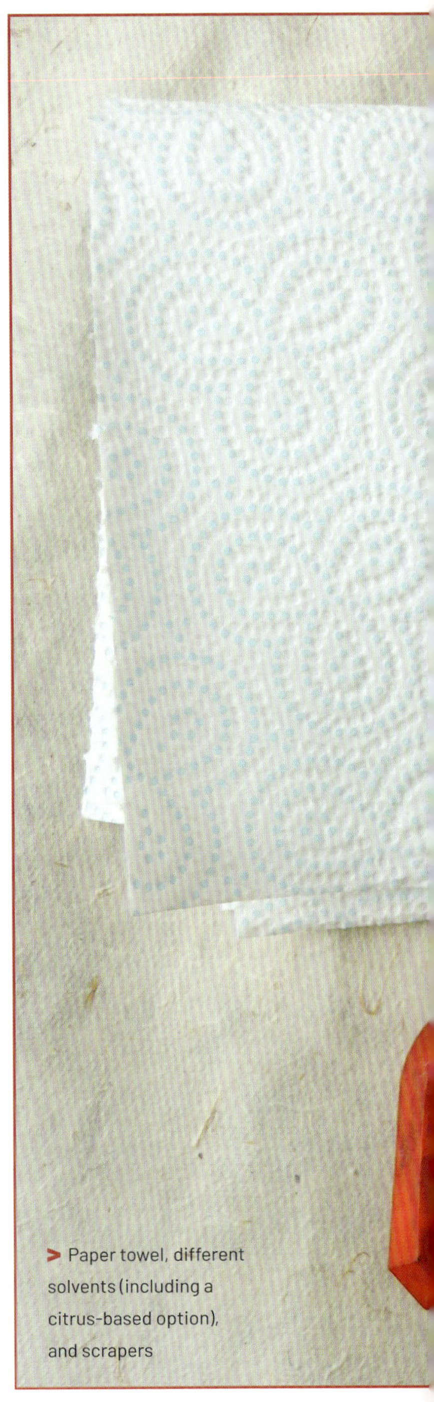

> Paper towel, different solvents (including a citrus-based option), and scrapers

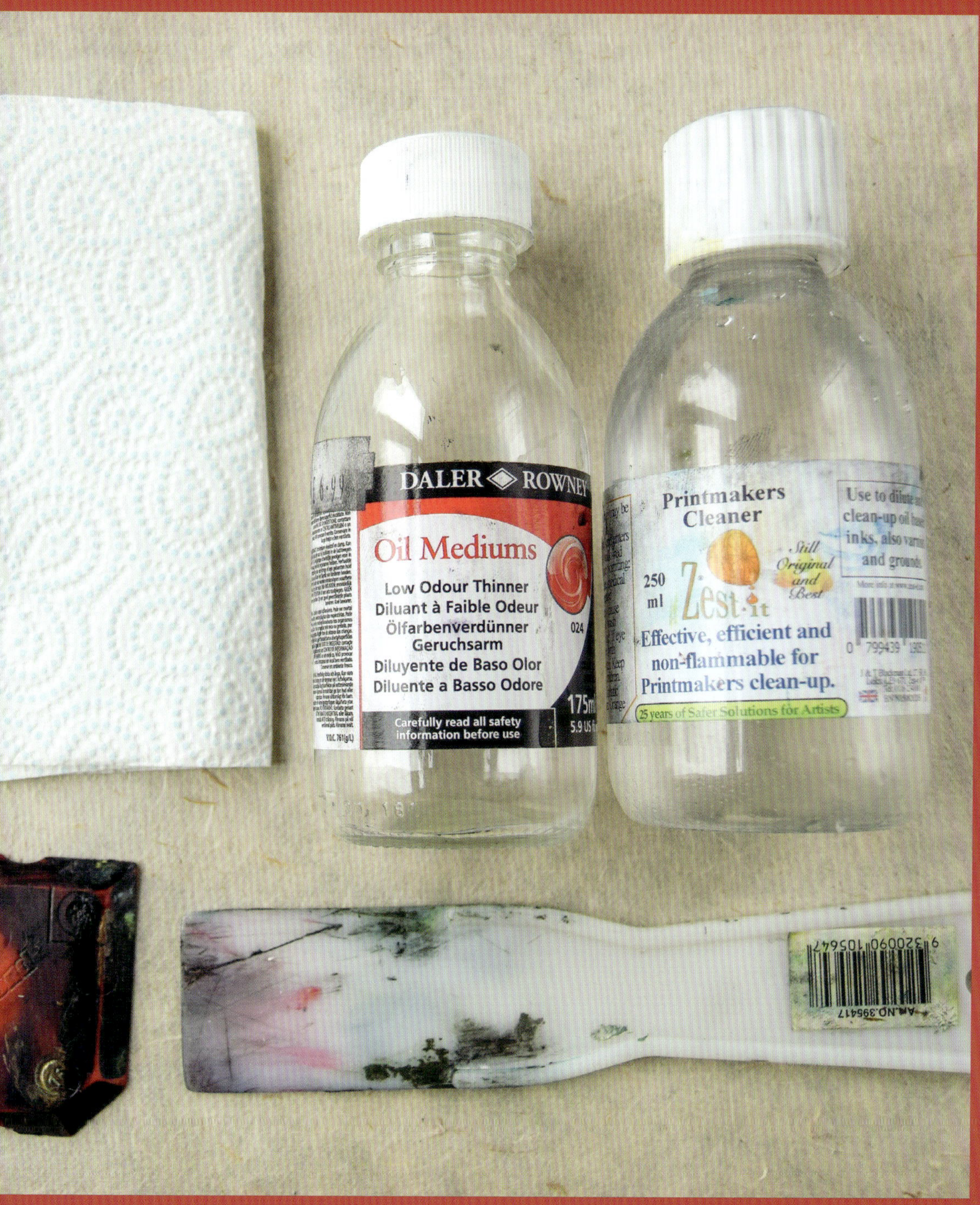
DALER ROWNEY
Oil Mediums
Low Odour Thinner
Diluant à Faible Odeur
Ölfarbenverdünner
Geruchsarm
Diluyente de Baso Olor
Diluente a Basso Odore
024
175ml
5.9 US fl oz
Carefully read all safety
information before use
Printmakers
Cleaner
250
ml
Zest·it
Still
Original
and
Best
Effective, efficient and
non-flammable for
Printmakers clean-up.
Use to dilute
clean-up oil based
inks, also varni
and grounds
25 years of Safer Solutions for Artists

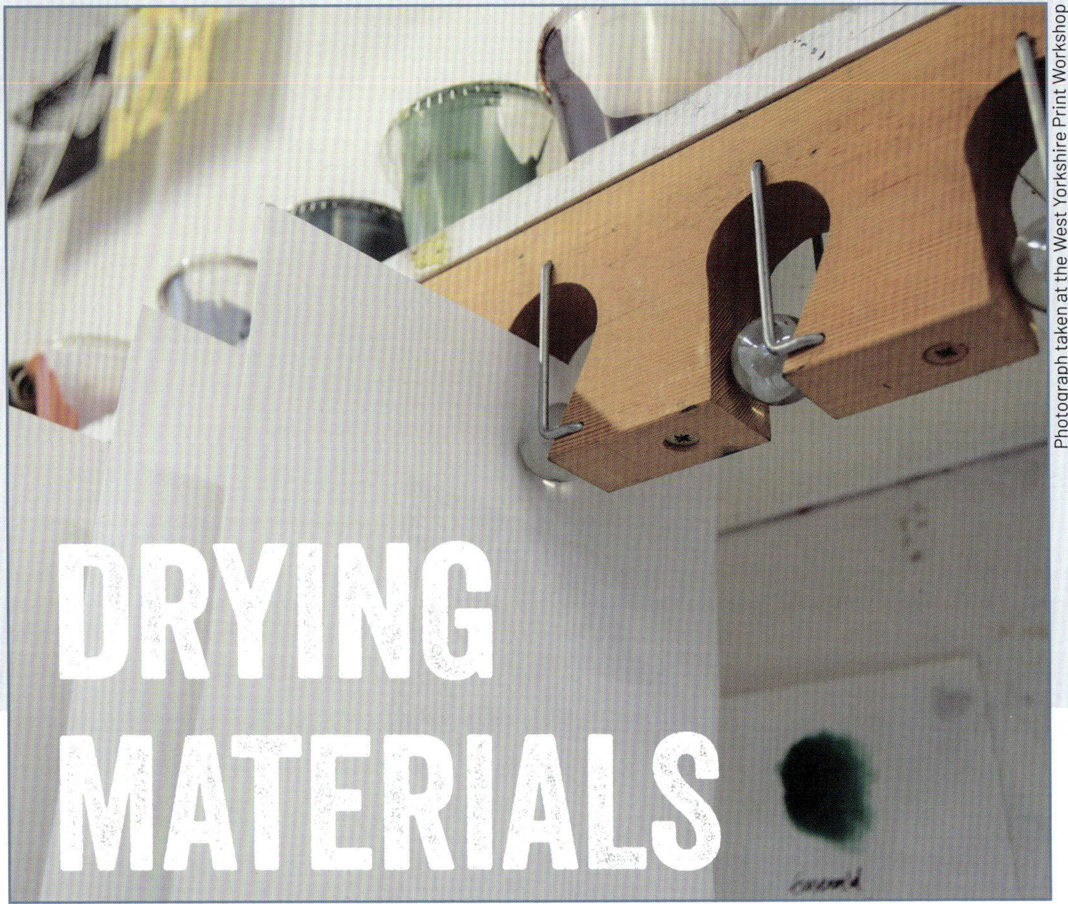

∧ A drying rack that uses marbles to grip the paper

The way you dry your prints will depend on the size of your workspace. These are the most common methods:

MARBLE-GRIPPING HANGER

Suspended from above, a marble-gripping hanger can hold a number of prints securely.

FLIP-UP DRYING RACK

Wall-mounted or freestanding, a flip-up drying rack can hold lots of prints. They don't take up too much space, though larger models can often be found in print workshops.

STRING & PEGS

A clothes line is a useful option if floor space is limited. Simply pin each end of the string to high points in your home or studio, then hang prints from it with pegs. If using clothes pegs, insert a small slip of paper between the peg and print to ensure the paper isn't marked or creased.

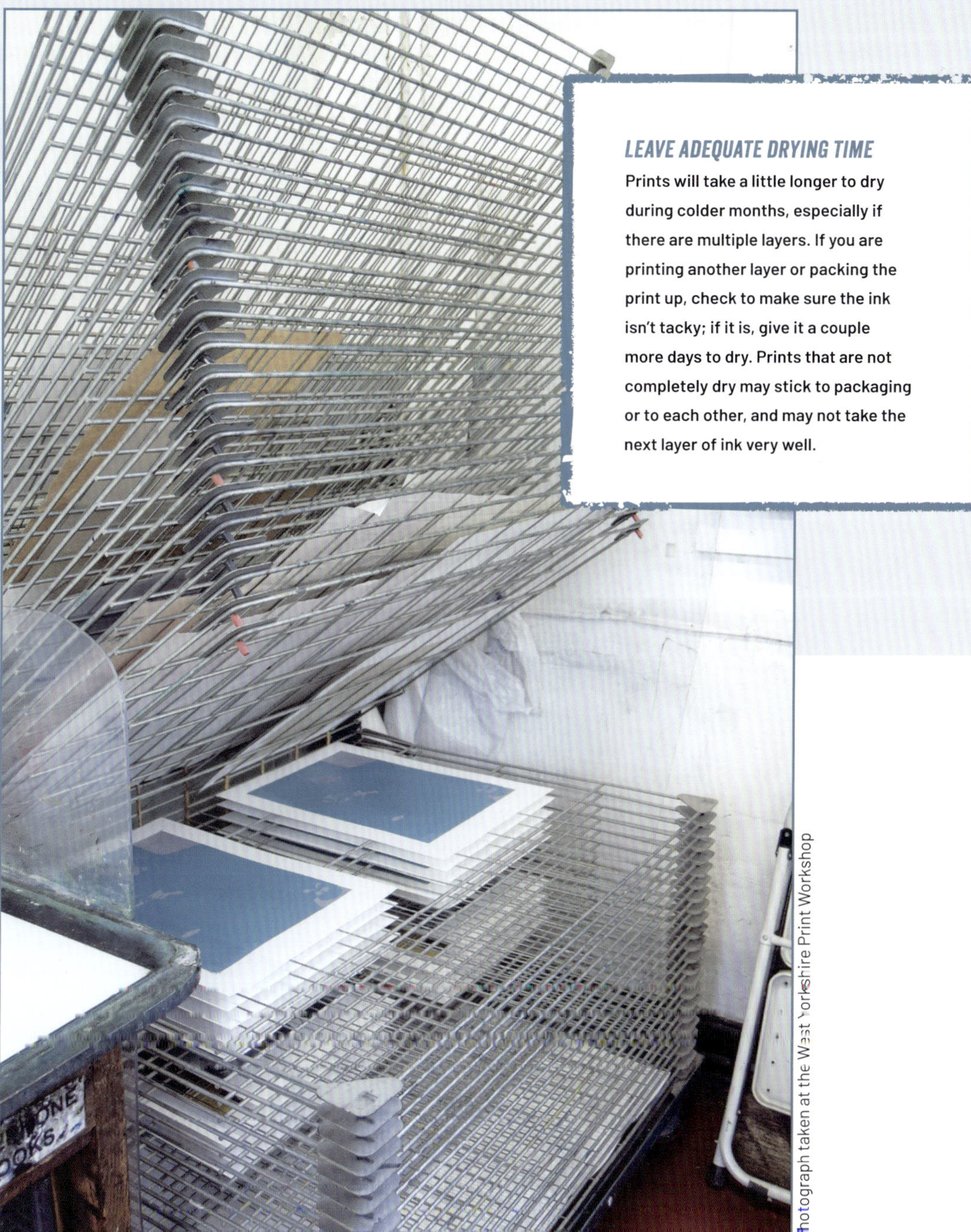

⋀ A large, metal flip-up drying rack

WORKSPACE

Every printmaker's workspace will be different, depending on what space you have available. When working from home, this can sometimes be very little. Here are a few recommendations for keeping your space organized:

PEG BOARD

These are great for hanging tools, inks, tape rolls, and rollers.

TOOL CABINETS

Often used by mechanics, these cabinets are useful for storing inks, tools, lino, and other materials.

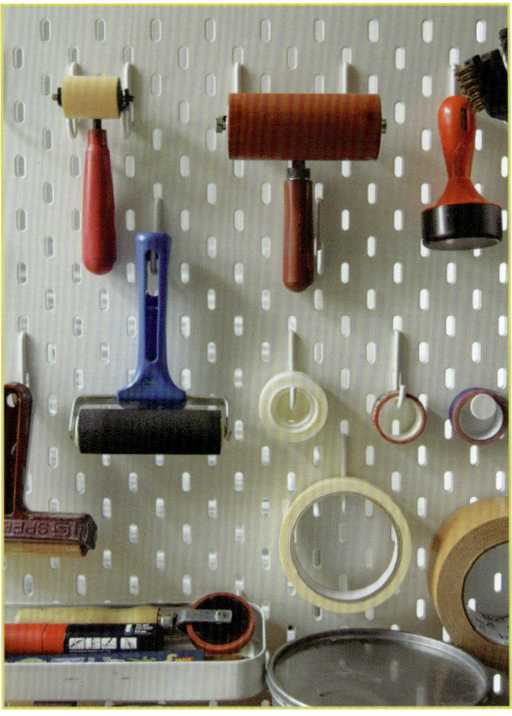

∧ Peg boards can be wall-mounted or clamped onto your desk

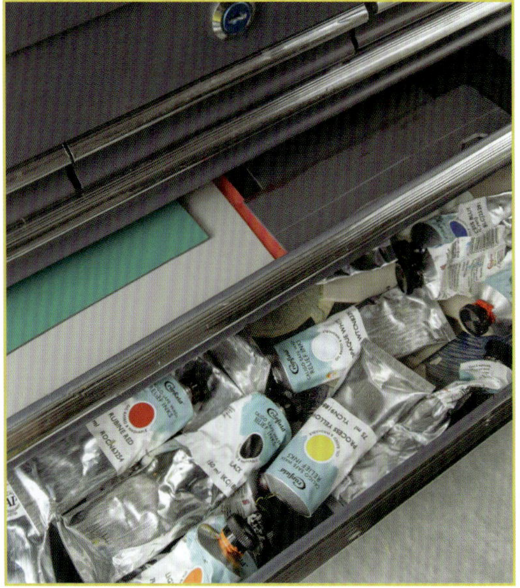

∧ Tool cabinets are robust units for storing tools and materials, keeping messy ink tubes out of sight

LIGHTING

Your workspace should be well lit when you're carving and printing. This is important for using any sharp tools safely, as well as enabling you to see your designs and ink colours accurately. A good sturdy lamp will help during late-night carving sessions.

PRINT STORAGE

Trays, shelves, or an architect's plan chest are useful for keeping your prints flat and dry.

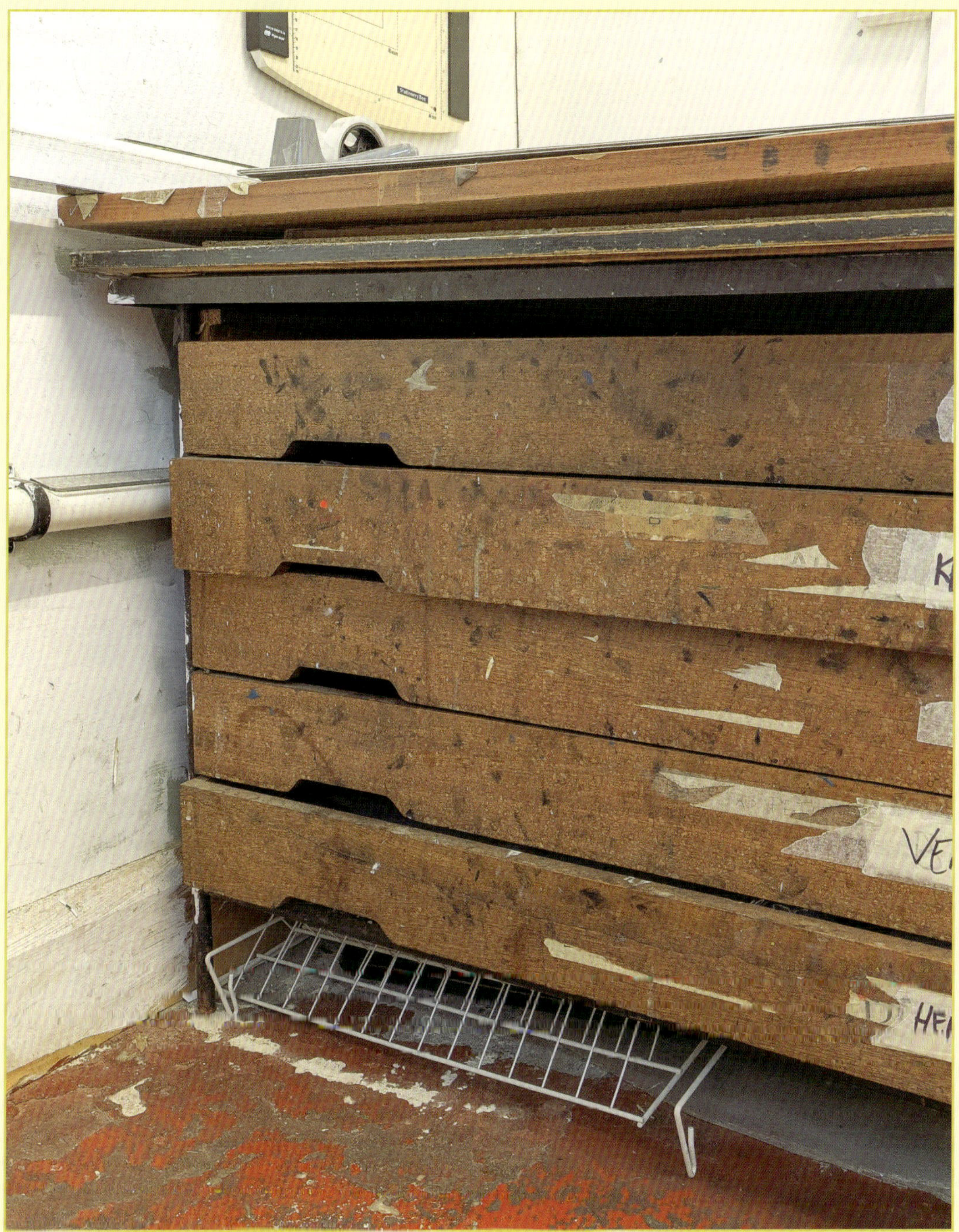

▲ Though expensive, plan chests are a great way to store lino blocks and prints, keeping them flat, dry, and secure

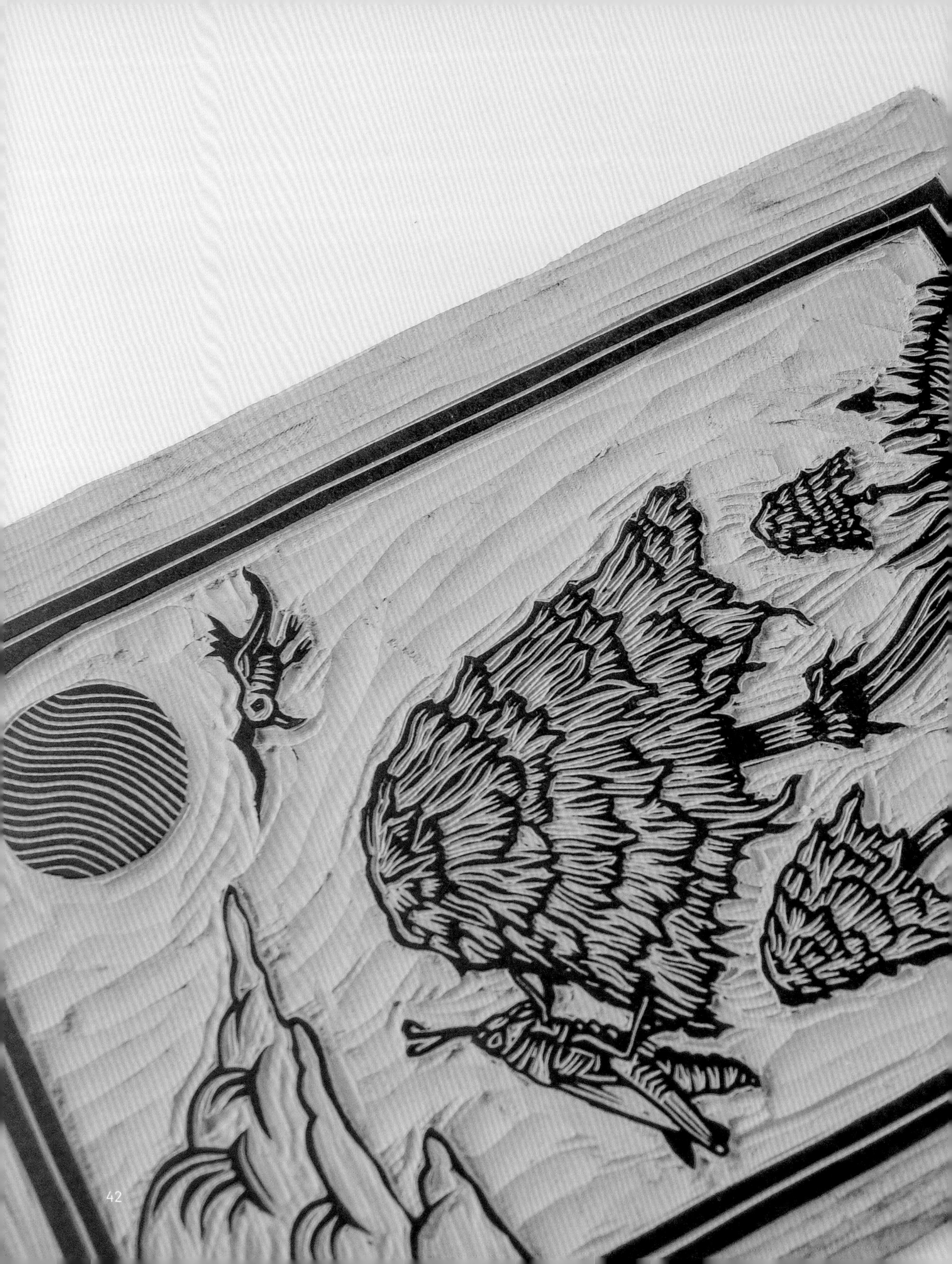

PROCESSES

BY GARETH BARNES (SPINDLE PRINTER)

DRAWING

Before you begin transferring designs to lino, carving them, and turning them into beautiful prints, you first need to come up with ideas to bring to life. This is the stage at which you can really let your creativity and imagination go wild.

Most printmakers sketch out ideas using a good old-fashioned pencil or pen, but using digital drawing software on a tablet (such as Procreate on the iPad) is becoming increasingly popular and has a few added benefits. While this isn't a book on how to draw, this chapter contains a few useful pointers that will help you turn your ideas into a finished design.

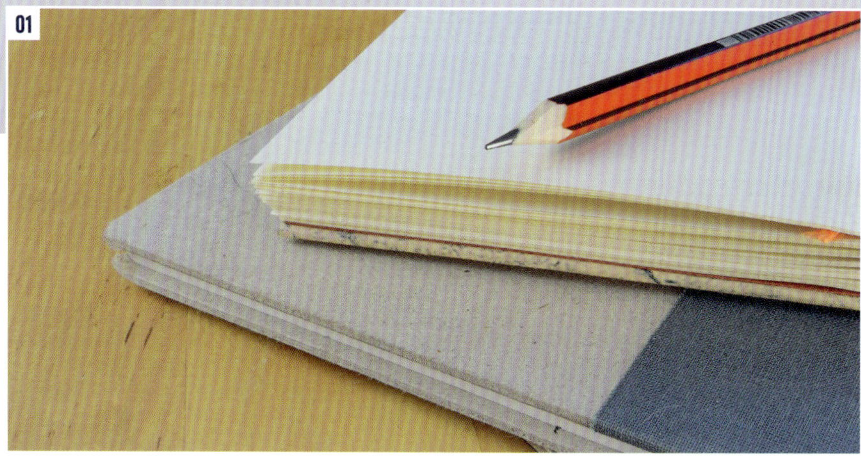

WORKING ON PAPER

01 Start by finding a sketchbook or sketchpad containing paper that feels good to draw on, such as a medium-weight cartridge paper that isn't too slick or smooth. These can be bought at any art or stationary shop.

Next, select an HB or 2B pencil. These are ideal for sketching out small design ideas (softer pencils will likely smudge). Alternatively, a fine ink pen can be used to draw ideas, or to go over pencil sketches to make them bolder and easier to trace later.

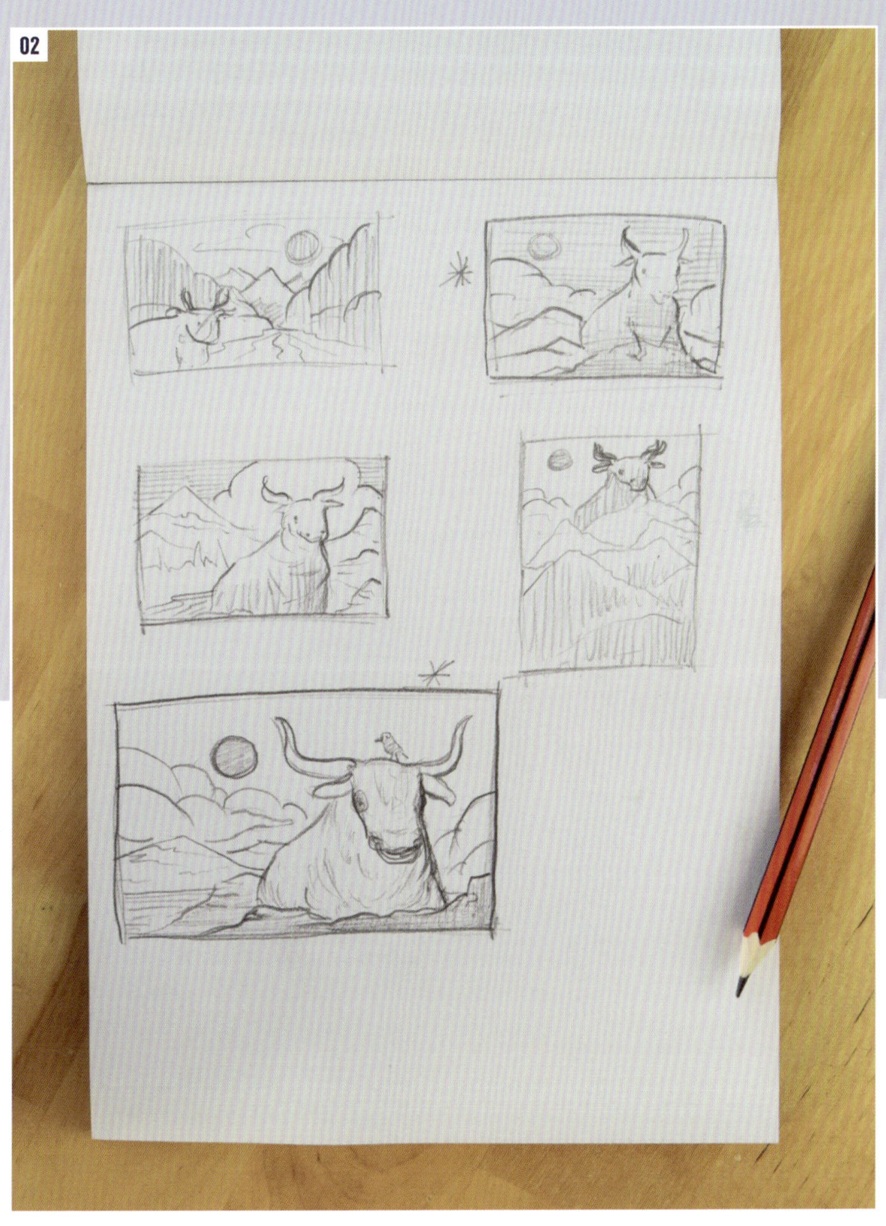

02 Every artist has their preferred way of transferring the
ideas inside their head onto paper. It can be useful to start by
sketching out small thumbnail drawings. These are a good way
to work out the basic composition with minimal detail.

CONTINUED >

03 You can then draw your preferred thumbnails on a larger scale, working in extra details. This is the step where you can start to figure out which areas might be lighter or darker.

04 Jotting down a few annotations or notes can be a useful way to record your thoughts and plan out the design.

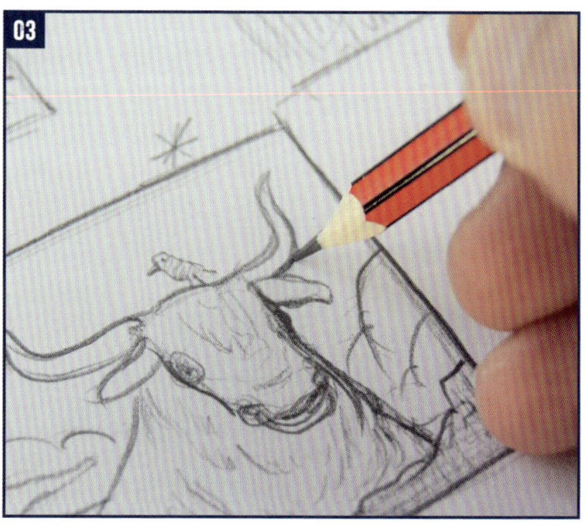

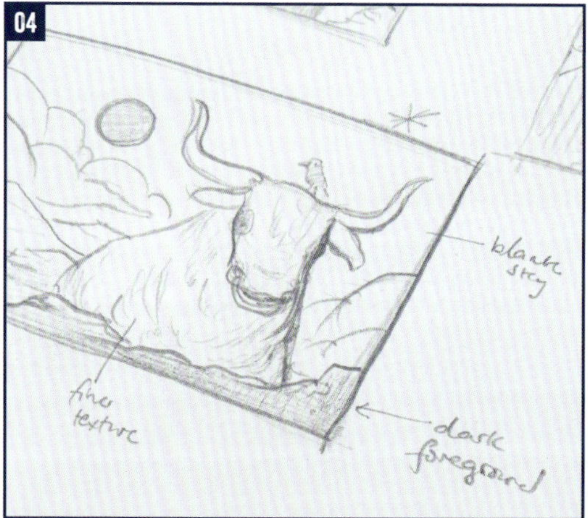

05 Once you're happy with your design, scale the drawing to full size. This is the stage when you can begin to work in more detail, light, dark, foreground, and background. You can also start to think about how you might carve it; whether you want to use textures or patterns in certain places, or make certain lines thicker, for example.

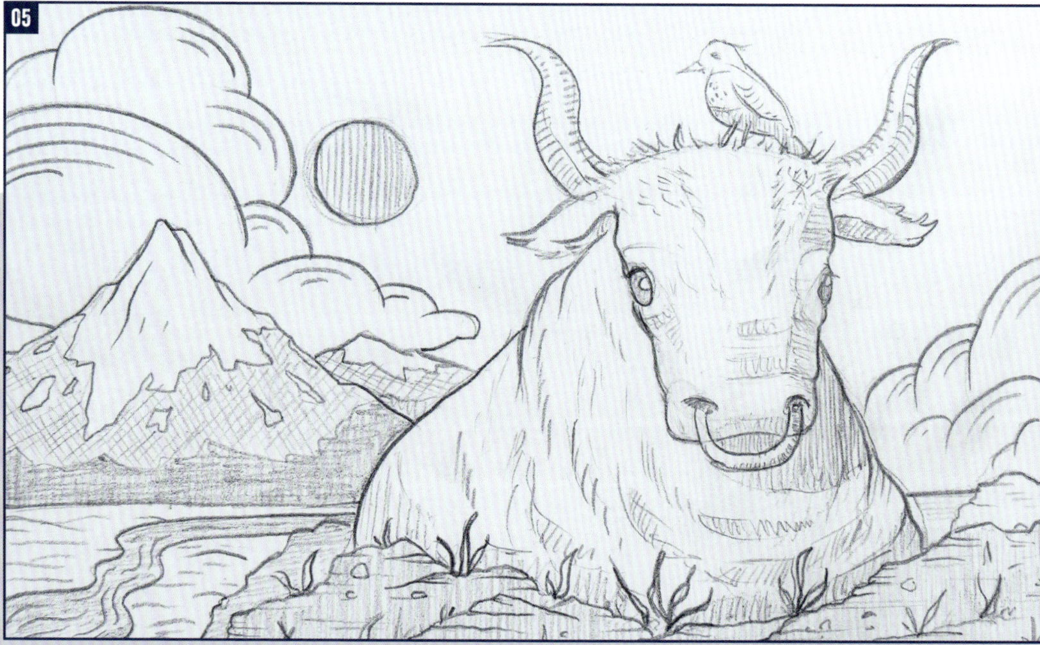

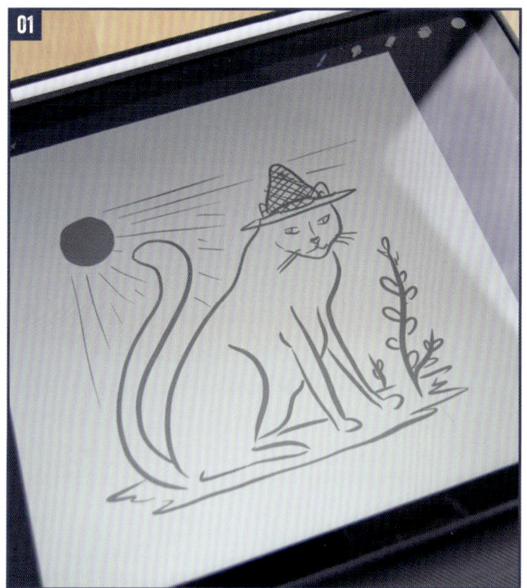

WORKING DIGITALLY

Using a tablet with a stylus (an electronic pencil) is another great way to sketch out ideas. There are several digital drawing apps available, each offering many tools, including the magic Undo function. Resizing and editing images is generally much easier when working digitally, plus designs can be easily reversed and printed out ready for transferring to lino.

01 Start by doodling a rough outline of your design, then slightly lower the opacity.

02 On a new layer, draw over the first sketch, refining the design, then lower its opacity. You can then delete or switch off the first layer.

03 Again, create a new layer and further refine the design, then switch off the previous layer. Continue these steps as many times as needed until you settle on a design you're happy with.

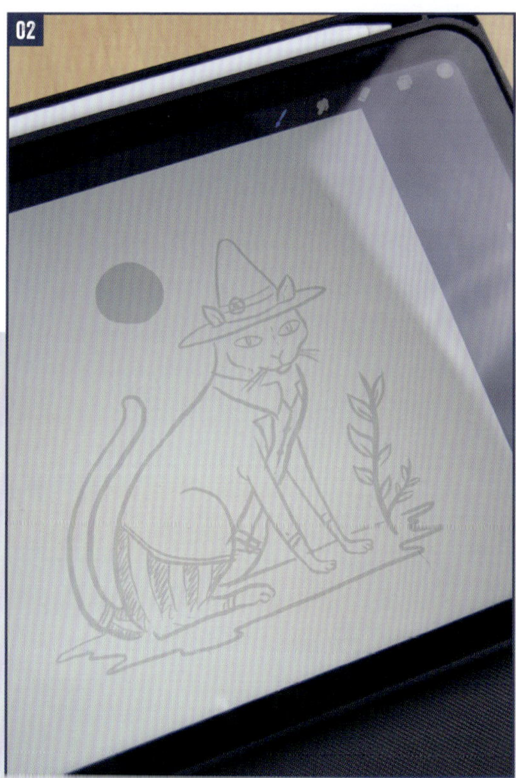

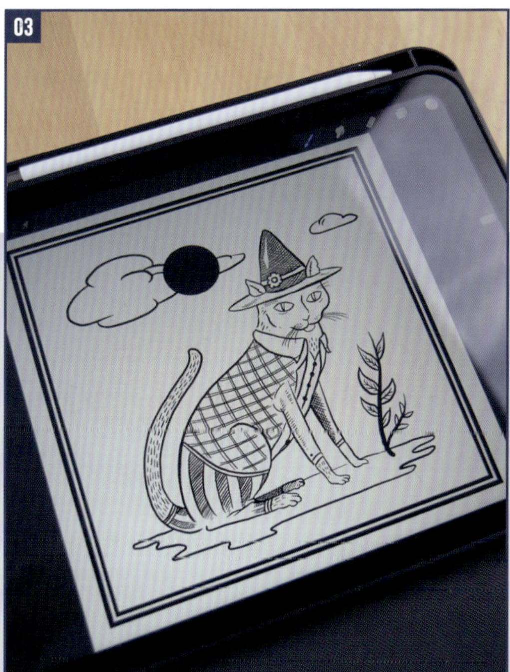

PREPARING THE LINO

Before you begin carving, there are a few tasks to complete to ensure the lino is prepped and ready. The steps below apply to all types of lino.

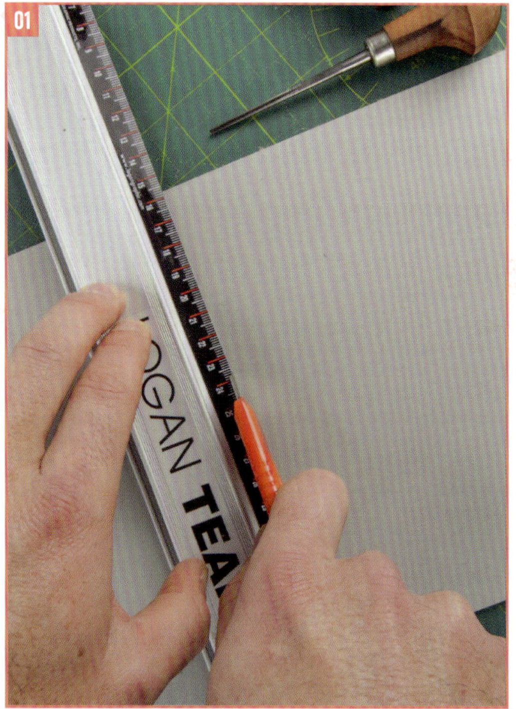

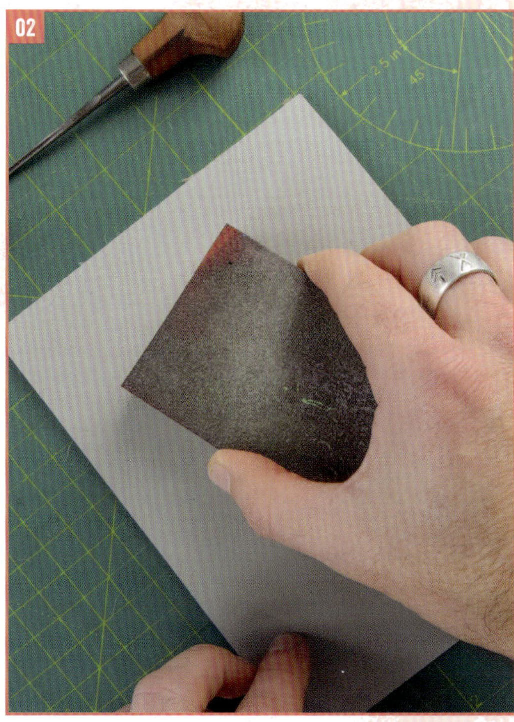

01 Using a large craft knife and steel ruler, cut the lino to the desired size. (Be careful not to cut your fingers!)

02 Use a fine-grit sanding block to gently sand the lino. This will help to remove any unwanted oil from the surface while also making it smoother, resulting in more even ink coverage.

03 Use ink or acrylic paint pens to coat the lino in a bright or dark colour. This will make it easier to see where you've carved.

04 Using a wide carving tool, bevel the edge of the lino by carving along it at a roughly 45° angle. This creates a softer edge, which is less likely to make a crease or impression on the paper during printing. You can skip this step if you want that effect, or if your design is going to go right up to the edge of the paper.

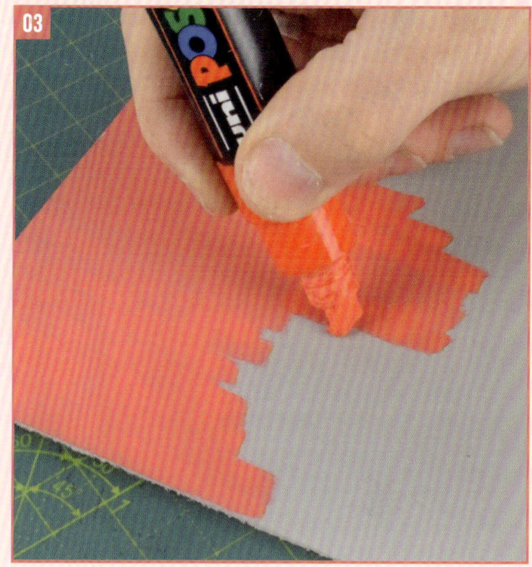

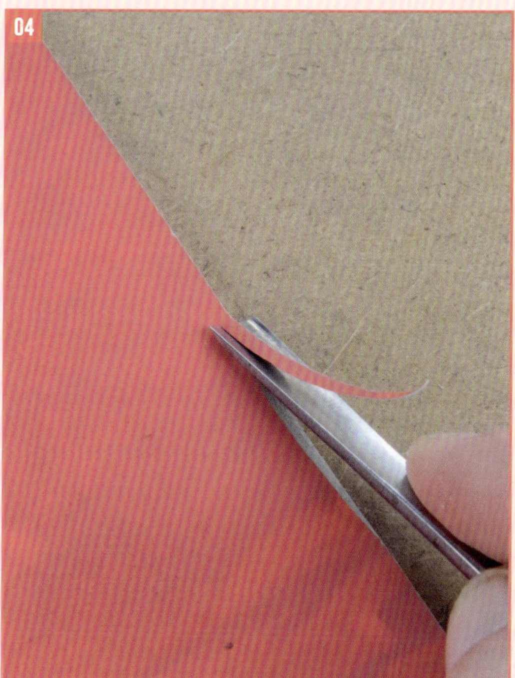

HESSIAN STRANDS

If using traditional hessian-backed lino, strands of hessian can sometimes stick out from the edge of the block. These can pick up ink when it's applied, which is then transferred to the paper, resulting in unwanted inky marks. Running a small flame along the edge before and after carving will get rid of these strands. Always take care to avoid burns and do not let children do this step.

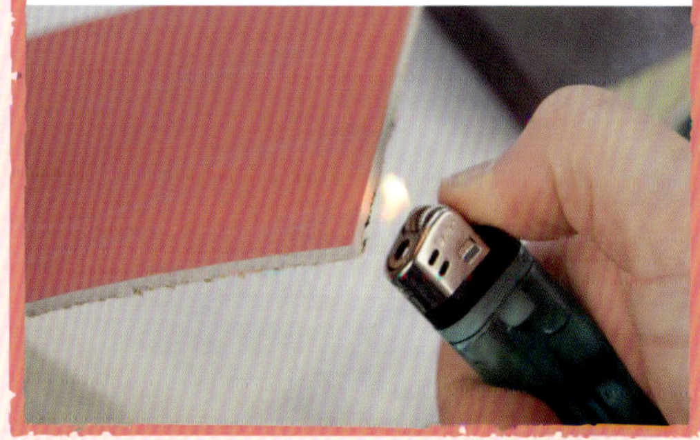

TRANSFERRING THE IMAGE

There are many different ways to transfer your design onto the lino block. Less commonly used methods include using heat, PVA glue, or gel mediums, but these can have patchy results and involve more materials than are necessary. The two methods detailed in this section are reliable and easy to follow.

If using the softer nylon lino, these methods will still work, but you will likely need to go over the design afterwards with a pen or pencil, or just draw the design directly onto the lino.

OPTION 1: USING A PHOTOCOPY OR PRINTOUT OF THE REVERSED DESIGN

You will need:

- Graphite or carbon paper
- Sharp pencil or ballpoint pen
- Masking tape
- Prepared lino

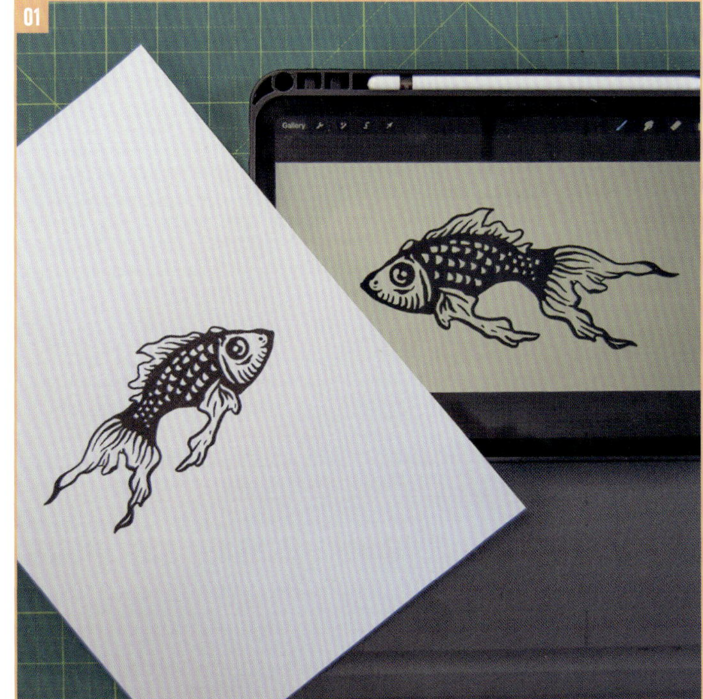

01 Print out or photocopy your design in reverse, making sure it's the right size to fit the prepared lino block.

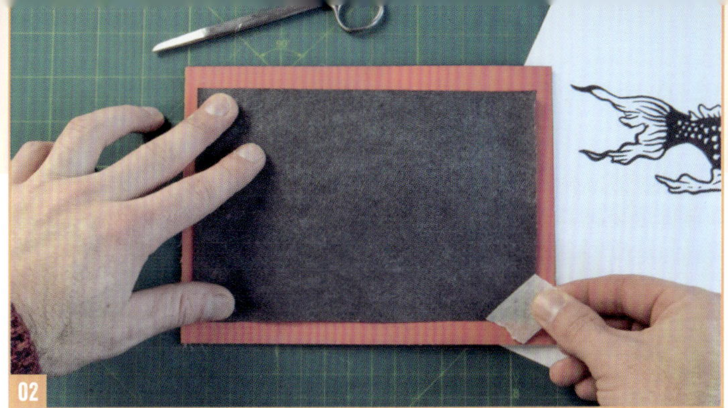

02 Cut a piece of graphite or carbon paper large enough to cover the image, then tape it to the lino with the shiny side facing down.

03 Securely tape the image to the lino.

04 Using a sharpened pencil or ballpoint pen, draw over the outline of the image.

05 Peel back the paper to check the design has transferred onto the lino as intended.

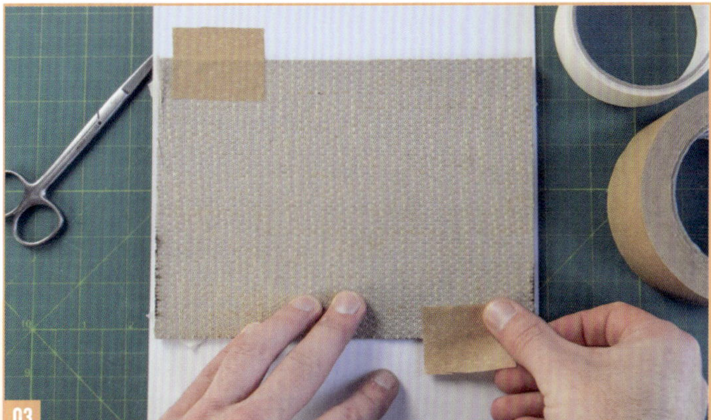

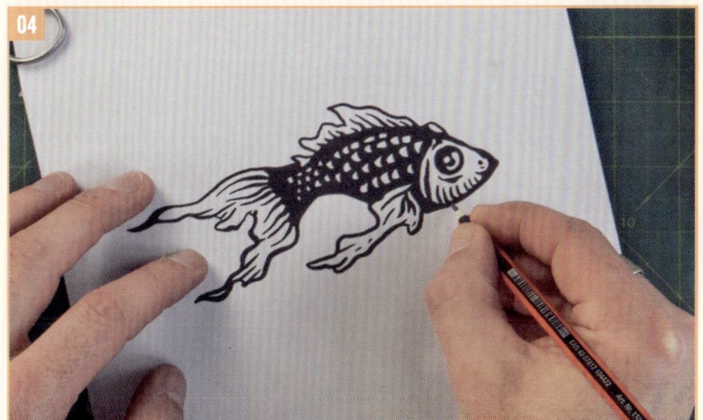

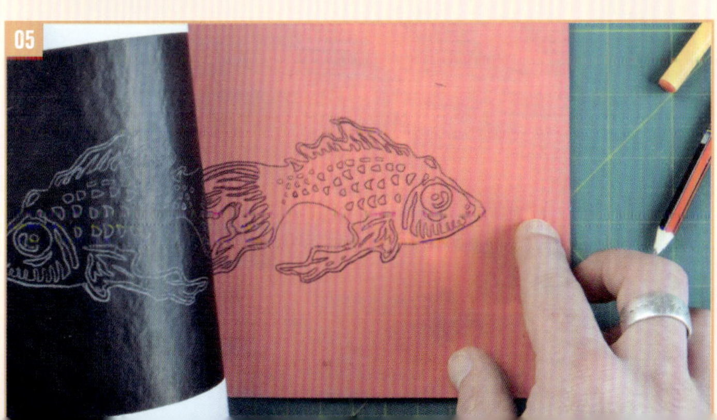

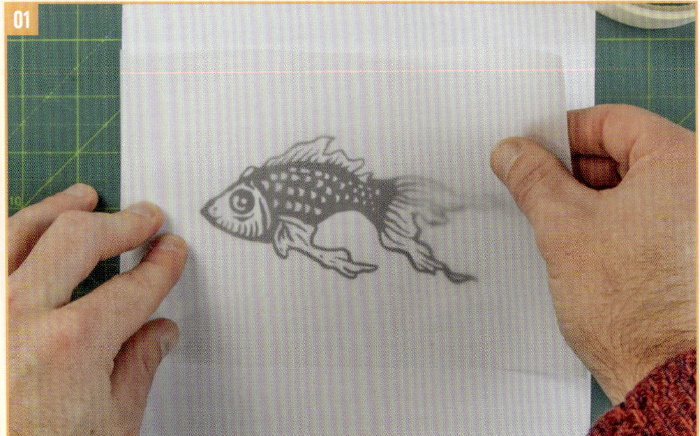

OPTION 2 : USING YOUR ORIGINAL DESIGN (NOT REVERSED)

You will need:

- Tracing paper
- Graphite or carbon paper
- Sharp pencil or ballpoint pen
- Masking tape
- Prepared lino

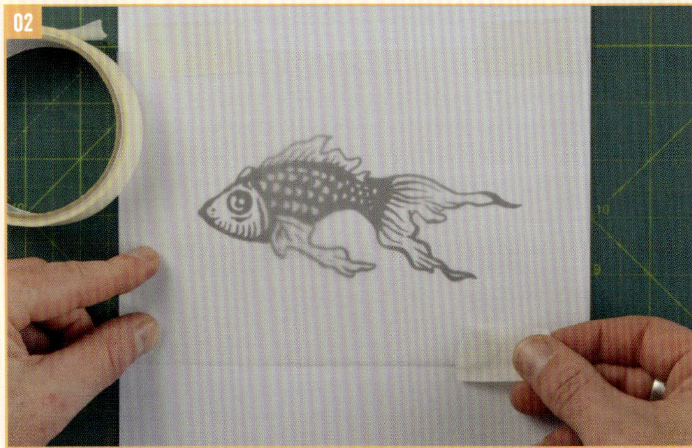

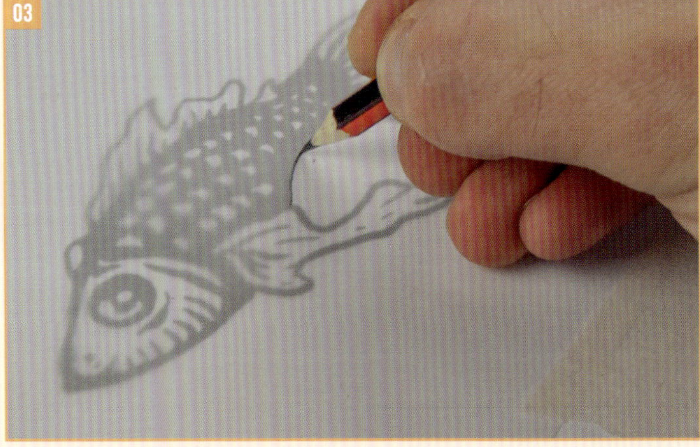

01 Cut a piece of tracing paper that is large enough to cover the design.

02 Securely tape the tracing paper down over your design using masking tape.

03 Using a sharpened pencil or ballpoint pen, firmly draw over the outline of the image.

04 Tape the graphite or carbon paper to the lino with the shiny side facing down.

05 Flip the traced image over and tape it down onto the transfer paper.

06 Draw back over the traced image.

07 Peel back the tracing layers and check the image has transferred successfully.

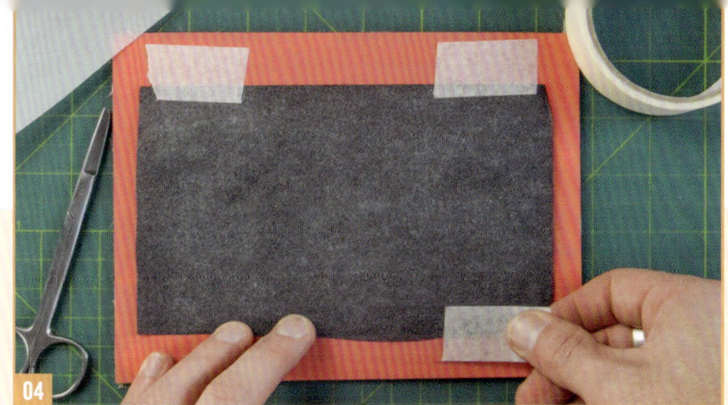

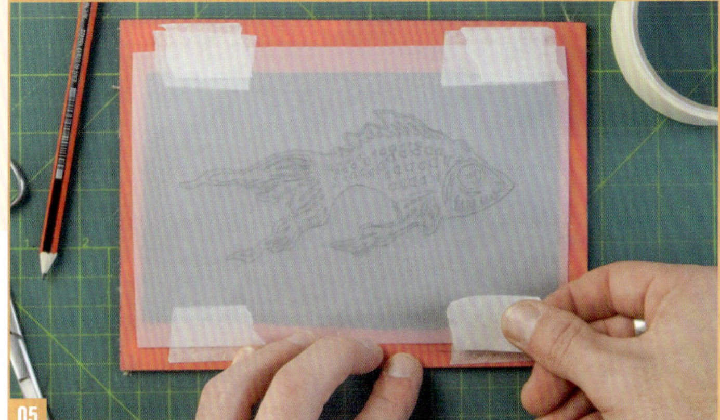

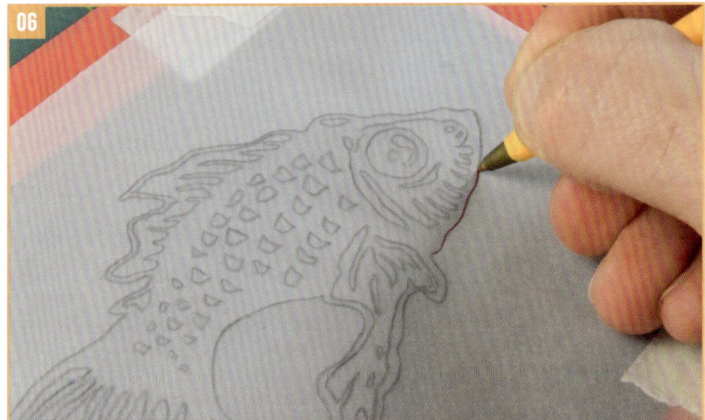

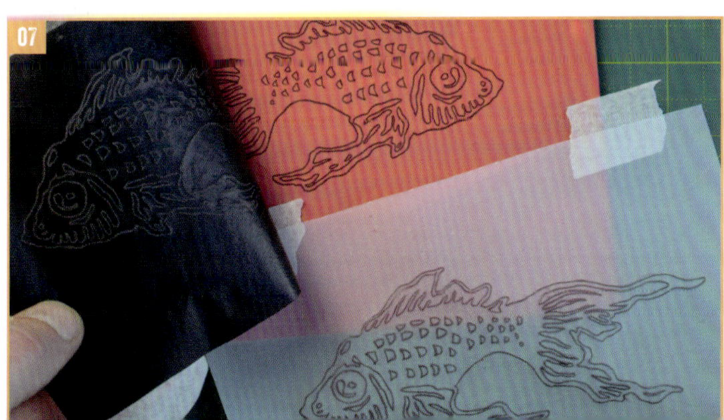

CARVING

Once you have transferred or drawn your design onto the lino, it's time to start carving. Whichever type of tool you choose (see page 17), it's a good idea to use a range of different shapes and sizes. This will allow you to be much more creative with the kinds of marks and lines you can make.

Creating a variety of marks can add interesting features, depth, tonal range, and textures, which can really enhance your prints. This section will explore some of the different marks and line work you can achieve when carving lino.

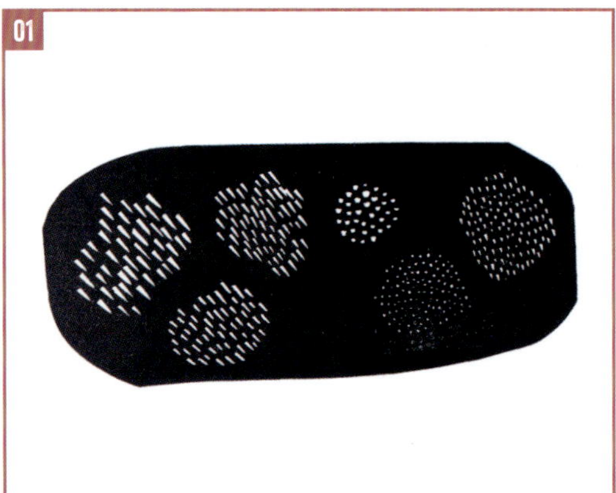

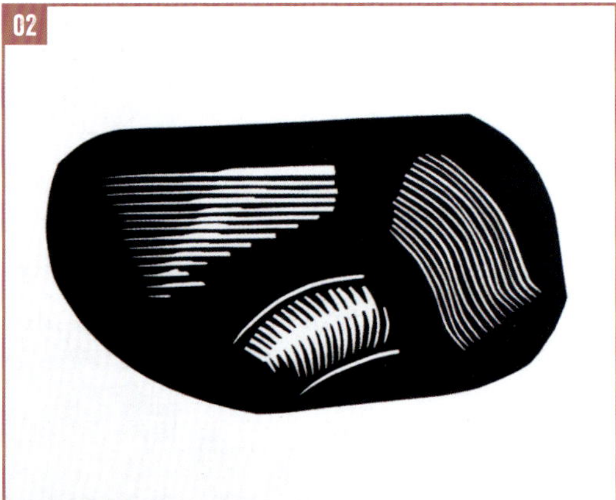

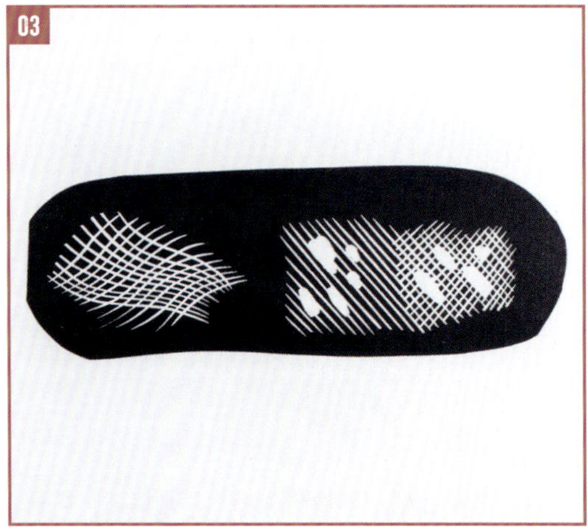

TYPES OF MARK-MAKING

01 Fine-tipped tools can be used to carve little dots or dashes, creating visually interesting textures or tones.

02 This type of line work creates beautiful patterns and textures. Varying the line thickness can give shapes form and depth.

03 Another way to add texture and variety is to cross-hatch the line work. You can then further carve into this to add a new layer of pattern or texture.

04 The shapes of the tools will naturally determine the types of grooves they carve, and sometimes these can be used to create interesting marks. The marks shown have been created using different-sized U-shaped tools.

05 Varying the line width can add form and depth, creating an obviously hand-carved look that makes your print more visually interesting.

06 Positive and negative elements can be used to great effect when you want to add depth to your images. In this example, showing a side-view of grass, the foreground is achieved by carving away that part of the image, leaving it white. The sky is then carved away too, leaving the the mid-ground grass as an area where ink will be added, which gives a sense of depth, light, and shadow.

07 Introducing bold and graphic elements into your work can take your designs to the next level.

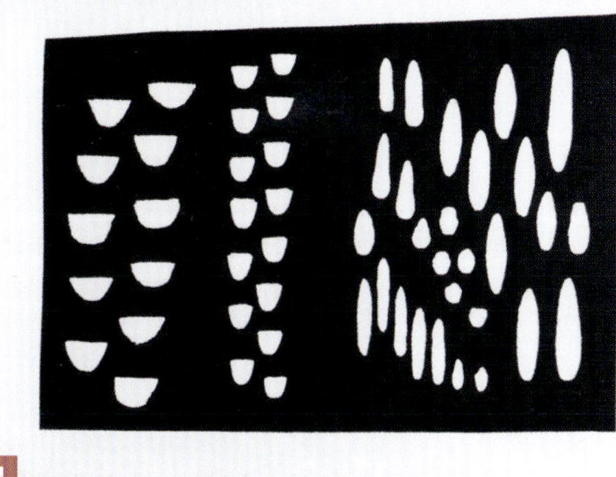

04

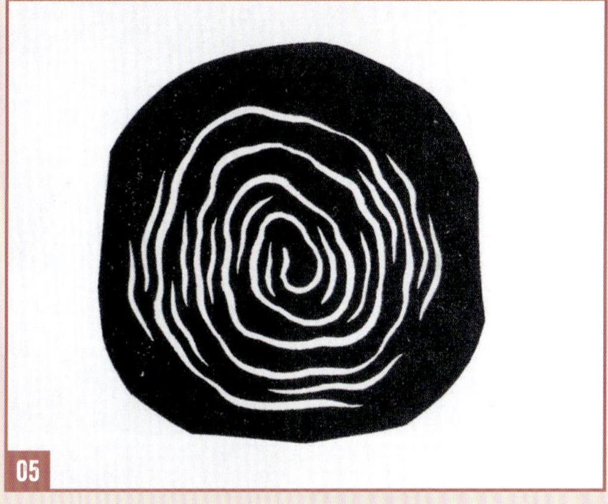

05

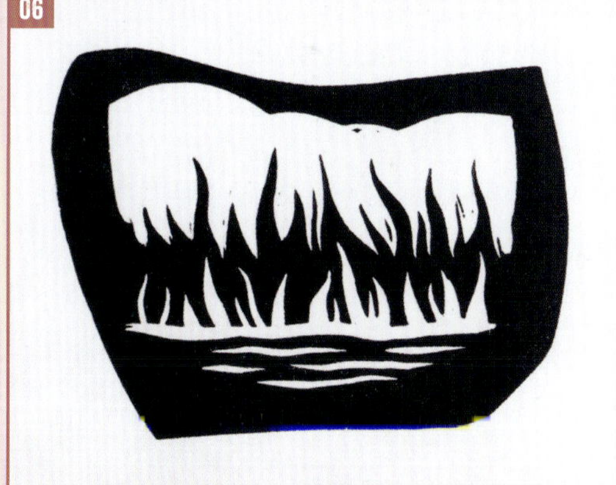

06

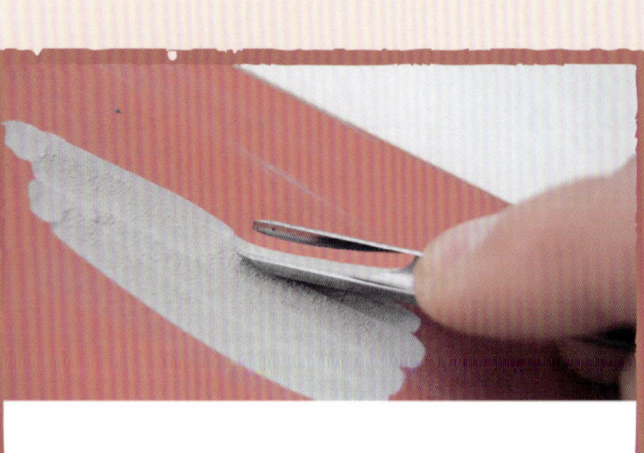

GOOD PRACTICE

To prevent injuries, remember to keep your tools sharp and to always carve away from yourself.

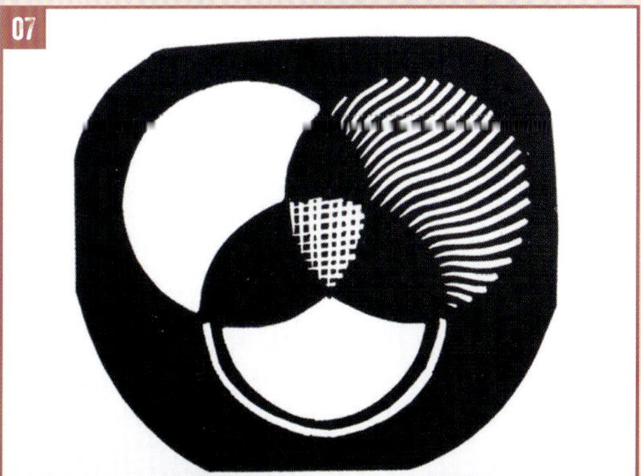

07

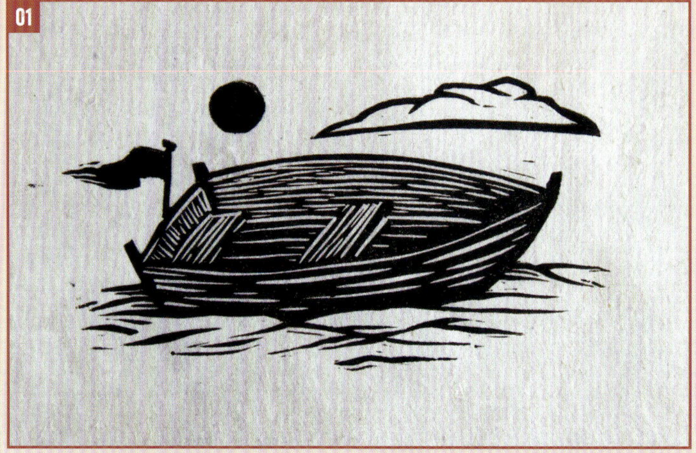

MARK-MAKING IN PRACTICE

01 Subtle variations of line thickness can create depth, giving a design a distinctive hand-carved look.

02 Crosshatching is a useful technique for giving objects form and shape.

03 Fine tools can be used to create a range of textures using dots or tiny dashes – a process called stippling.

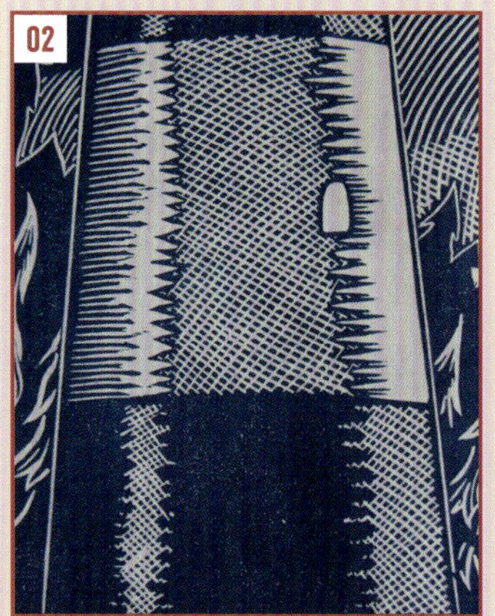

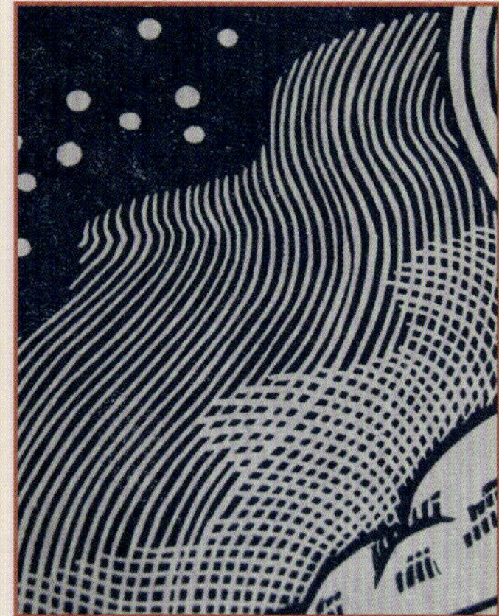

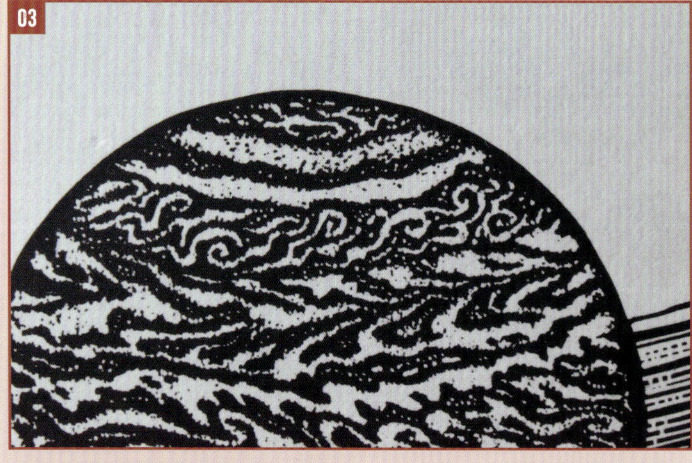

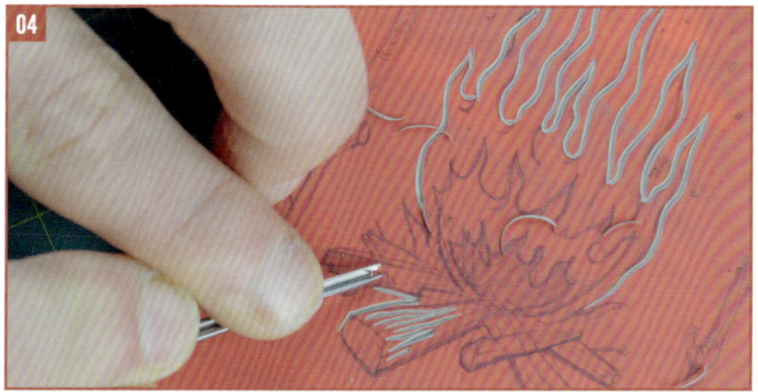

04 Some printmakers like to add line work and textures as they carve.

05 As you carve your design, you may want to check your progress midway through to make sure it's looking as intended and that no sections have been missed. Here are a couple of ways to do that:

a. Lay a thin sheet of paper over the lino, tape or hold it down firmly, then go over it with the side of a pencil lead, graphite stick, or pastel. This will reveal the carved image.

b. Alternatively, tip some cornflour (or similar) onto the lino and scrape across using a flat edge, filling the carved spaces. This will create a contrasting view of the carved image, providing a good idea of how it will look when printed.

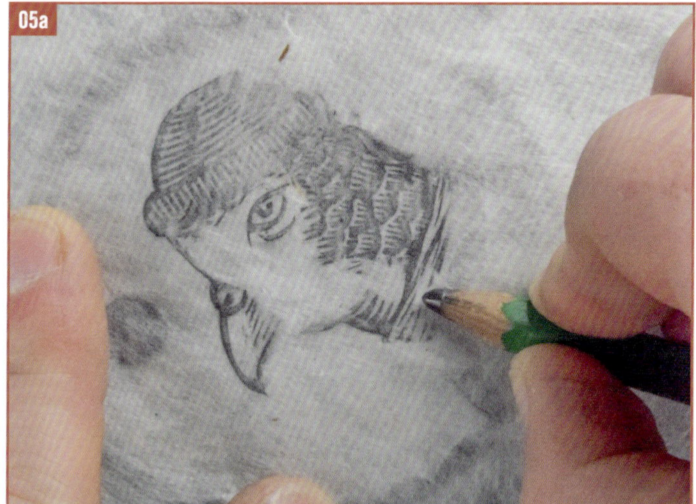

PREPPING PAPER

Once you have chosen your paper (see page 22), decide on size and prepare it for printing.

PAPER SIZE

When choosing paper size, leave a reasonable amount of space around the image. This will provide more flexibility when framing and mounting the print, allowing you to decide how closely you wish to crop the image. It's generally easier to find a frame for the standard paper sizes in your country, but there are no rules. Printmakers create artwork in many different sizes and formats.

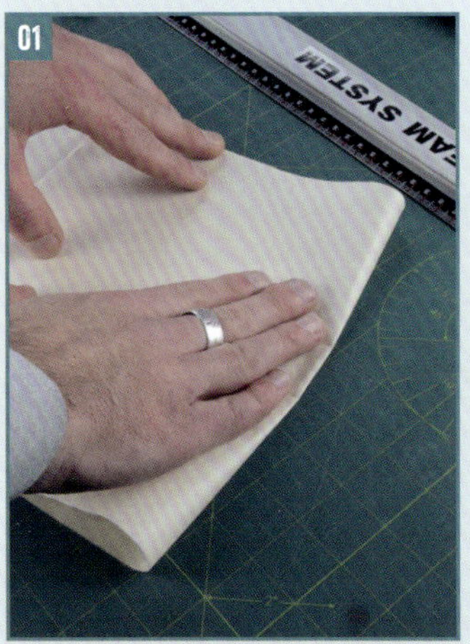

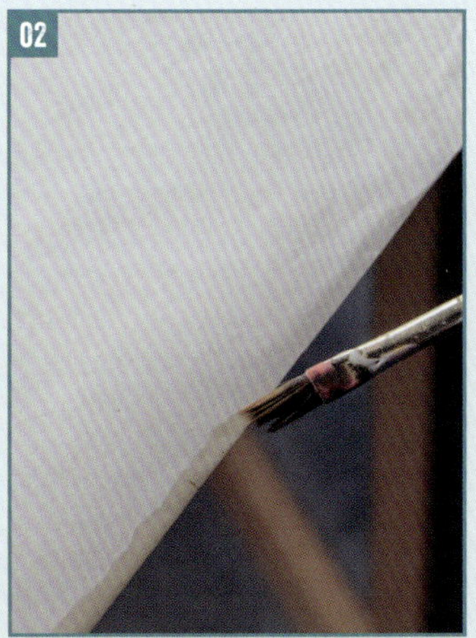

PAPER EDGE

Hard- or clean-edged paper is cut with a craft knife or scalpel, creating a straight, neat finish. Deckled edges have a feathered, torn, or handmade look to them, which is often kept visible when the print is framed. While you can buy special rulers that create a deckled edge as you tear the paper along them, you can easily create this effect without one.

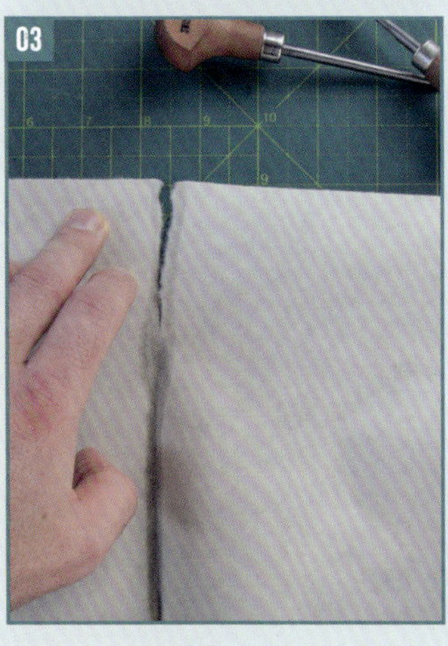

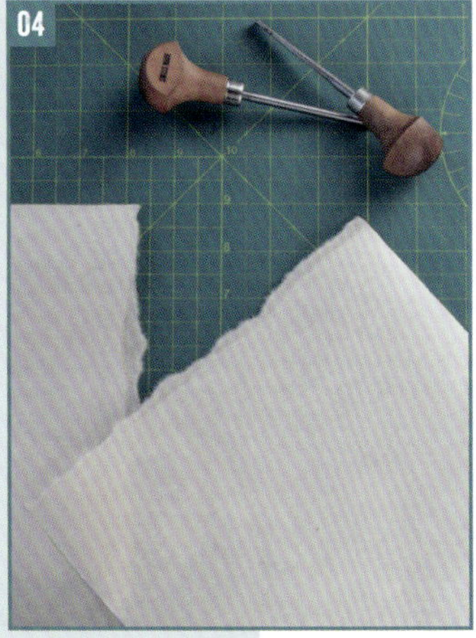

01 To create a deckled edge, start by folding the paper along the line you want to tear.

02 Add a little water to a small paintbrush and gently run it along the folded edge, leaving a thin line of moistened paper.

03 Unfold the paper, then carefully tear it apart along the moistened crease.

04 Leave the paper to dry before using.

REGISTRATION

While this isn't the most exciting stage, it is one of the most important if you want consistent print placement. This is especially vital when creating prints with multiple layers. Skipping the registration process at the start can lead to layers not lining up, prints looking wonky, and a lot of frustration.

The first step is to 'tab' your paper. As discussed on page 25, there are two useful tools for this: registration pins and tabs. This section will demonstrate how to use them.

01 Lay your prepared sheet of paper in the centre of a piece of board (or directly onto the bed of a press if you're using one). Place the registration pins about 5 mm from the paper edge at one end, then secure them with strong tape.

02 Snap plastic registration tabs onto the pins.

03 Tape the tabs to the paper using a low-tack masking tape. This will be easier than standard tape to remove later, and therefore less likely to damage the paper.

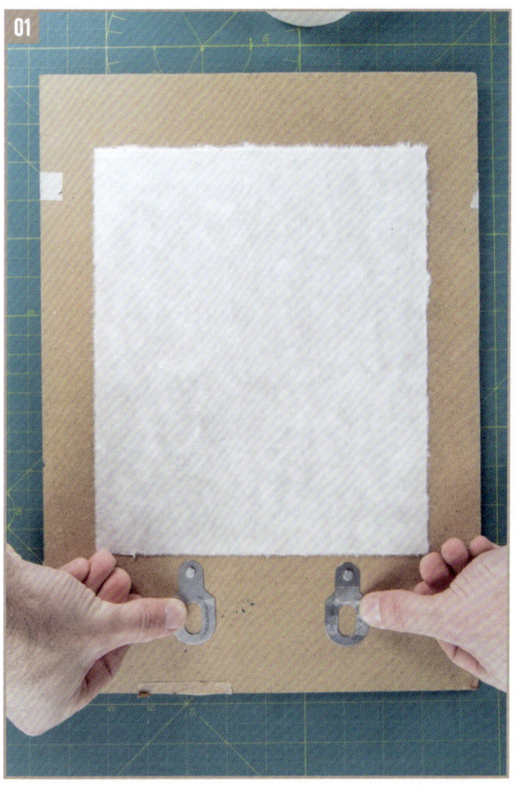

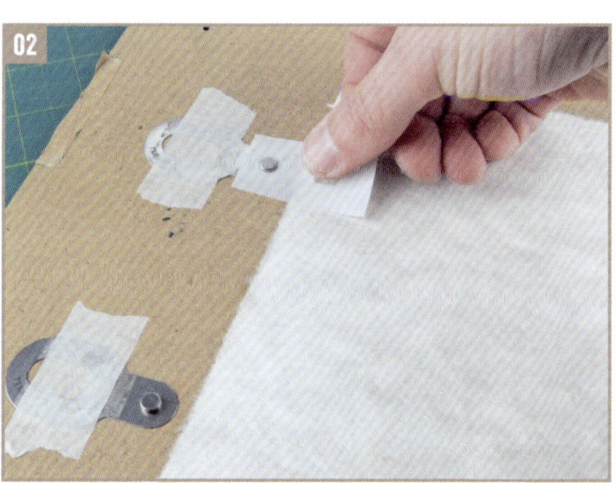

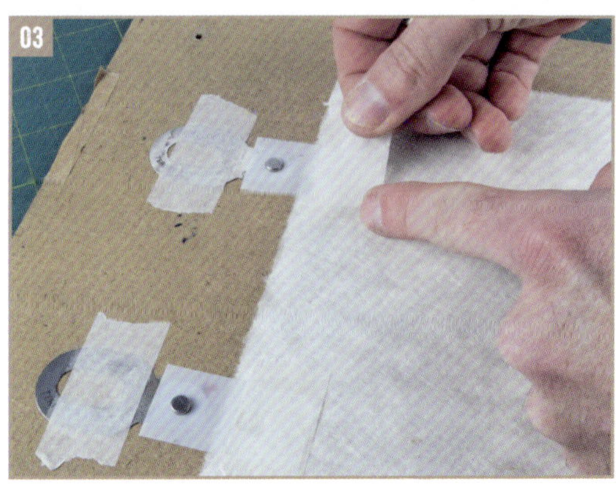

CONTINUED >

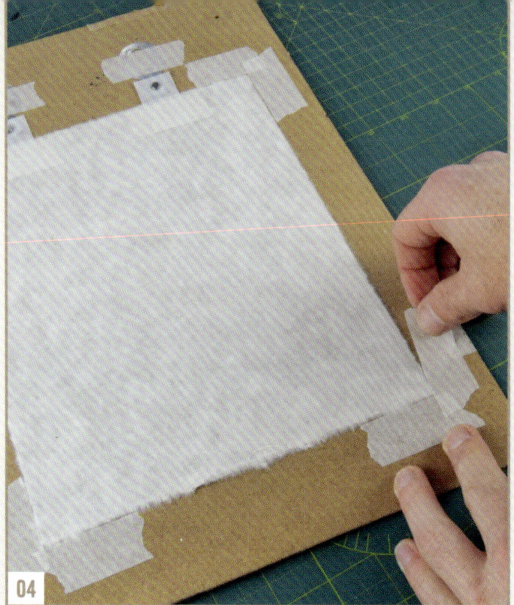

04 Next, you'll need to mark where the paper falls, as you'll soon be removing it from the board. An easy way to do this is to mark the corners with tape, as shown.

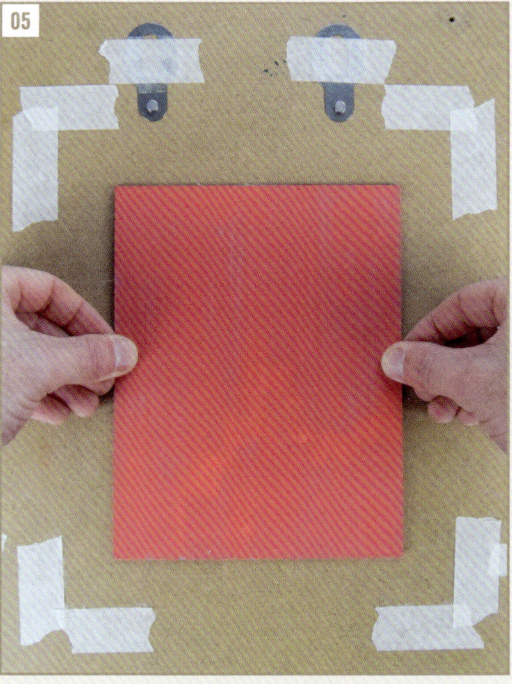

PRINTING GUIDE

Cut out a piece of paper, card, or plastic the same size as your paper, then mark out where the lino block sits on it. You can then use this as a guide each time you print. It's also handy to have when tearing paper to the right size from a larger sheet.

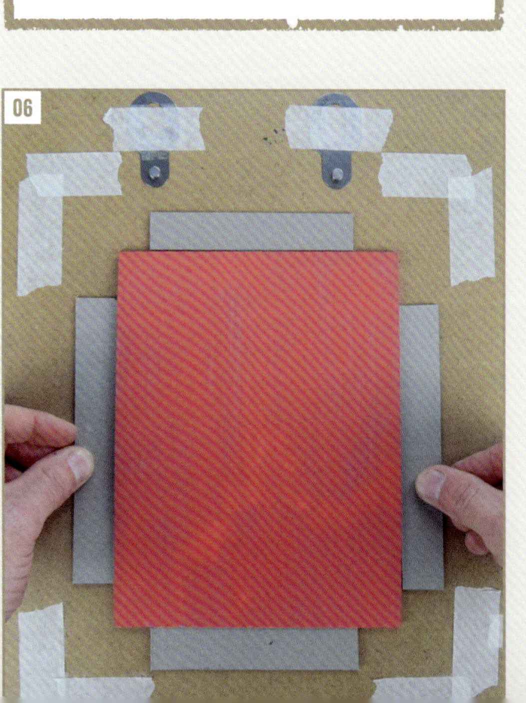

05 Once you've removed your paper, position the lino block where you want the design to print (typically in the middle). Use a ruler to help with this if you want exact results, or simply go by eye.

06 To stop the lino from moving, either glue or tape it down; or, if you want to be able to remove the block for carving and inking, use thick card strips to create a frame that holds it in place. You can then take the lino out, ink it, and fit it back in for each pressing. This is a good way of securing the lino if your design is carved right up to the edge and you don't have space for taping it.

MIXING & ROLLING INK

The inking stage can be messy, so it's worth investing in an apron before you start. Although most inks can be washed off of your hands easily enough, you may want to buy some disposable gloves too.

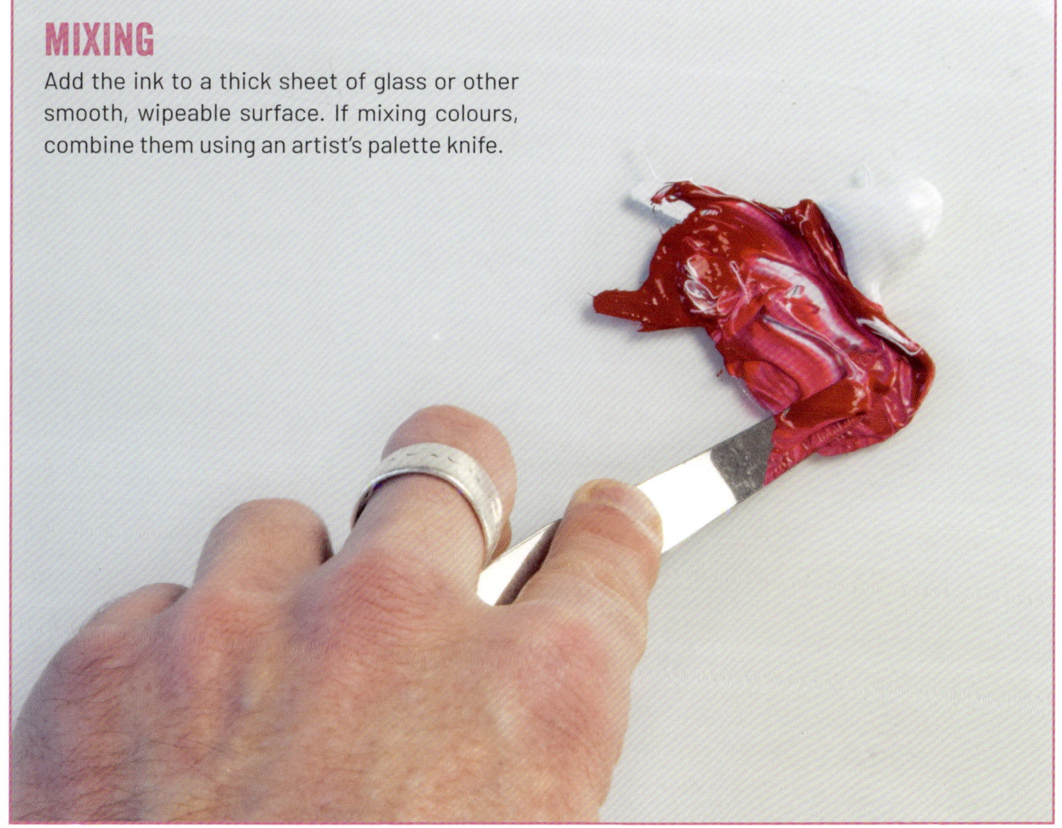

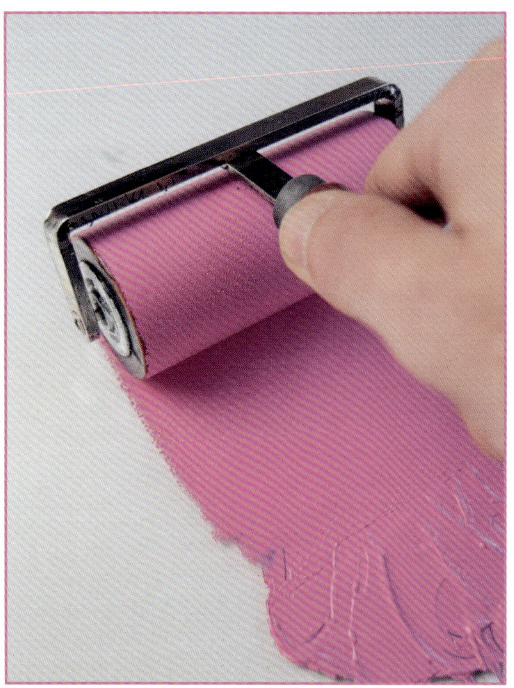

∧ When picking up ink from the mixing surface with the roller, make sure you roll outwards from the edge of the main 'blob' of ink. This ensures you don't pick up too much.

ROLLING

It's useful to invest in a range of roller sizes (see page 18). When choosing which roller to use, select one that is roughly the same width as the lino block you are inking. This will ensure the ink is applied evenly, without patchy areas.

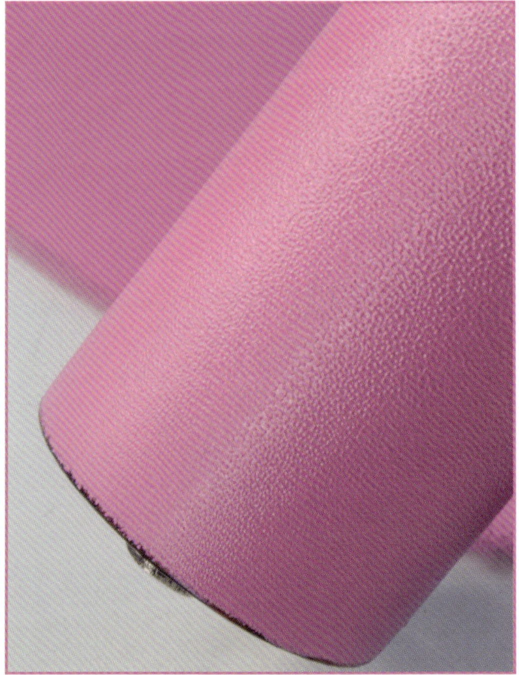

∧ It takes practice to learn how much ink to apply to the roller. As a general rule, it's better to apply too little than too much. If the ink is too thin, you can always add more and press the print again, but too much ink can result in messy edges and a loss of detail. This image shows the amount of ink you want to aim for.

TACKY INK

If the ink is too thick and tacky, as can happen in colder months, a liquid called 'tack reducer' can be added. This will loosen up the ink, making it flow better.

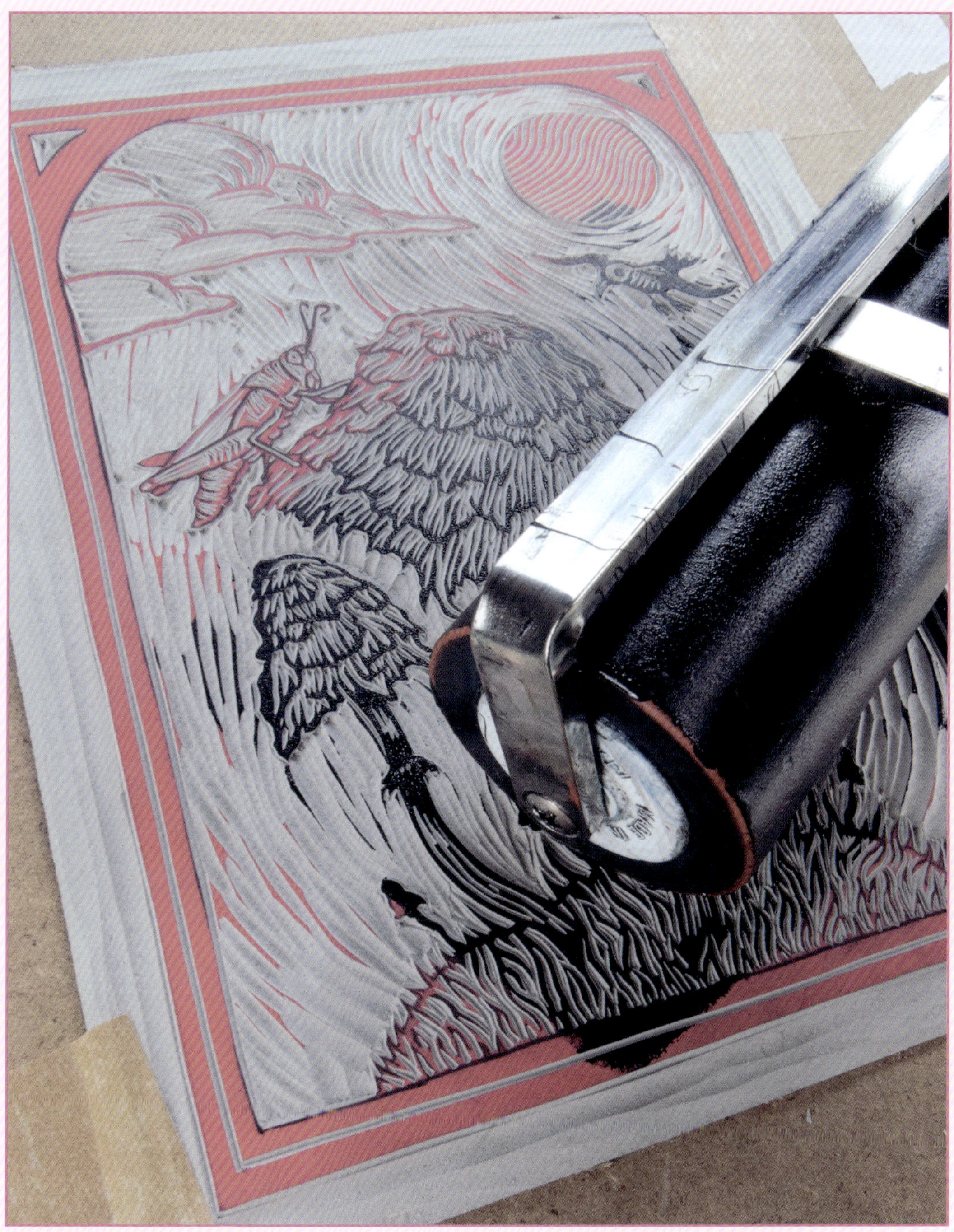

▲ Roll the ink across the lino block, making sure to cover it evenly. Only a little firmness is needed when rolling.

INTRODUCING COLOUR

Understanding the basics of colour theory and mixing colours will open up a host of creative possibilities. Familiarize yourself with what inks you need to combine to achieve certain colours – this will save you both time and ink. You probably know most of the basics already, but let's refresh!

MIXING PRIMARY COLOURS

The primary colours are cyan (blue), yellow, and magenta (red). Mixing two of these together, in different combinations, will create secondary colours: orange, green, and purple. Mixing all three together will create brown. By combining equal amounts of a primary with a secondary colour – for example, yellow and orange – you will create tertiary colours. In this case, yellow-orange.

01 Blue mixed with red will create purple. By adding more of one of the colours you can change how blue or red that purple appears.

02 Blue mixed with yellow will create green. Adding extra blue will create more of a teal colour, whereas adding more yellow will create a lighter 'grassier' green.

03 Red mixed with yellow will create orange. Adding more of either colour will lighten or darken the orange.

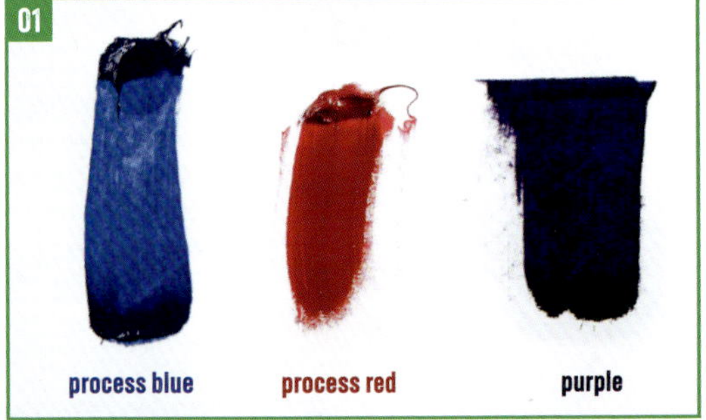

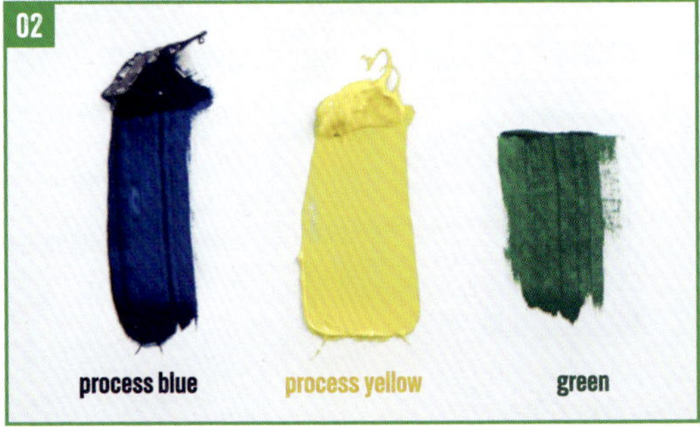

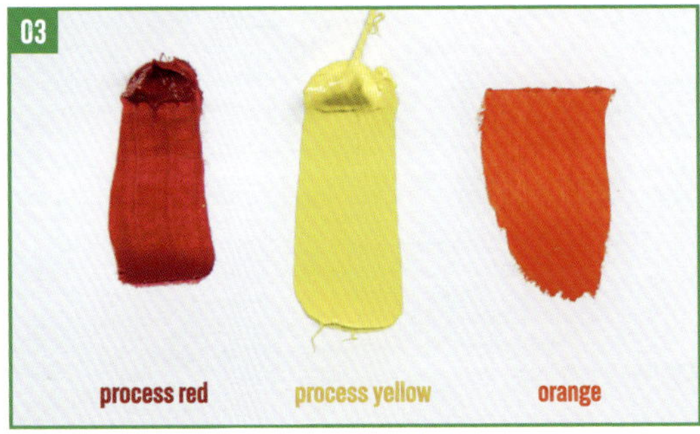

TINTS & SHADES

Adding white to a colour will create lighter tints, which will of course vary depending on the amount of white introduced. The more you mix in, the lighter and fainter the colour will become. Mixing in black will create darker shades of the original colour, becoming increasingly darker the more black you introduce.

ORDER OF MIXING

If you wish to mix a pale-to-medium colour, start with a lighter colour ink, gradually adding in the black ink until you reach the desired colour. Starting with a dark ink when trying to mix a light colour will only result in wasted ink, as you will need to use an awful lot of light ink to reach the desired colour. Conversely, if you want to mix a dark colour, start with the darker ink and gradually add in the lighter colour.

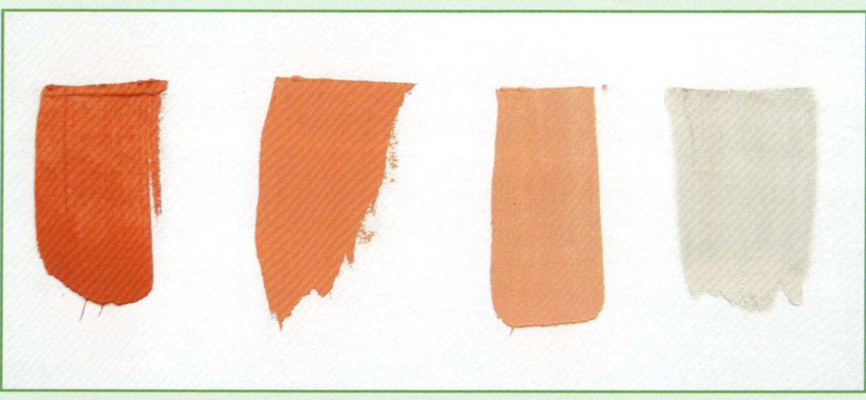

⋀ Adding white to orange to create various tints of orange

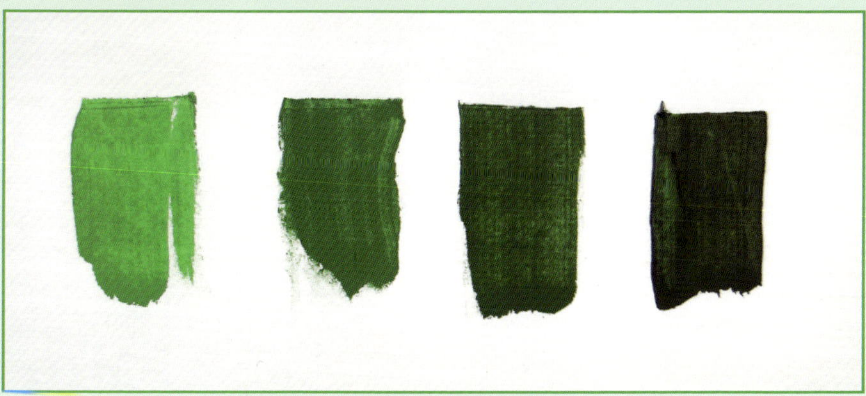

⋀ Adding black to green to create various shades of green

PRESSING

There are a few different methods you can use to press your print, including budget-friendly spoons and barens, table-top folding presses, and large cast-iron presses. All of these produce great results, so the one you opt for will depend on your budget, workspace, type of paper, and personal preference. This section will explore some of the more accessible pressing methods.

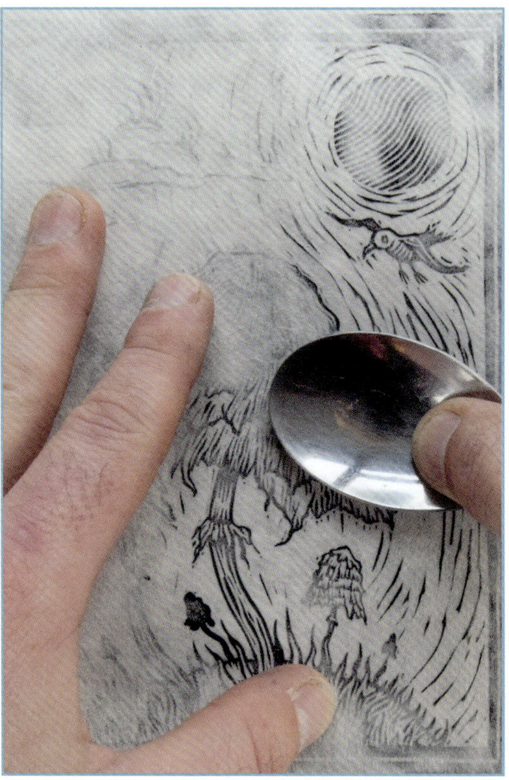

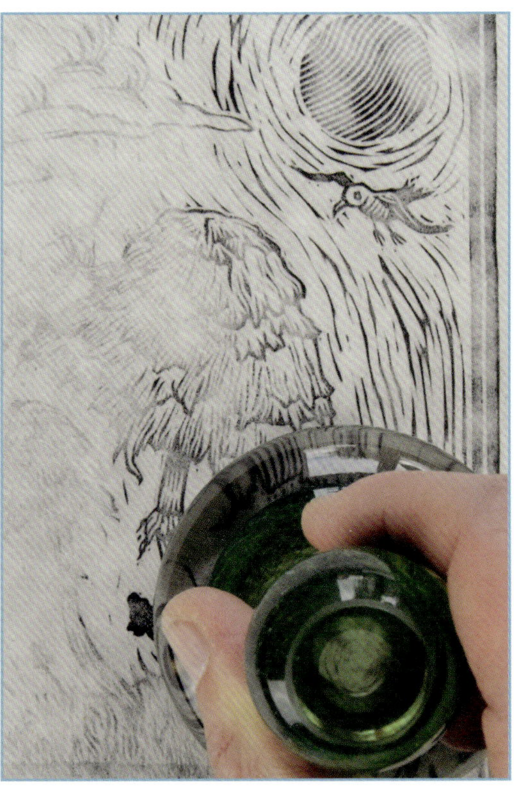

SPOONS

To transfer a print using a spoon (metal or wooden), press firmly with the curved side facing down. Spoons work best when using thinner paper and can be hard work if printing onto thicker paper, or when pressing large prints.

BARENS

Barens come in various shapes, materials, and sizes. This glass baren is naturally heavy, which means it doesn't need as much pressure as lighter options. Like most barens, it has a handle to grasp as you move it over the paper.

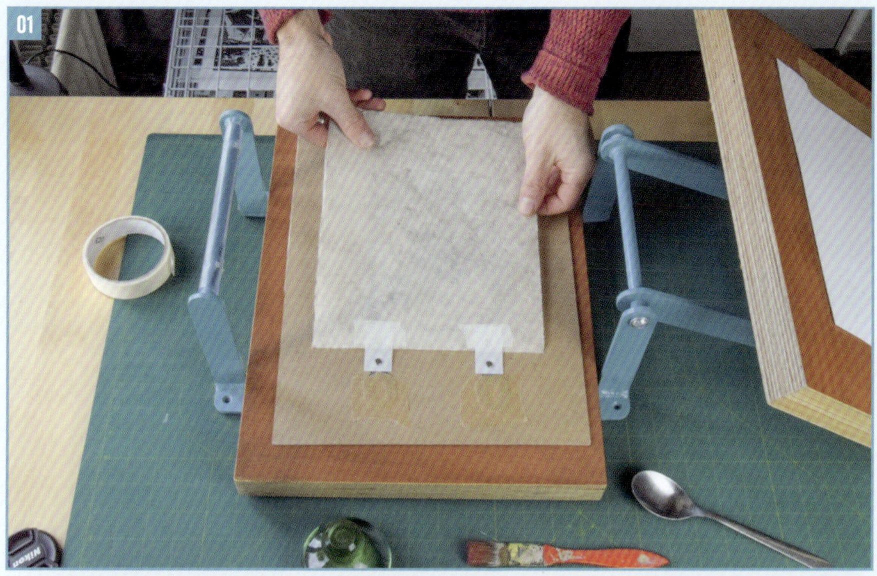

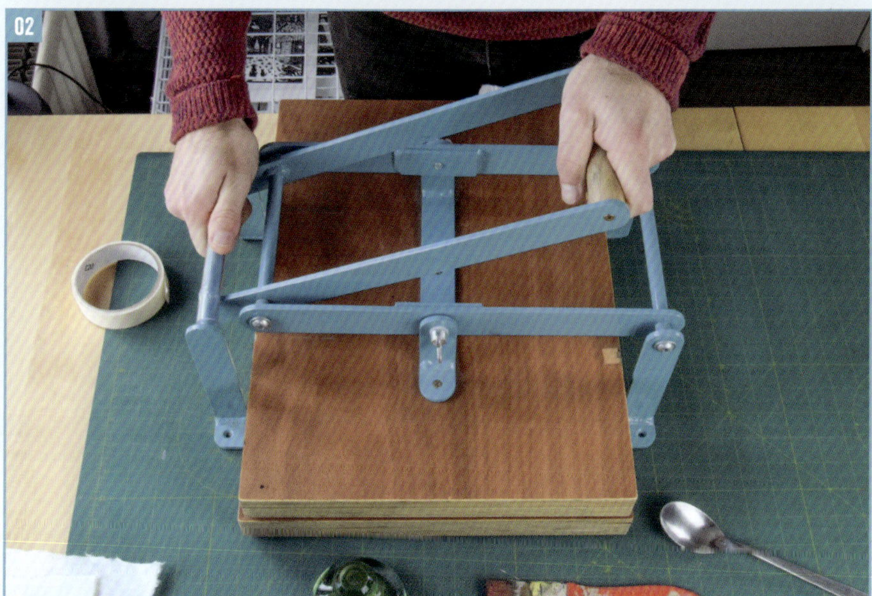

TABLE-TOP FOLDING PRESS

01 Start by opening the press and positioning the registered lino block in the centre of the base. Next, clip on your paper.

02 Fold the top half of the press back over and press down firmly on the handle. The two halves of the press will sandwich the paper and lino, applying pressure and transferring the ink.

CONTINUED >

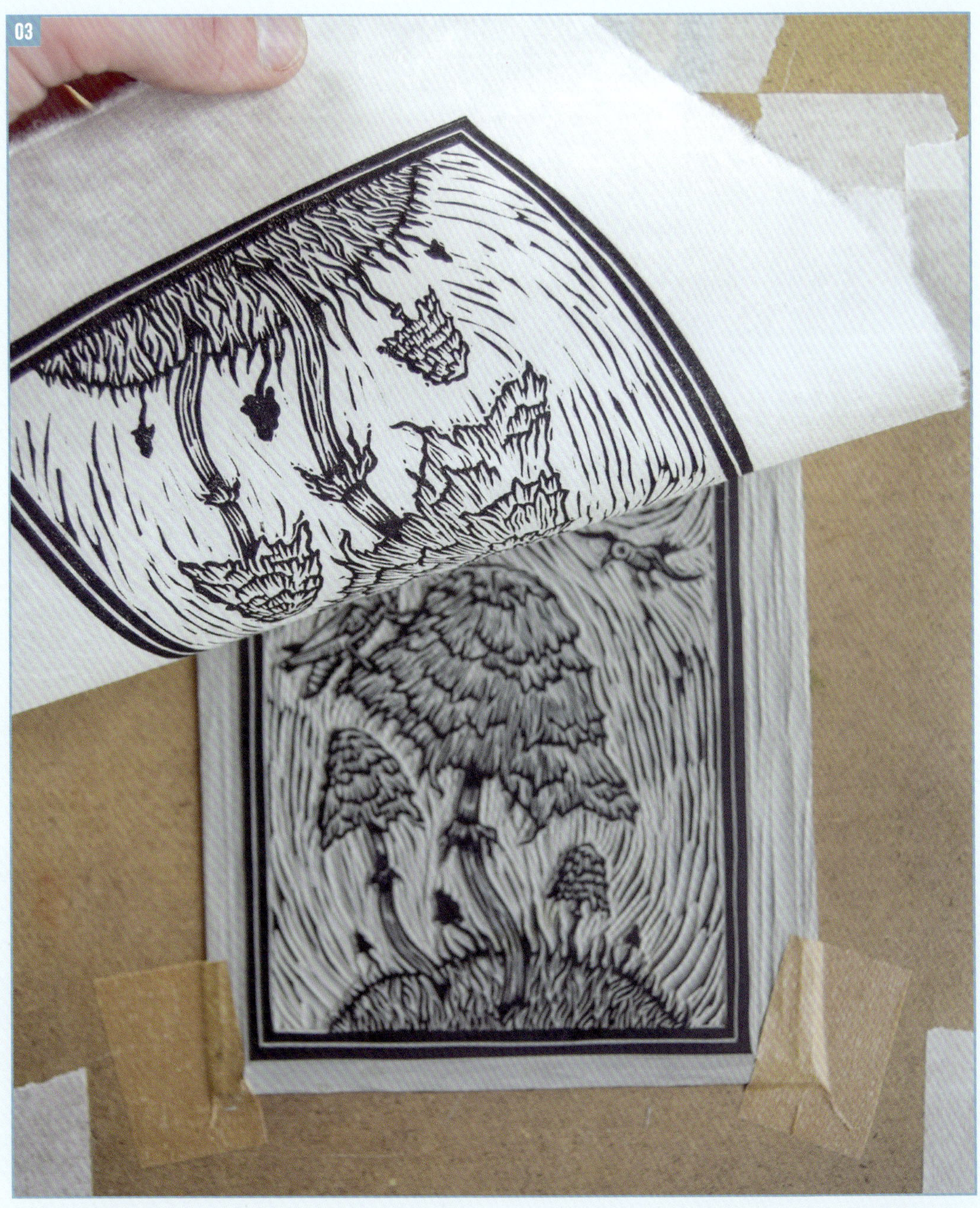

03 After pressing the print, open the press, peel back the paper, and check that the ink is evenly transferred. Roll on more ink and press again if needed. If small areas of the image need more pressure, you can use a baren or spoon to go over them.

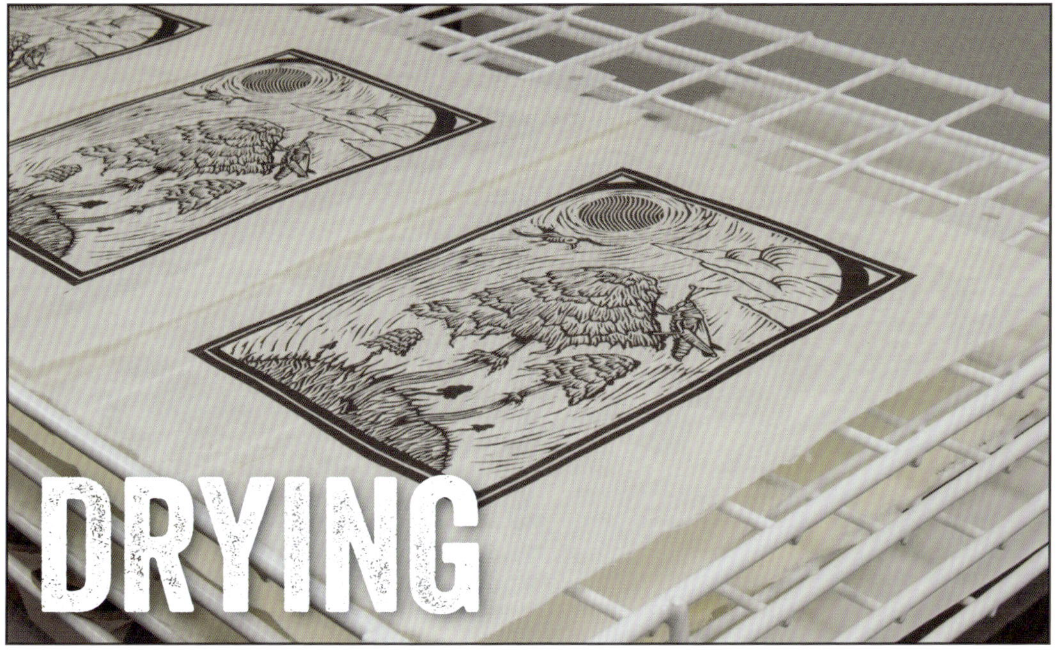

DRYING

Various drying options were covered on page 38. The key points to remember are:

- Allow prints plenty of time to dry. The drying time will vary depending on the type of paper used, the type and thickness of the ink, and the temperature of the room. Check back after a day or two. If the ink is still a little tacky, it needs more time. Multi-layered prints will generally need longer.

- Don't let prints dry with inked areas overlapping, as this risks them sticking together.

- Prints will dry faster in warm, dry environments with air circulation. Ensure drying prints have enough space between them to allow air to circulate.

- Drying catalysts, such as cobalt driers, can be used to speed up the drying process. These are added to the ink before printing. They are not compatible with all inks, however, so check the inks you're using first.

REMOVING TABS

Once the prints have dried, remove the registration tabs. Running a hairdryer over the tape for 10–15 seconds will make them easier to remove and less likely to damage the paper as they come away.

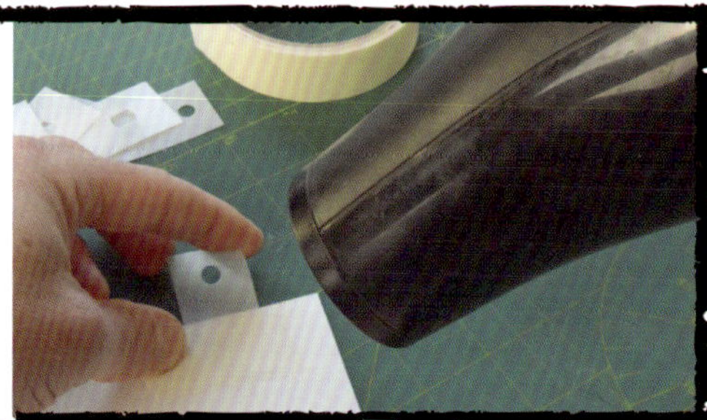

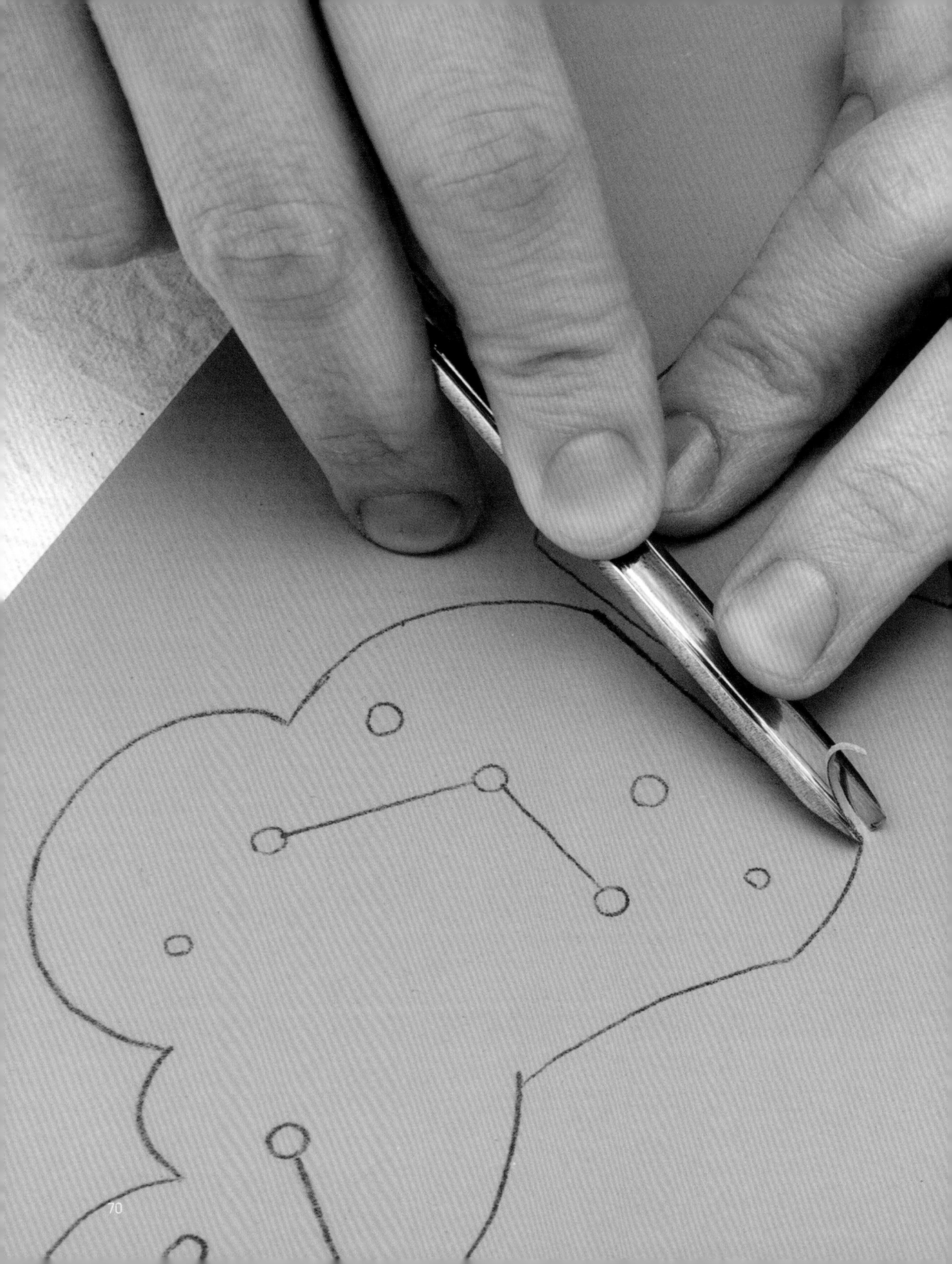

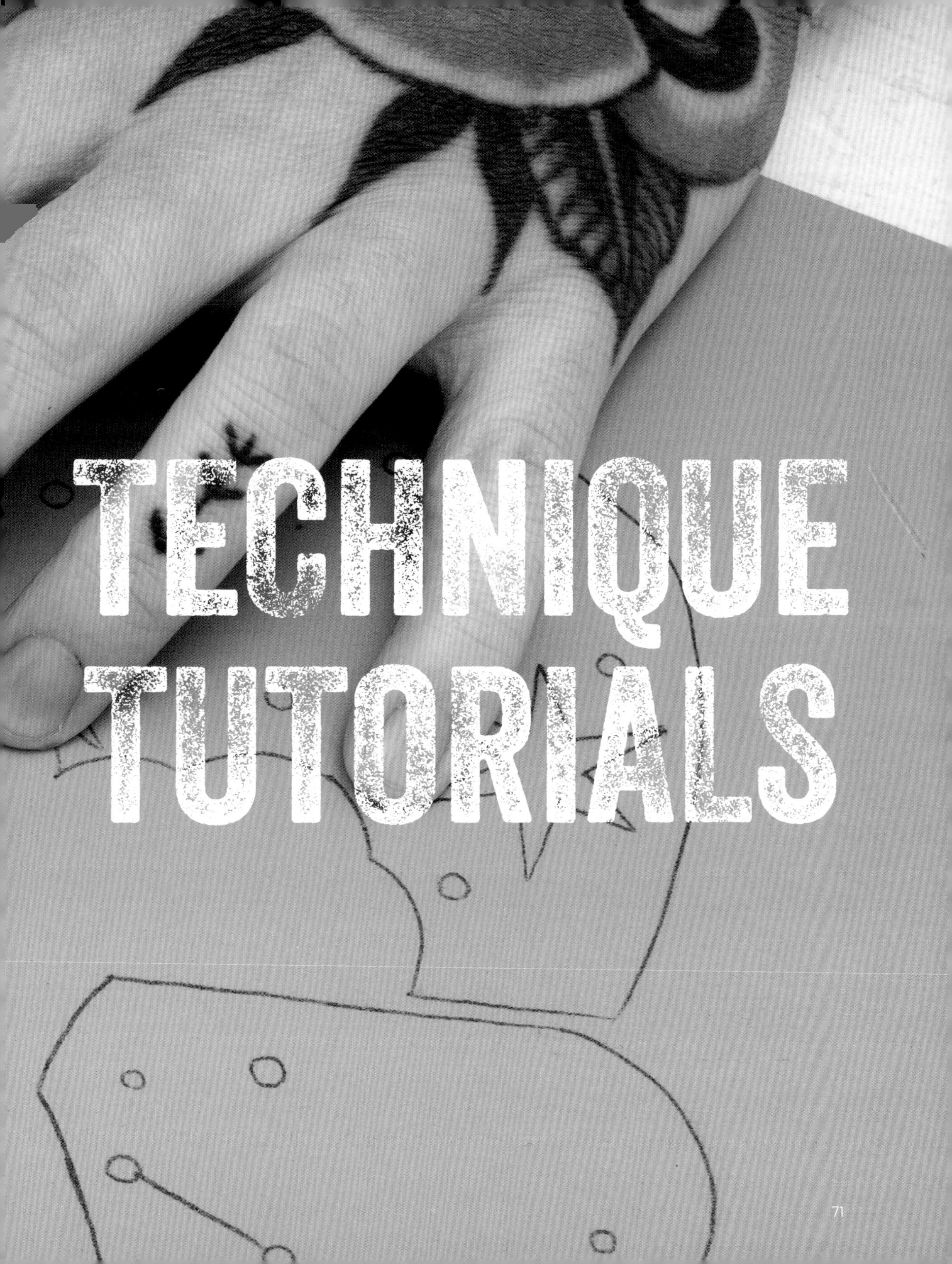

TECHNIQUE TUTORIALS

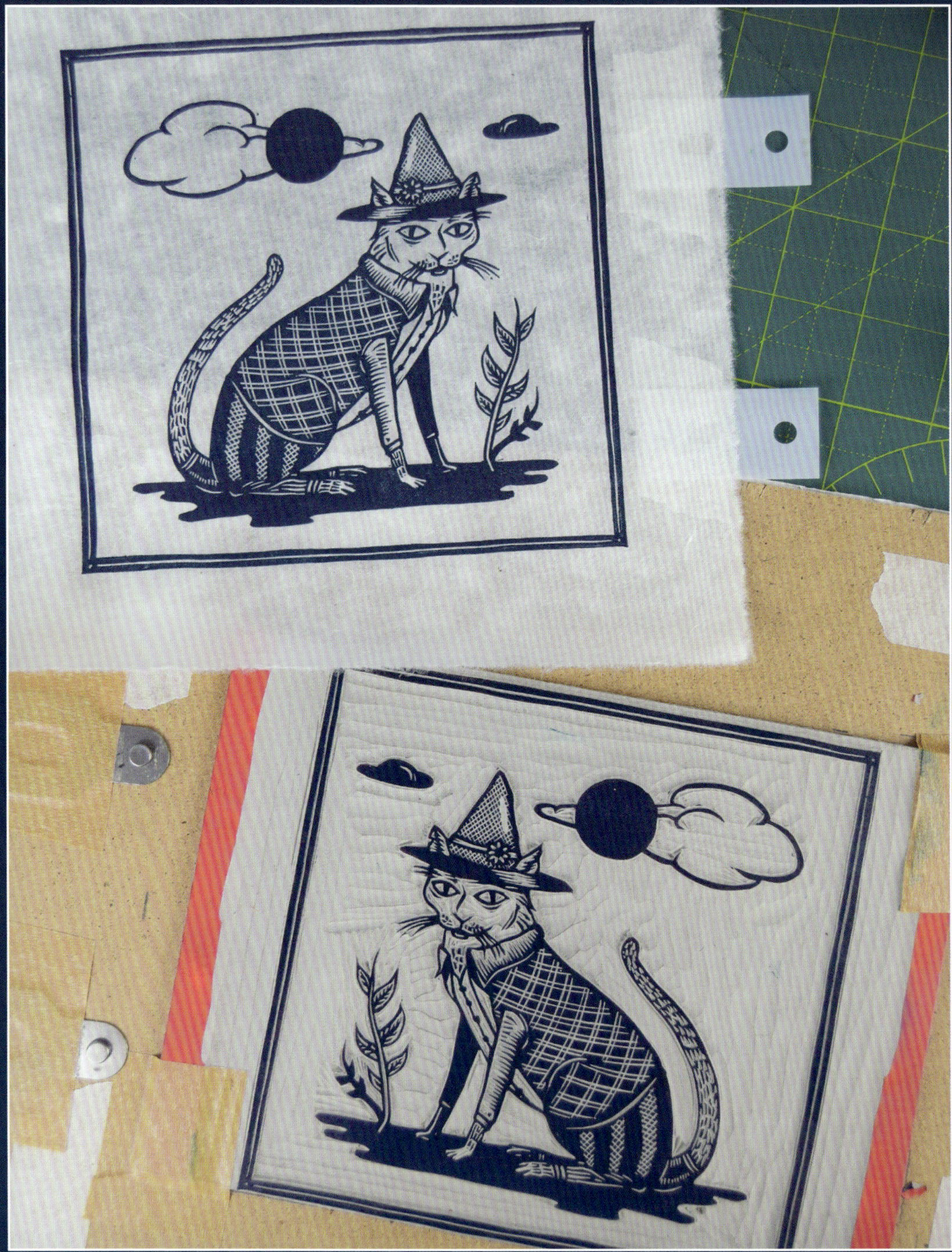

SIMPLE SINGLE-COLOUR PRINT

WITCH CAT

BY GARETH BARNES (SPINDLE PRINTER)

There's no better place to start than with the basics. This tutorial will show you how to create a relatively simple, yet no less effective, single-colour linocut print. Practising with single-colour prints is a great way to hone your skills and get to grips with the linocutting process. Assemble the materials you need, then follow along at your own pace. You will have the most success if you take the time to master the fundamentals before progressing to more complicated techniques.

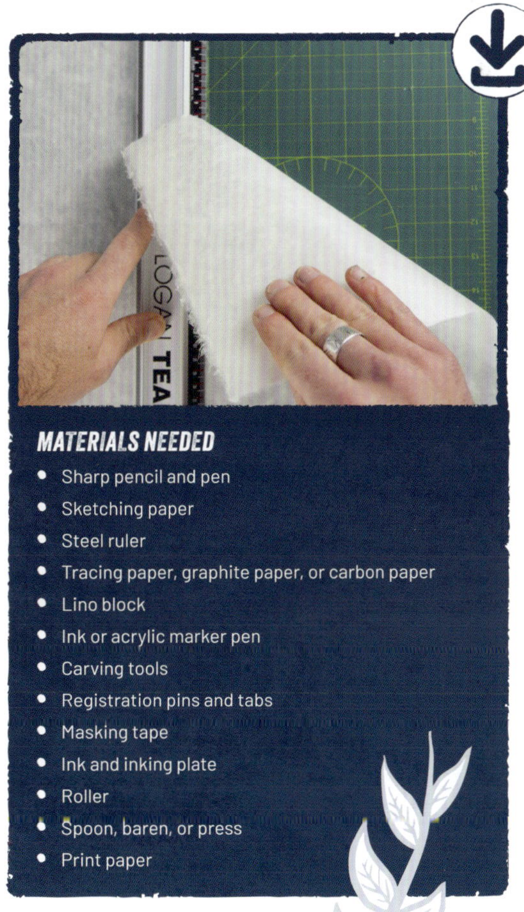

MATERIALS NEEDED

- Sharp pencil and pen
- Sketching paper
- Steel ruler
- Tracing paper, graphite paper, or carbon paper
- Lino block
- Ink or acrylic marker pen
- Carving tools
- Registration pins and tabs
- Masking tape
- Ink and inking plate
- Roller
- Spoon, baren, or press
- Print paper

01 DRAW THE IMAGE

Draw out your design, whether on paper or digitally. Some printmakers like to draw in all of the details and line work at this stage, while others prefer to add details as they carve. Some detail will be added to this design as it's carved, but not too much. (See how this design was developed on page 47.)

SIMPLE VS DETAILED

Single-colour prints are relatively simple in terms of the process, but whether you carve a simple or detailed design is up to you. Some printers naturally gravitate towards more intricate, complex images, while others prefer bolder, more graphic pieces. Neither style is better than the other – create what makes you happy!

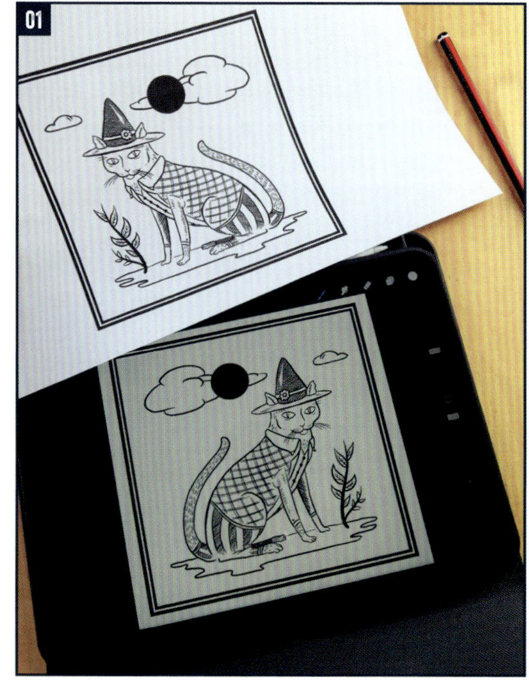

∧ The image is reversed and printed off at the correct size

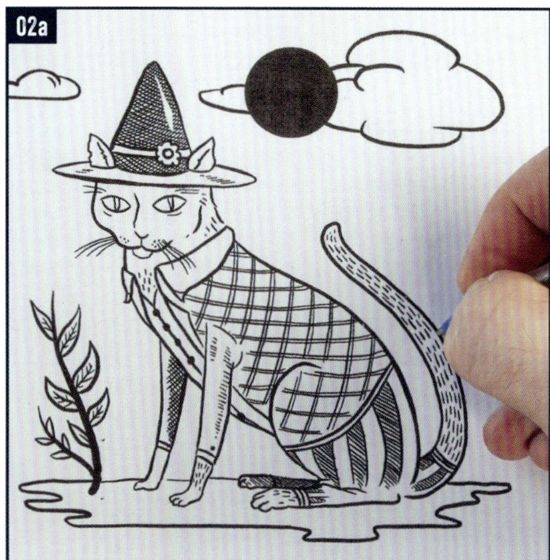

∧ Tracing over line work with a blue pen – the blue stands out from the original black lines so you can see where you've already traced

02 TRANSFER THE IMAGE

Use graphite paper and a pen to transfer the reversed image onto the lino. If needed, use a pencil or pen to make some of the transferred lines darker and neater, or to add to the design.

∨ By taping the drawing and transfer paper down, you can easily peel it back to check it's transferred fully

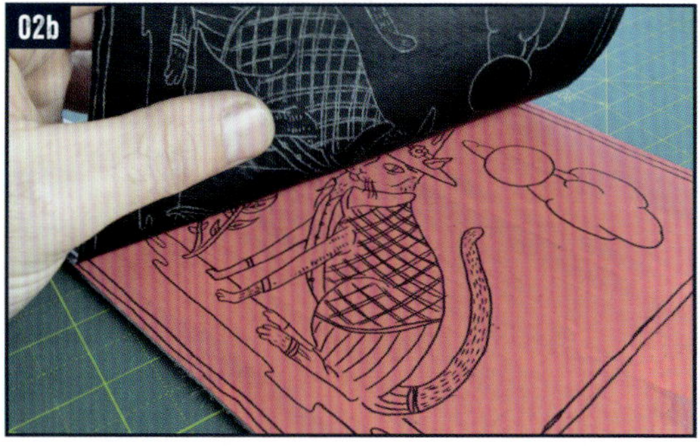

03 CARVE THE OUTLINE

Using a small V-shaped tool, carefully carve around the outside of your design. These carved outlines will act as a sort of barrier. When using a bigger tool to clear large areas of unwanted space, the outlines will tell you where to stop, preventing you from accidentally taking out a chunk of the design.

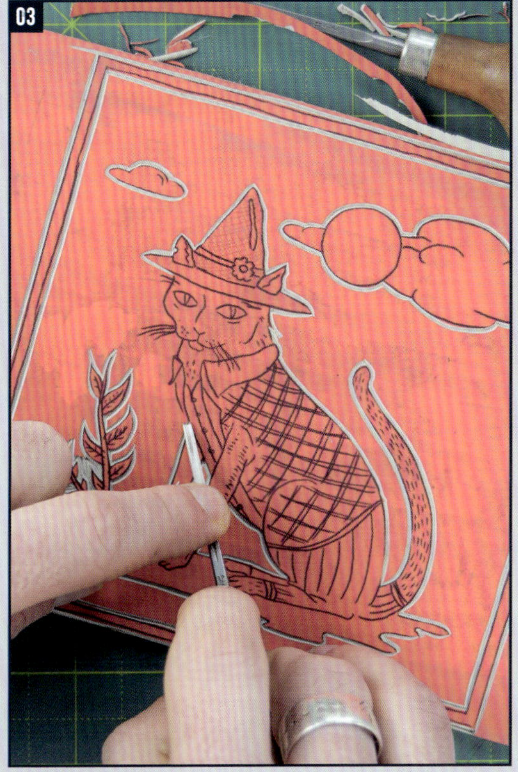

The smallest V-shaped tool is well-suited for carving the outline

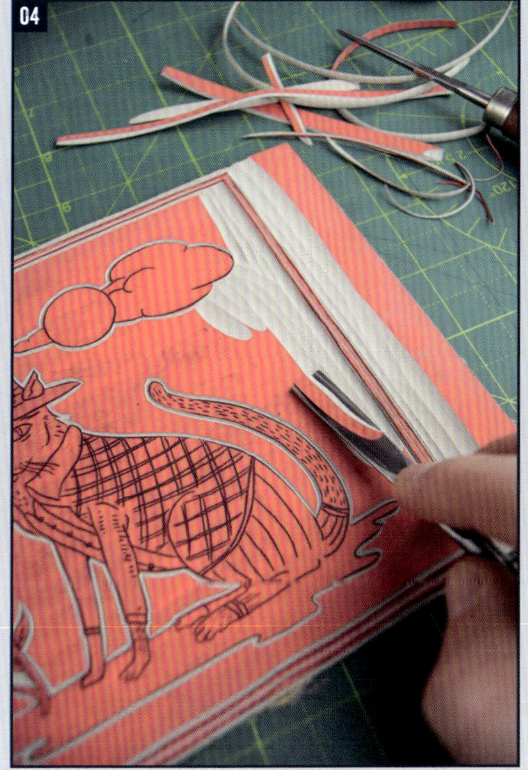

Clearing inside and outside the frame using a wide U-shaped tool

04 CLEAR LARGE AREAS

Use a wide, shallow U-shaped tool to clear the unwanted space around the design. Carve it as flat as possible to prevent any inky marks in these areas. While larger tools allow you to quickly carve out big areas, take care and don't rush.

05 WORK IN DETAILS

Use a cross-hatching technique to give the hat some textile-like texture. Next, use a medium-sized U-shaped tool to carve out a slither of lino as a highlight, giving the hat shape a sense of depth and form.

> Cross-hatching (carving lines in one direction, then carving a second set of lines over the first set in a different direction) is a great way to add texture and variety in your mark-making

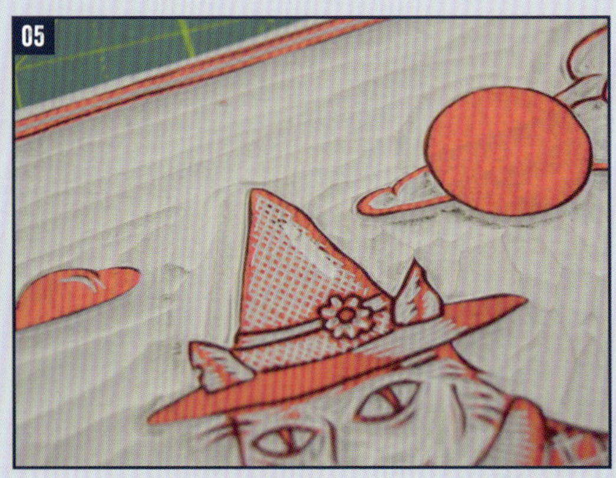

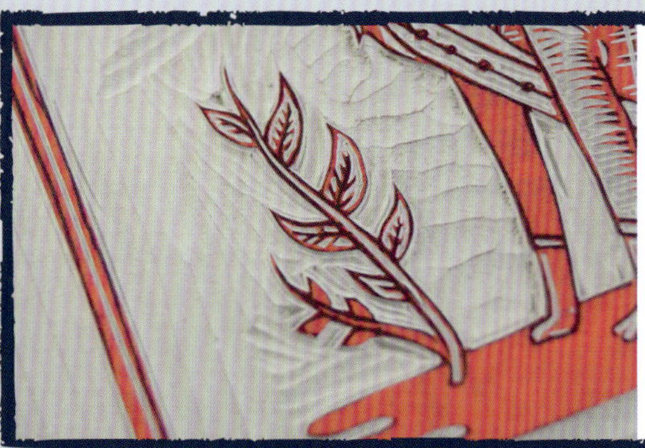

ADDING DEPTH

A simple way to add depth to an object is to make the foreground brighter than the background. Notice how the larger stem of the plant is carved into, whereas the smaller stem isn't. This makes it look like the smaller stem is farther away, in shadow, creating a sense of depth.

06 PREPARE THE PAPER

Choose your paper, keeping in mind how you plan to press it. Mitsumata paper has a warm off-white tone, subtle texture, and a handmade feel, plus at 60 gsm is light enough to be easily pressed with a spoon. Tearing along the edge of the paper with a ruler, rather than cutting, will keep the edges slightly fluffy. Next, use tape or pen to mark on the printing surface where the paper will sit. This will make tabbing each sheet a little faster.

> Tearing along a ruler gives the paper a softer edge, and adding registration tabs ensures it will line up correctly with each print

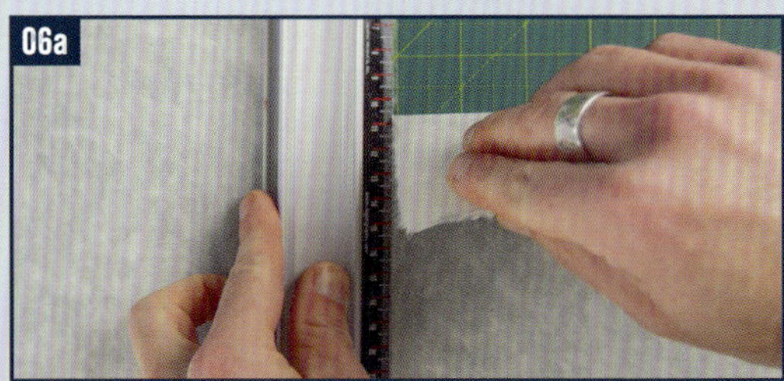

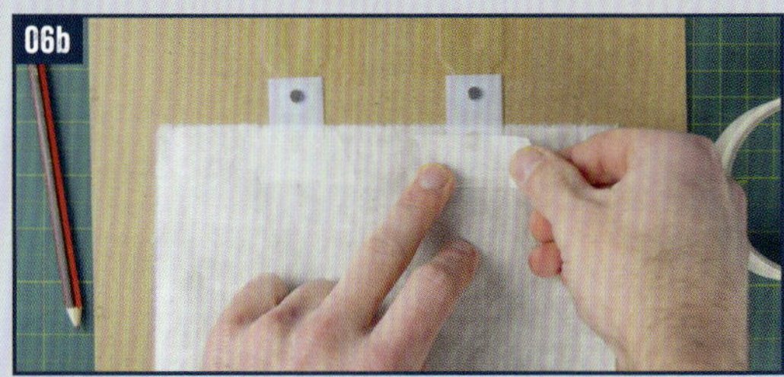

07 REGISTER & SECURE THE LINO

Position the lino block in the centre of the taped area. Next, use strong tape to secure the lino to the printing surface – 3 mm board in this case.

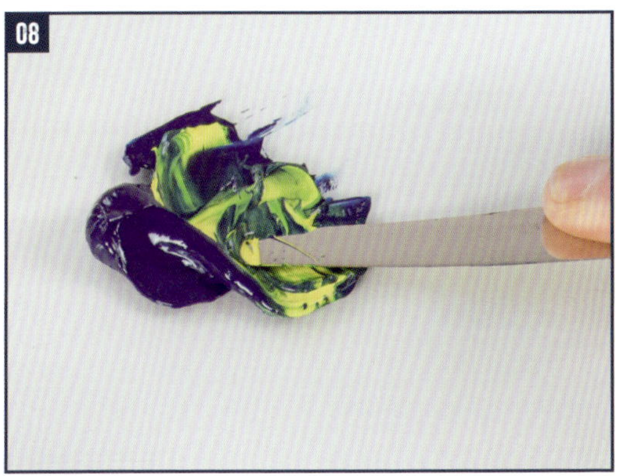

> A few pieces of strong tape will keep the lino from sliding around

08 MIX THE INK

This 60 gsm Mitsumata paper has a light, warm tone that will pair well with a dark teal or turquoise colour, which can be mixed from blue and yellow. As the intended colour is dark, start with blue and gradually add in the yellow. Mix and adjust until you create the desired colour.

< Use a palette knife to mix the inks together

09 ROLL ON INK

Apply ink to the roller, then roll it over the lino until every part of the raised surface has ink on it. The roller used here is roughly the same width as the design, so it should transfer the ink smoothly, without streaks or uneven patches. Try to keep your roller as level as possible. If you hold it at an angle, you might roll ink onto the carved-out areas. If you do, either stick a bit of tape over it, rub it off, or carve it away.

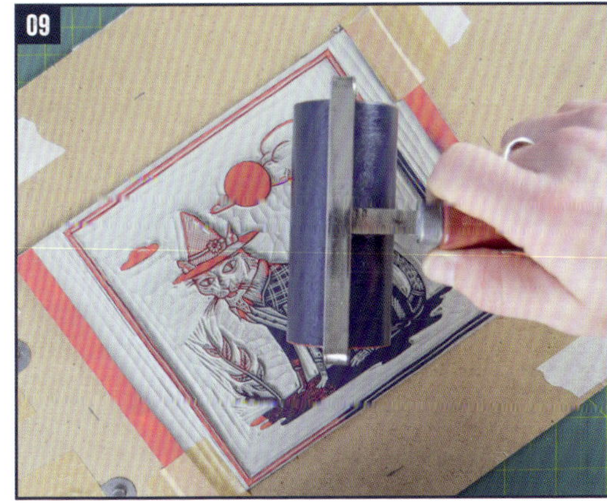

> It's better to ink the lino too lightly than too heavily – too much ink risks losing the details

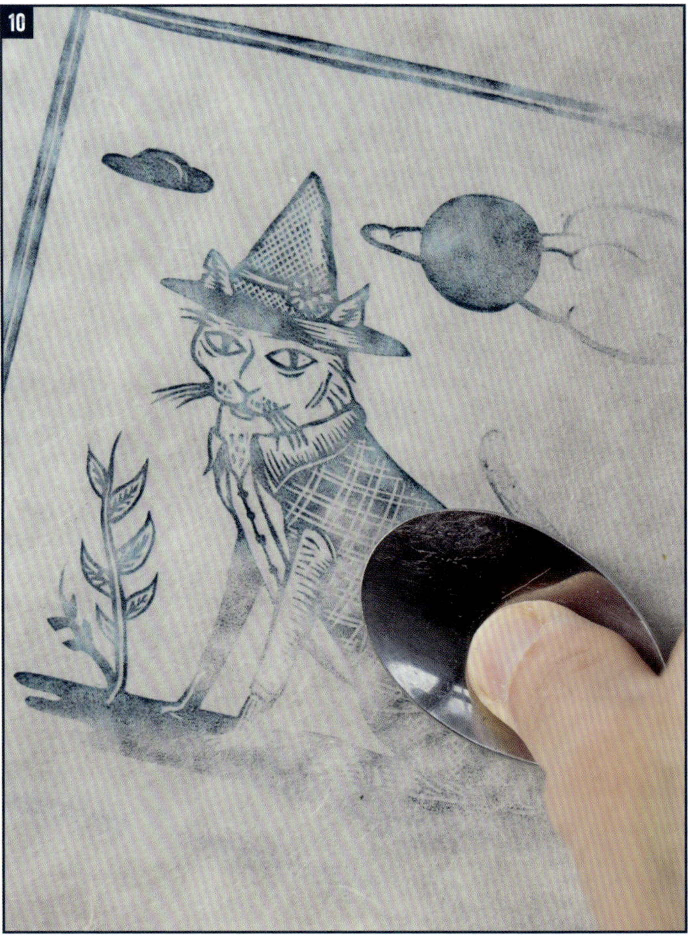

10 PRESS PAPER TO LINO

Click your paper onto the registration pins, lay it across the inked lino, and press it. Use the back of a small metal spoon for this if the paper you're using is lightweight.

< If using lightweight paper, you may see the image appear on the reverse as you press

11 CHECK YOUR PROGRESS

After the first press, carefully peel back the paper and check if the design has printed evenly. If it appears patchy or too light, simply re-ink the lino and press it again. Because the lino is taped in place and the paper connected to the pins, the print shouldn't become blurred or misaligned. It can sometimes happen if the paper is very thin and flexes a little while you press, but shouldn't occur too much if you're careful when pressing.

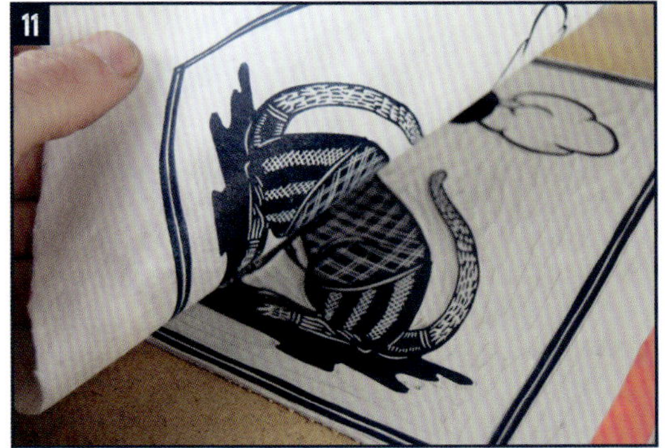

∧ Checking to see if the design is evenly printed

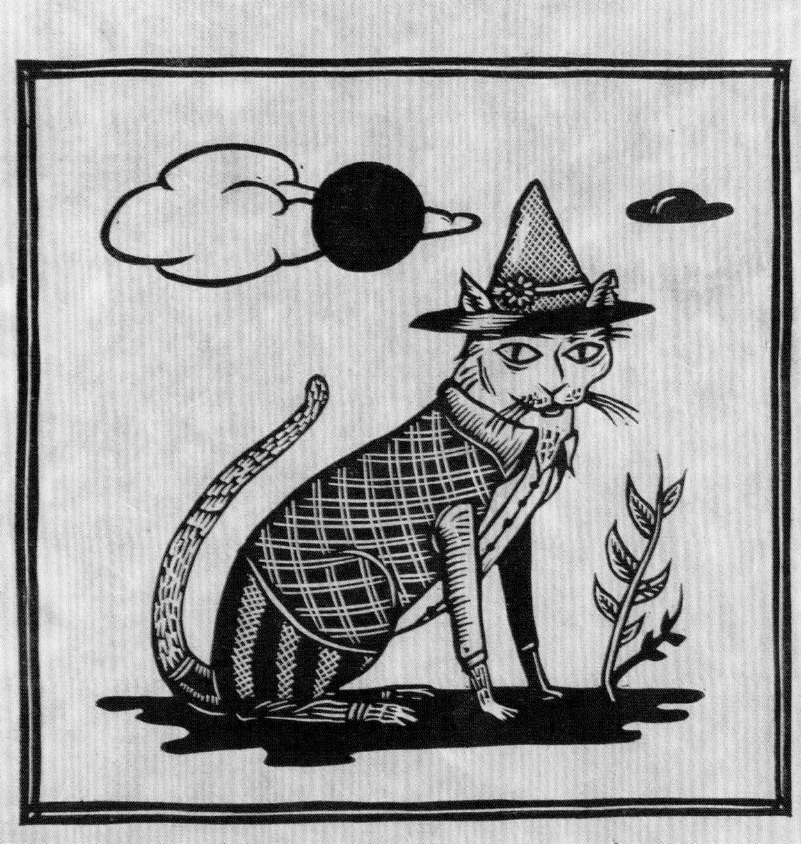

Witch cat | The line work is crisp and bold, the details are clear, and the teal contrasts nicely with the warm paper

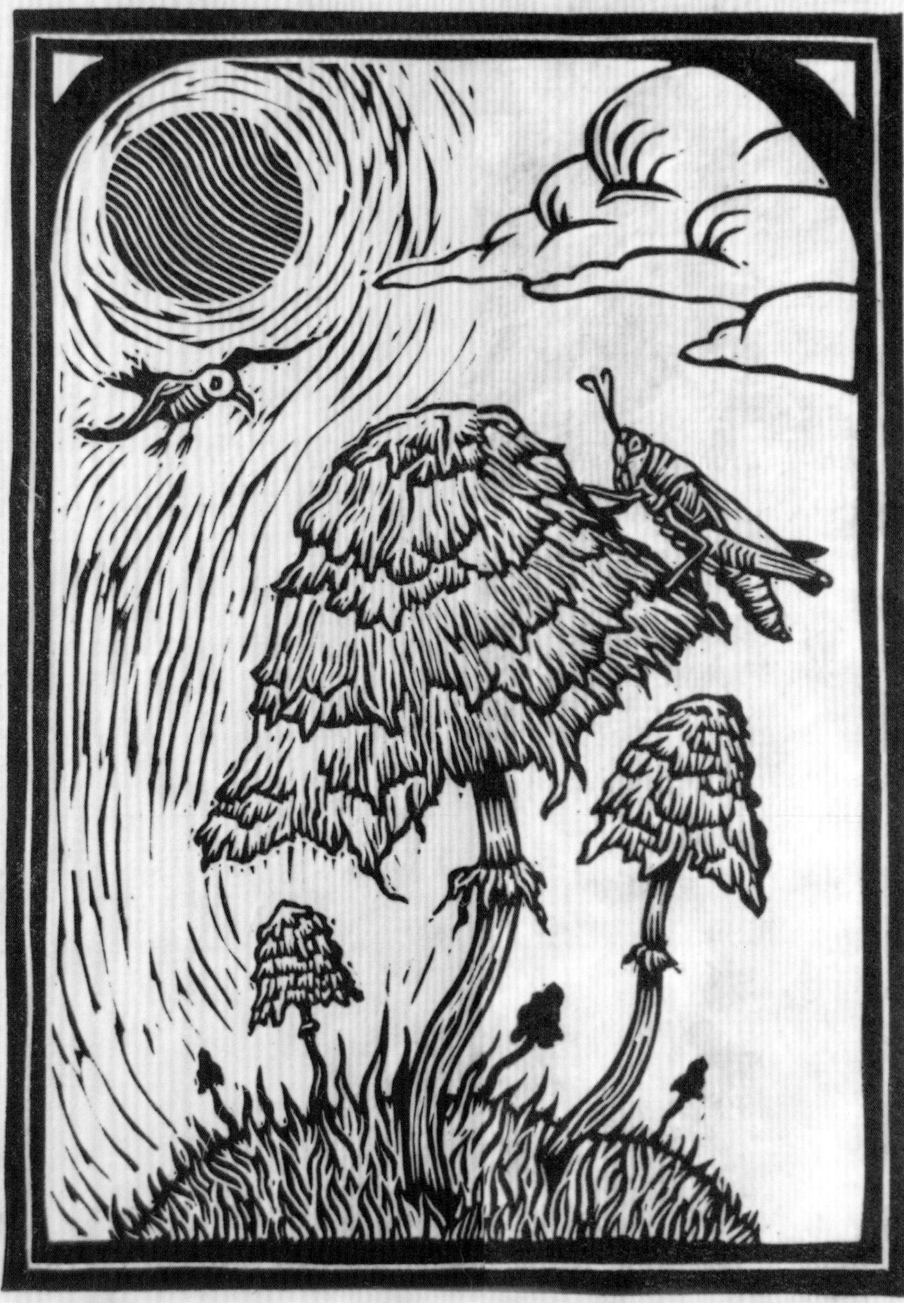

NOISY VS CLEAN PRINTS

MUSHROOMS

BY GARETH BARNES (SPINDLE PRINTER)

Carving lino can often leave little ridges and peaks – pointy lines between the carved grooves that can pick up ink when it's applied. Some printmakers like this textural decoration and will deliberately carve loosely to include the tool marks and 'noise' in their designs. Other printmakers prefer very 'clean' neatly printed designs without any rough ink marks or messy textures. They will remove any ridges using a broad, flat carving tool before inking. There are also many printmakers who lie somewhere in between, aiming for generally crisp, clean prints, but allowing for a few marks here and there.

This tutorial will demonstrate what is meant by 'noisy' and 'clean' prints, and how you can achieve both techniques.

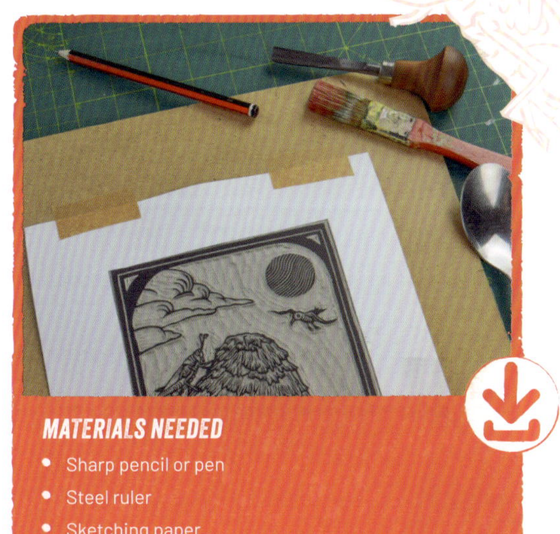

MATERIALS NEEDED

- Sharp pencil or pen
- Steel ruler
- Sketching paper
- Tracing paper, graphite paper, or carbon paper
- Lino
- Ink or acrylic marker pen
- Carving tools
- Registration pins and tabs
- Masking tape
- Ink and inking plate
- Roller
- Spoon, baren, or press
- Print paper

NOISY PRINT

01 DRAW THE DESIGN

Start by drawing your design either on paper or digitally. Make sure there's plenty of space in the background that can be left textured (noisy) or carved flatter (clean). If working digitally, reverse the design and print it. If working on paper, you will need to reverse the design using the method demonstrated on page 50.

> The digital drawing and reversed print-out, with lots of empty background space

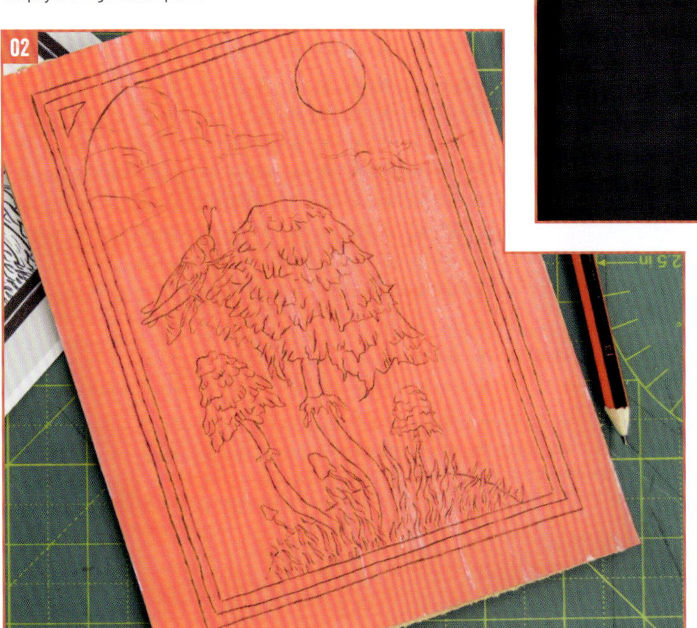

< Red ink is used to coat the lino before the design is transferred

02 TRANSFER TO LINO

Before transferring the design, lightly coat the lino with either ink or acrylic marker and let it dry. This will allow you to see where you've carved. Next, use graphite paper to transfer the reversed image directly onto the lino, or use the other transfer method (see page 52). Now go over the lines with a pen, adding further details. Leave a little space around the edge of the lino so it can be taped down at the printing stage.

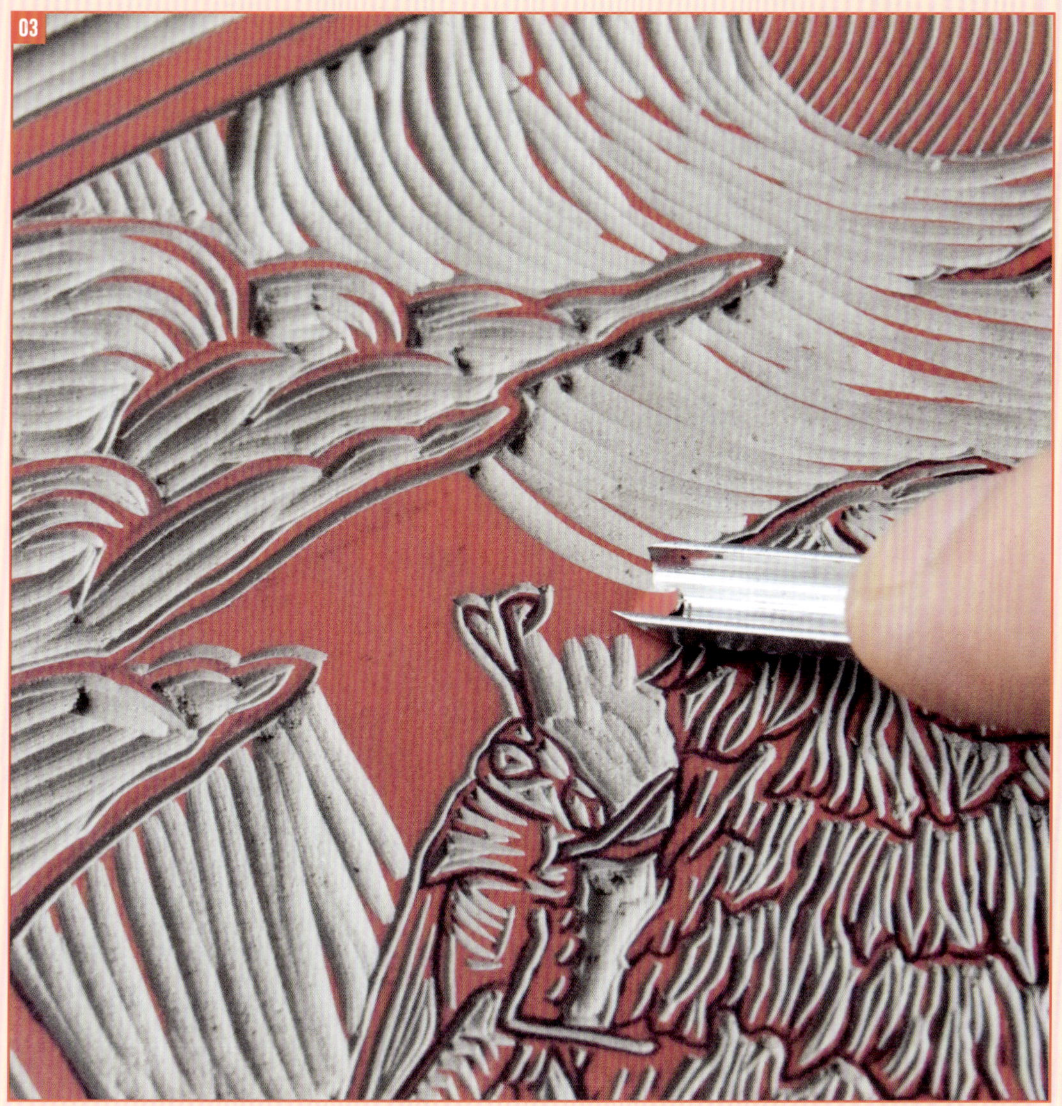

∧ Using a large U-shaped tool to loosely carve away lino

03 CARVING

Consider how you wish the finished print to look. Do you want to see inky marks and noise across the whole image, or only in certain areas? Would you prefer the marks to be random, or to have a direction? Do you wish to see bold or smaller, subtler marks?

To create a noisy texture, use a range of carving tools (except the broad, flat type) to carve into the space around the main design. By purposefully not being too tidy, you will end up with little ridges that will capture ink and add texture.

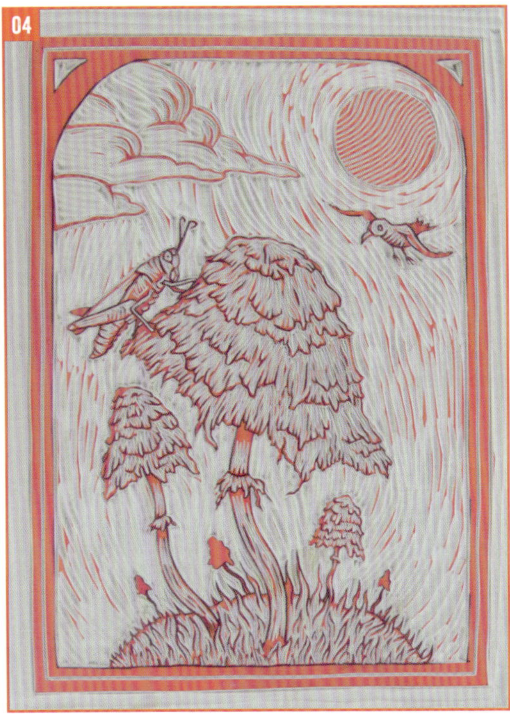

04 REVIEW THE LINO

Once you've finished carving, look over the lino block to check it's ready for printing. This is the time to make any adjustments. For example, you may feel there's too much noise and want to carve more away to balance out busy areas with emptier ones. How much noise you include, and how you integrate it into the image, is up to you.

< The noisy areas are carved in one direction, with the marks flowing towards and around the sun

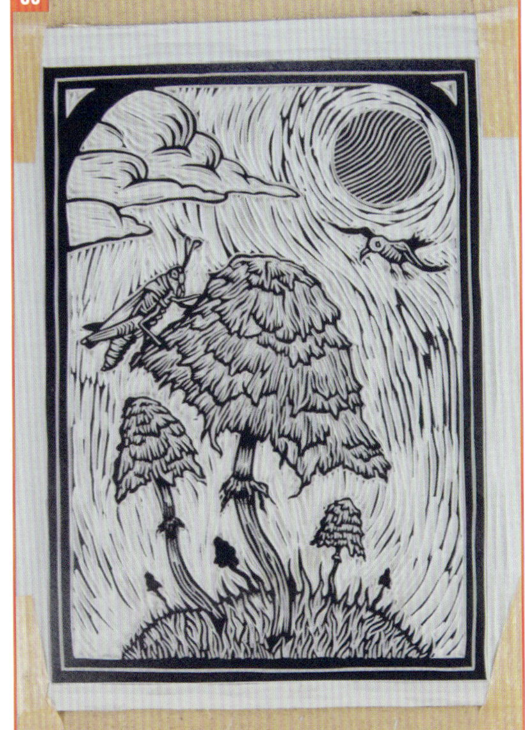

05 INK THE BLOCK

Roll on your ink of choice. If your lino is light in colour, darker inks will make the carved design stand out, especially any 'noisy' textures left in the background. This will give you a clearer idea of what the final print will look like, although in reverse. Once happy, press the design.

> Freshly inked, observe how the busy texture adds to the design

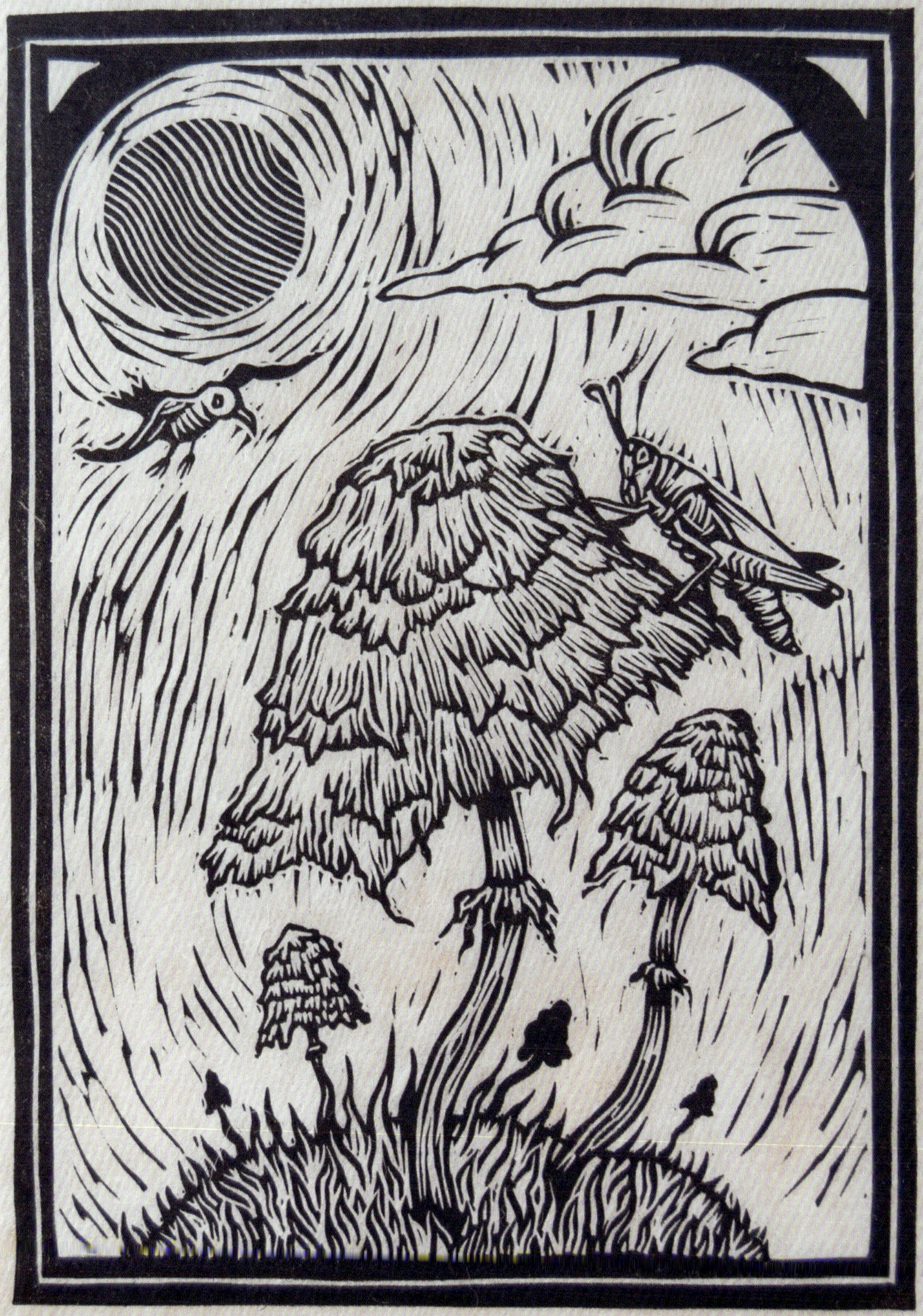

Noisy, textured print | The textured background gives the final print a beautiful, hand-carved feel

CLEAN PRINT

01 CARVE FLAT AREAS

To create a version where the background is clean and ink-free, use a broad, flatter U-shaped tool to carve the lino as flat as possible. Broader tools are great for removing pointy ridges of lino left from carving with smaller tools. They will make the surface more level, meaning fewer unwanted inky marks are printed.

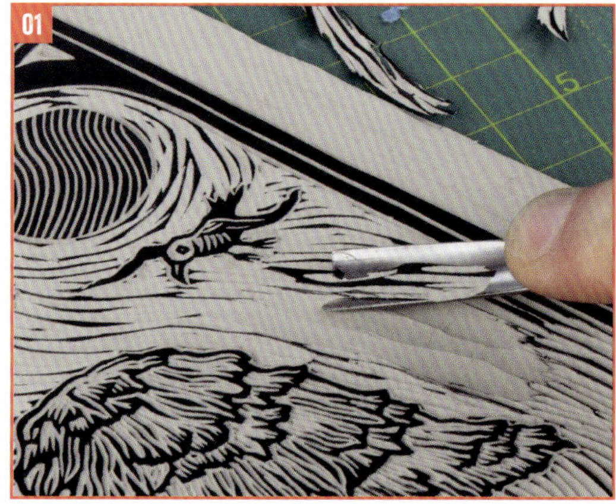

> Using a broad carving tool to remove the textured ridges in the background

02 INK & CHECK THE SURFACE

Ink the lino using a roller that is broader than the block. This will reduce the chance of accidentally rolling ink into carved areas, which can happen if the roller is too narrow and tilts slightly as you roll. Once inked, inspect the areas you want to remain free of ink. Carve away any ridges that have picked up ink, then print.

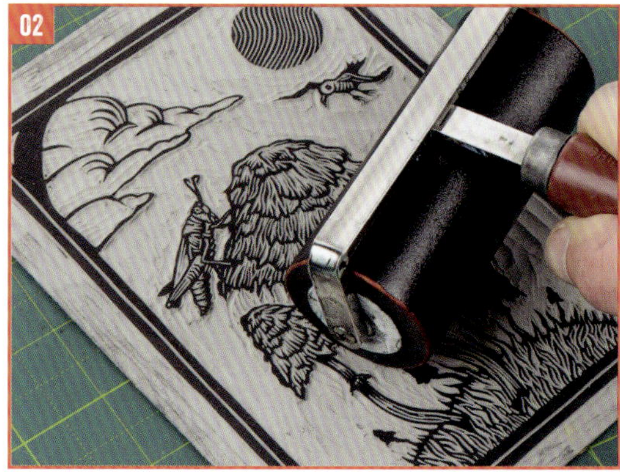

> Using a broad roller to apply ink evenly to the lino

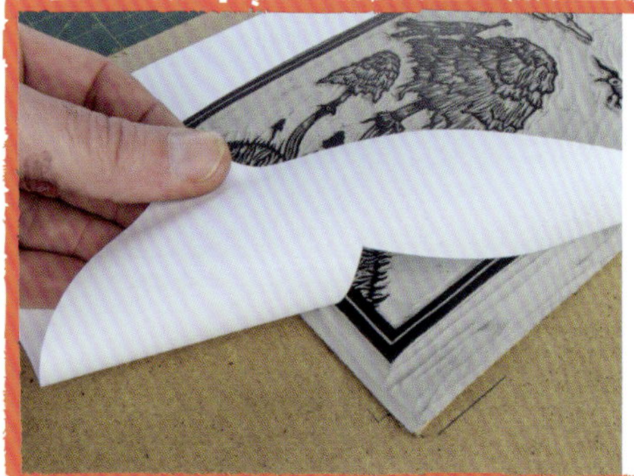

MASKING

One method to prevent unwanted marks on a print is to mask off areas of the lino. Even if some of the ridges do pick up ink, the mask will cover them so they won't be printed. For this design, mask off the area outside of the border with paper. Tape it down on one side only so you can lift it out of the way while inking the block.

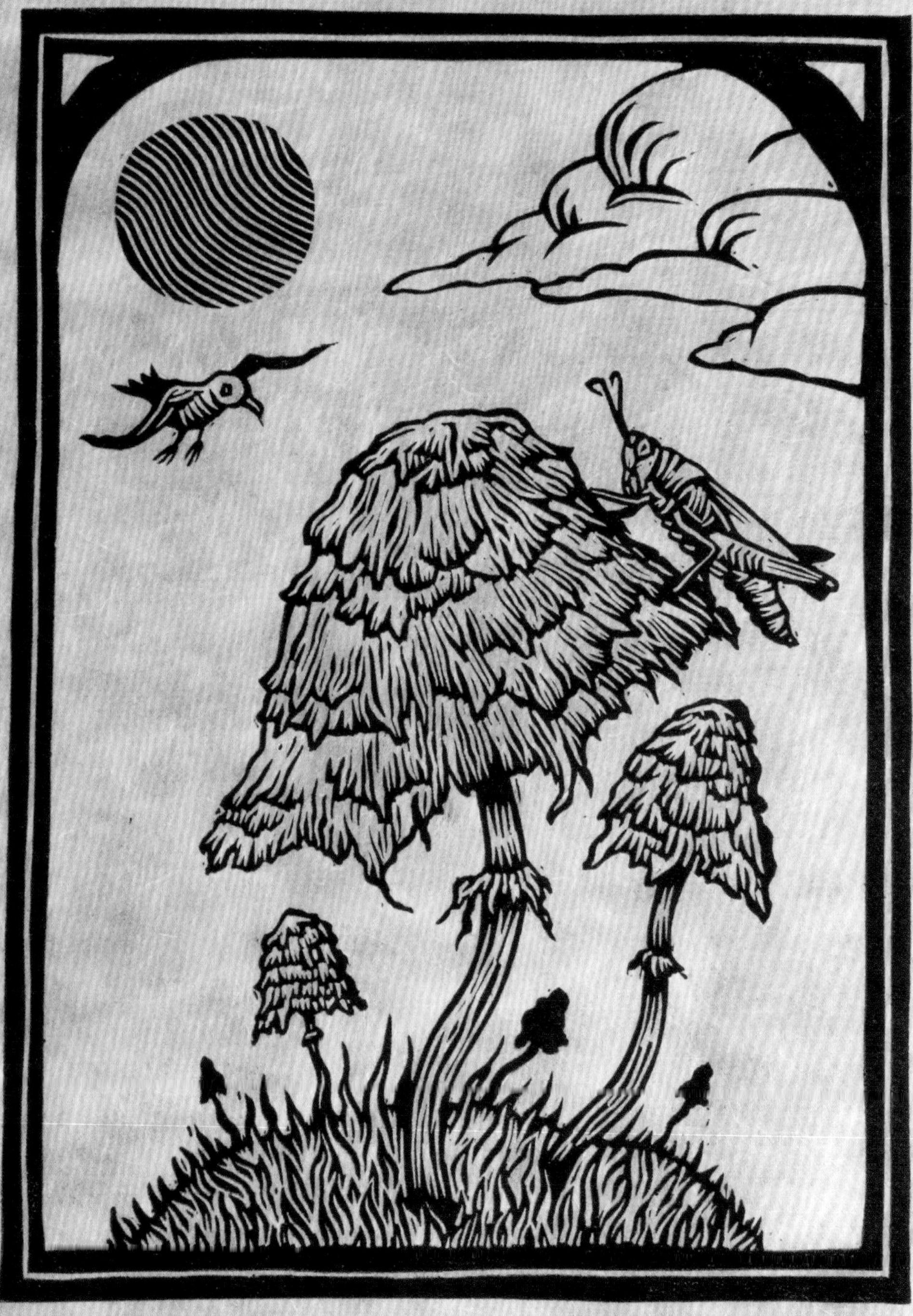

Clean, neat print | In this print there is more space around the different elements, which makes them stand out and have more impact

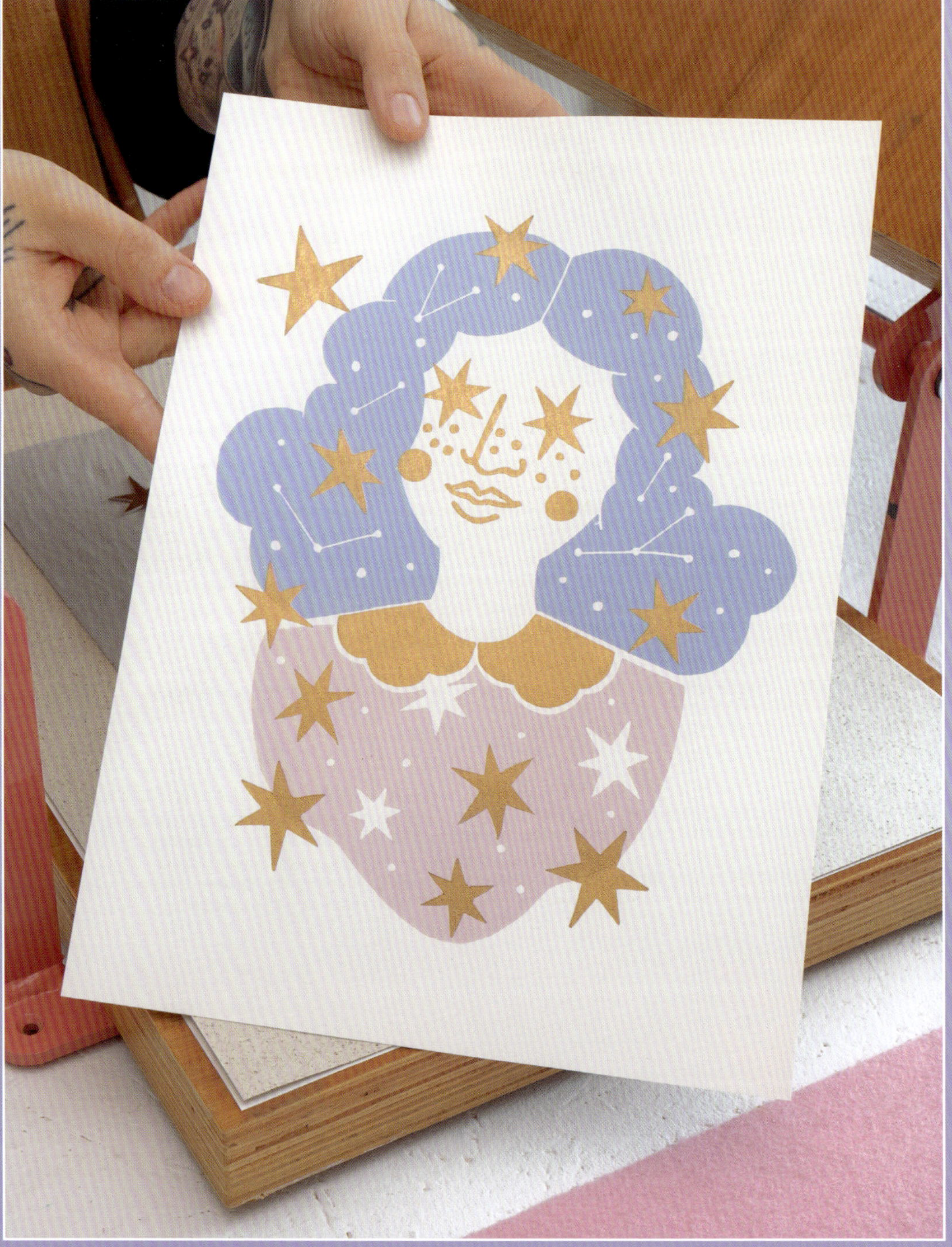

MULTI-BLOCK PRINT

LADY NIGHT SKY

BY ANNA HERMSDORF

Multi-block linocut prints are created by carving a design over two or more lino blocks. Each block is inked with one or two different colours, then printed in layers to produce the final print. This tutorial will show you how to use two traditional hessian-backed lino blocks and three colours to create a cosmic portrait, featuring stars and constellations. You can reprint the image as many times as you like with the same or different colour combinations. A table-top press is used to print the image in this demonstration, but you can create the same effect using a board with a baren or spoon.

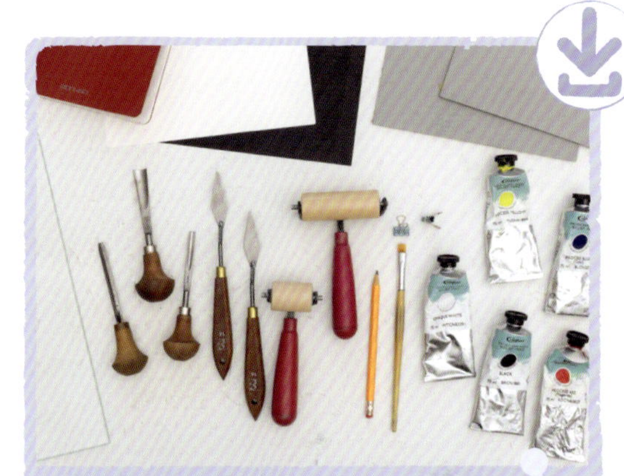

MATERIALS NEEDED

- Pencil and eraser
- Sketching paper
- Carbon paper
- Small clamps
- Two lino blocks (21 cm × 29.7 cm)
- Carving tools of various sizes
- Inks (black, white, cyan, magenta, process yellow, gold)
- Two palette knives
- Glass or acrylic plate
- Two rollers (narrow and wide)
- Small brush
- Print paper (the same size as the lino blocks)
- Press (or baren or spoon)

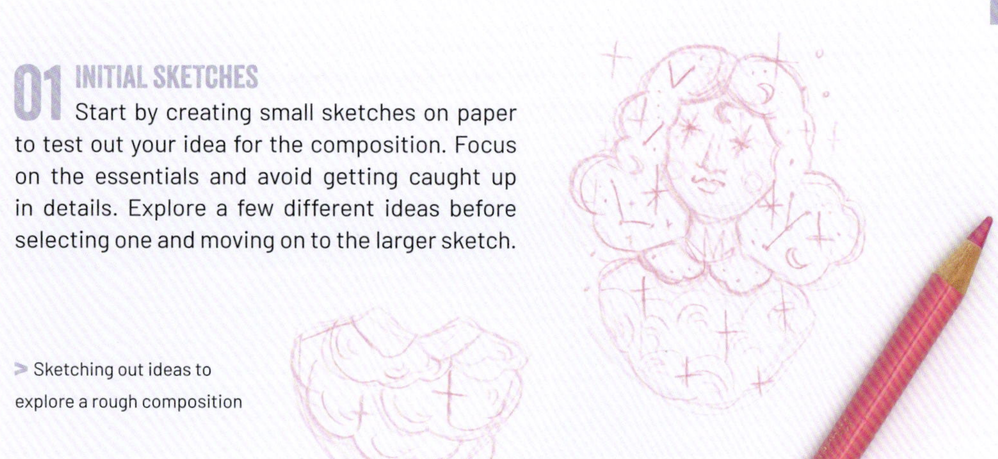

01 INITIAL SKETCHES

Start by creating small sketches on paper to test out your idea for the composition. Focus on the essentials and avoid getting caught up in details. Explore a few different ideas before selecting one and moving on to the larger sketch.

> Sketching out ideas to explore a rough composition

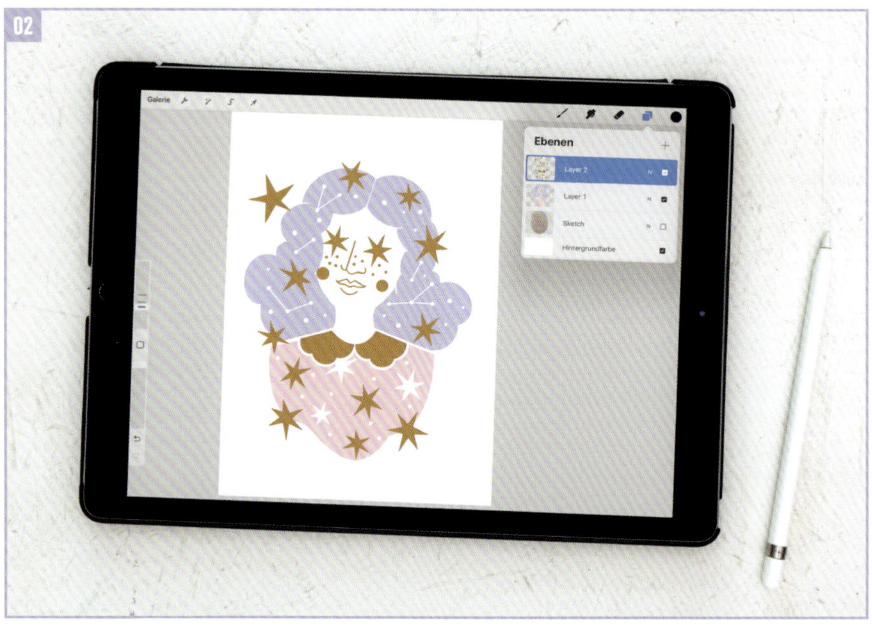

< Redrawing and refining the design in a digital drawing app

02 REFINING THE DESIGN

Take a photo of the sketch and open it in a digital drawing app, such as Procreate. Create a digital version of the sketch, then define the layers (which parts of the design will go on which block) and choose the colours. If you don't have access to digital painting software, redraw and refine your sketch at the intended size on paper and test out different colours.

03 PRINT OUT & TRANSFER

Use the digital software to scale the design to the exact same size as your lino blocks. Next, flip the design horizontally to make a mirrored version, then print out the two separate layers. Once you have two greyscale printouts, transfer each one to a separate lino block using carbon paper and small clamps to hold the printout in place. Precision is important when transferring the artwork – the printouts and lino blocks being the exact same size will help to ensure accuracy, as you can line up the edges. This is an alternative to using registration tabs and pins.

> The first layer transferred to the lino block using carbon paper

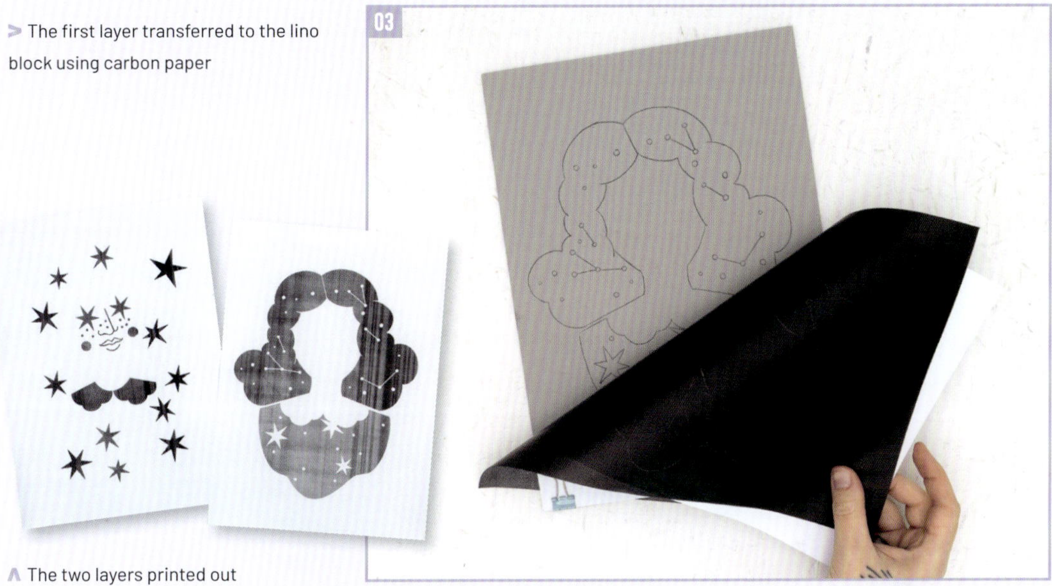

∧ The two layers printed out

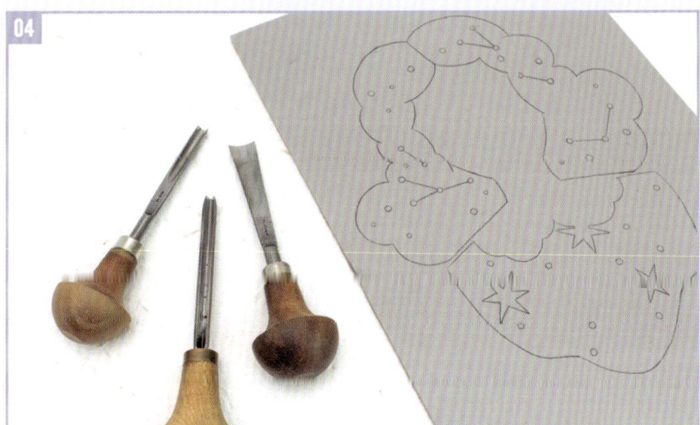

∧ Pfeil carving tools, sizes L9/5, L12/4, and B7/14

04 CARVING TOOLS

You will need three sizes of carving tool for carving this print into the lino: a versatile V-shaped tool for both fine and broader details, plus a wider U-shaped tool and flat U-shaped tool for carving the background. Feel free to use other sizes too, but these three form a solid basic set.

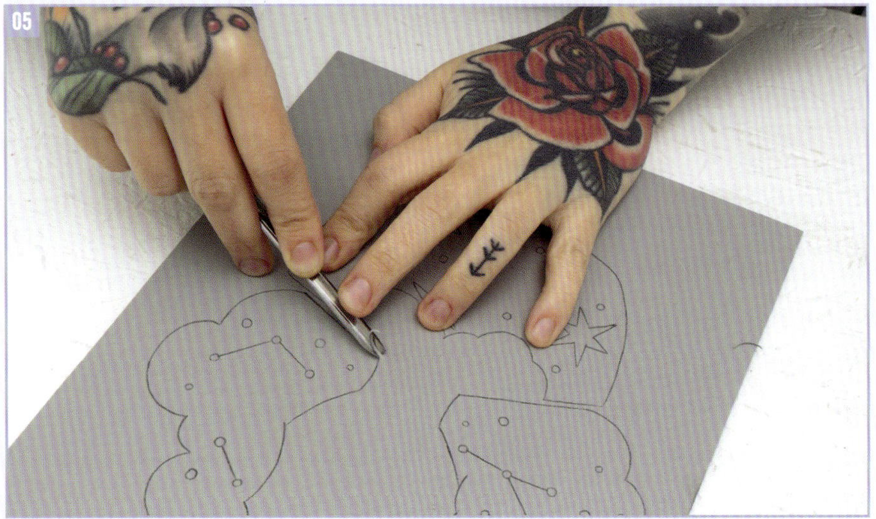

‹ Using the different tools to create sharp edges and a clean background

05 CARVING THE FIRST LAYER

Start by using the V-shaped tool to carve an outline around each of the different elements. Next, use the U-shaped tool to widen this outline, creating a safety zone around the areas you wish to keep intact. Finally, use the wide U-shaped tool to clear away large areas of the background. To clean up the edges, use the V-shaped tool to carve along the outer lines, creating sharp contours.

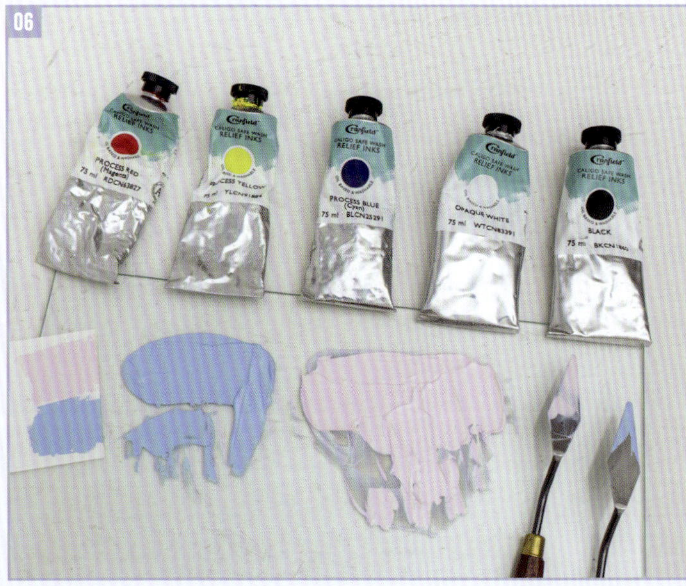

06 MIXING COLOURS

Light blue and pink will be used for the first layer. To create a blue with a slight purple tint, mix white and cyan with a touch of magenta. For the light pink, combine white and magenta, adding some yellow to create a warm tone. Test out both shades on a piece of paper before printing.

‹ Five colours are all you need to create a wide range of shades

07 ROLLING OUT THE INK

Use a palette knife to apply the ink to a glass plate, spreading it out so it roughly matches the size of the rollers. Next, use the rollers to pick up some ink and roll it out to create a smooth, uniform layer. Roll from front to back and left to right to ensure consistent application and distribution on both the plate and rollers.

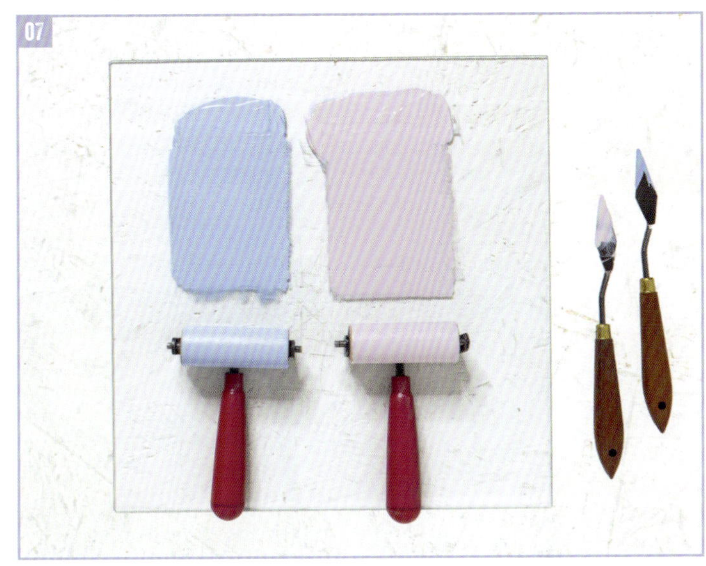

> Rolling the ink smoothly and evenly onto the glass plate

08 INKING THE BLOCK

Position the lino block in the centre of the press bed (or board if using a spoon or baren). The woman's hair will be blue and her clothing pink. To ensure an even application of ink on the lino, begin rolling from the centre outwards. Roll from bottom to top, and from left to right, to evenly ink the block. Try not to touch the background, but if you do, use a short, stiff brush to wipe off the excess ink.

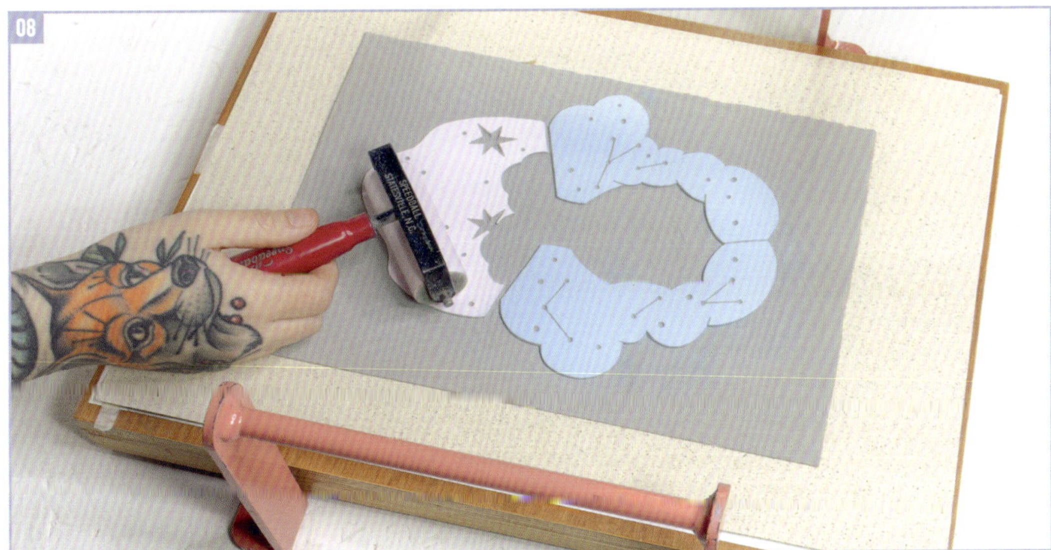

∧ Inking the block evenly, rolling outwards from the centre

09 REGISTRATION

Once the ink is evenly spread, align a sheet of paper over the lino block. Smooth 130-180 gsm drawing paper is used for this print. Again, the paper being the same size as the lino block will help you with correct placement. Don't trim the design, as this will cause misalignment during printing. Place the paper at the lower edge of the lino block first, then hold it in place while gently lowering it.

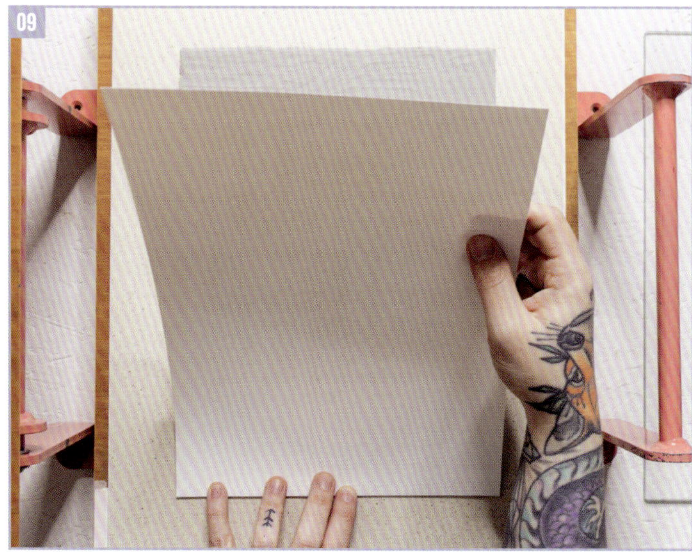

> Carefully aligning the paper over the inked lino block

10 INK DISTRIBUTION

Once the paper is in place, place the press's felt mat on top, close the press, and apply firm pressure, pulling the lever three to five times. Alternatively, you can use a baren or spoon. The ink does not always distribute perfectly, so carefully check the print before lifting the paper fully. This will allow you to adjust the pressure or add more ink if necessary.

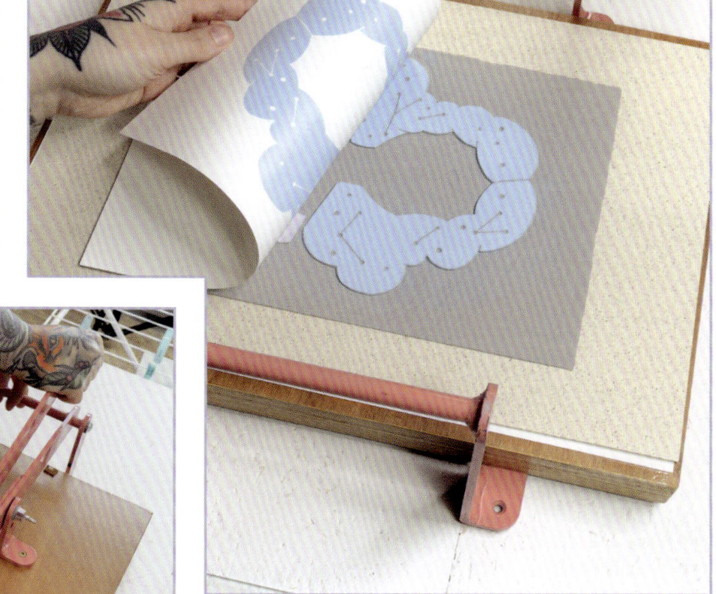

∧ Checking the ink distribution

11 DRYING

Once happy with the print of the first layer, lift the paper and set it aside to dry. If securing with pegs, make sure they don't apply too much pressure, as this could leave marks on the paper. Let the prints dry for two to seven days – depending on how much the colours on the second layer will overlap with those on the first – before printing the next layer.

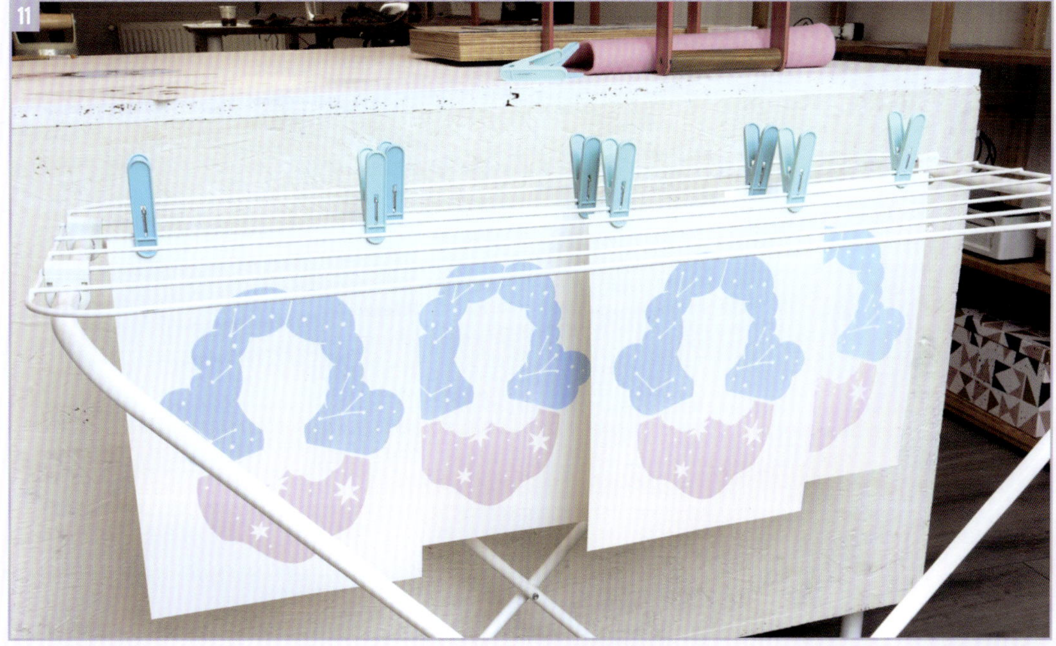

∧ A small drying rack is an excellent space-saving solution when drying prints

12 THE SECOND PRINT LAYER

While waiting for the first layer to dry, carve the second layer on the second lino block, following the process in step 05. Once the first layer is dry, ink the second lino block ready for printing. This time there is only one colour – gold – so no mixing is necessary. Use a small roller to ink each part of the design, wiping away any splashes with a brush.

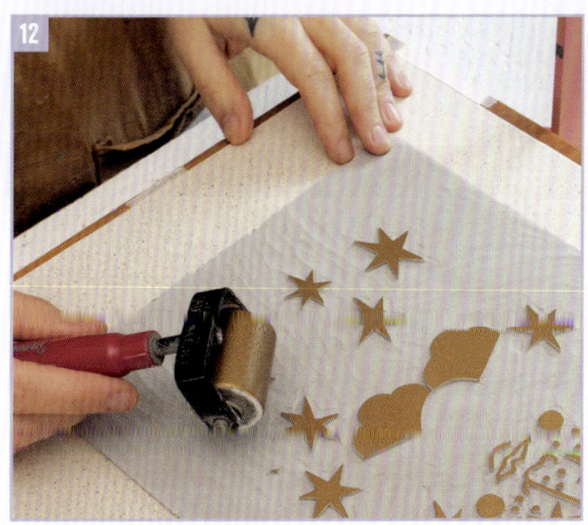

> Inking the second layer

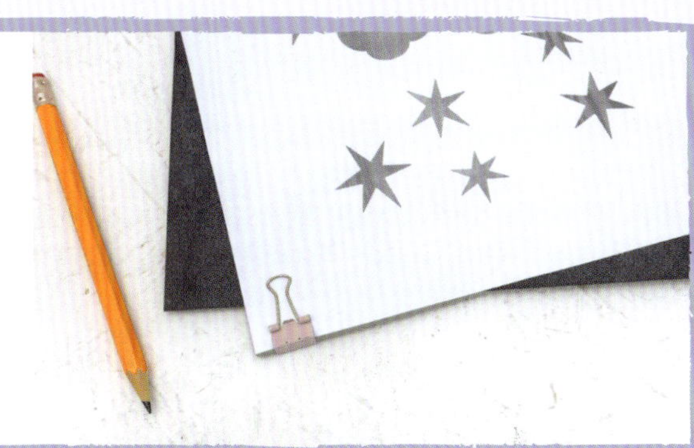

WORK ACCURATELY

Layering multiple lino blocks requires precise work. This is easier when printing onto pre-cut paper bought from a print shop, but harder when using handmade paper with a deckled edge. For the latter, you should use registration tabs to help you.

13 REGISTRATION & PRINTING

Now you'll need to carefully align the printed first layer over the inked second-layer block. Again, line up the lower edge of the paper first, then slowly lower it into place. This particular design allows for slight misalignment, so it's not a problem if the registration isn't perfect. Such designs minimize frustration while still achieving a great result. Follow the process in step 10 to print, then leave to dry.

< Carefully aligning the dry print along the edge of the block

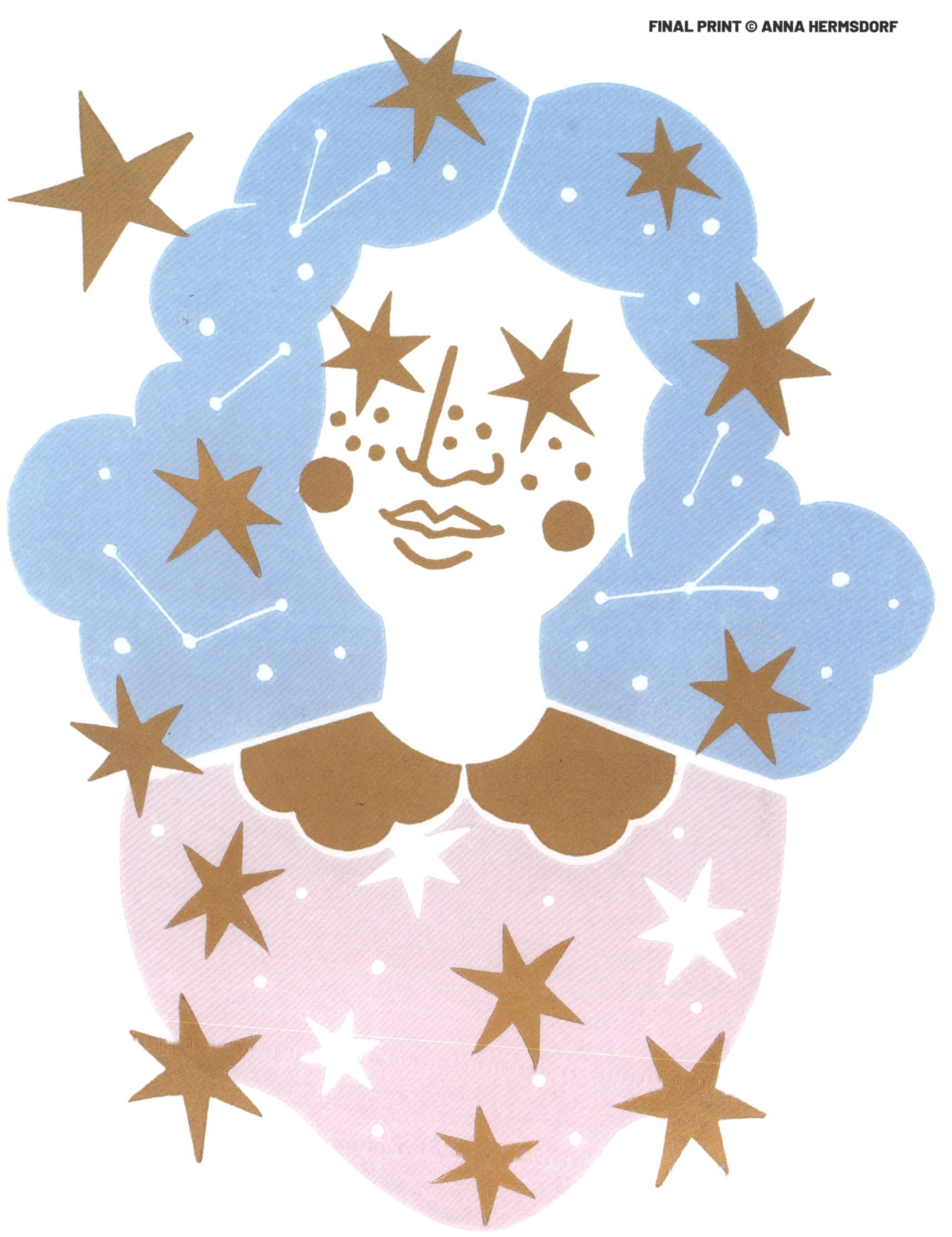

Lady Night Sky | Though it may look complex, this two-layer cosmic portrait is relatively easy to achieve

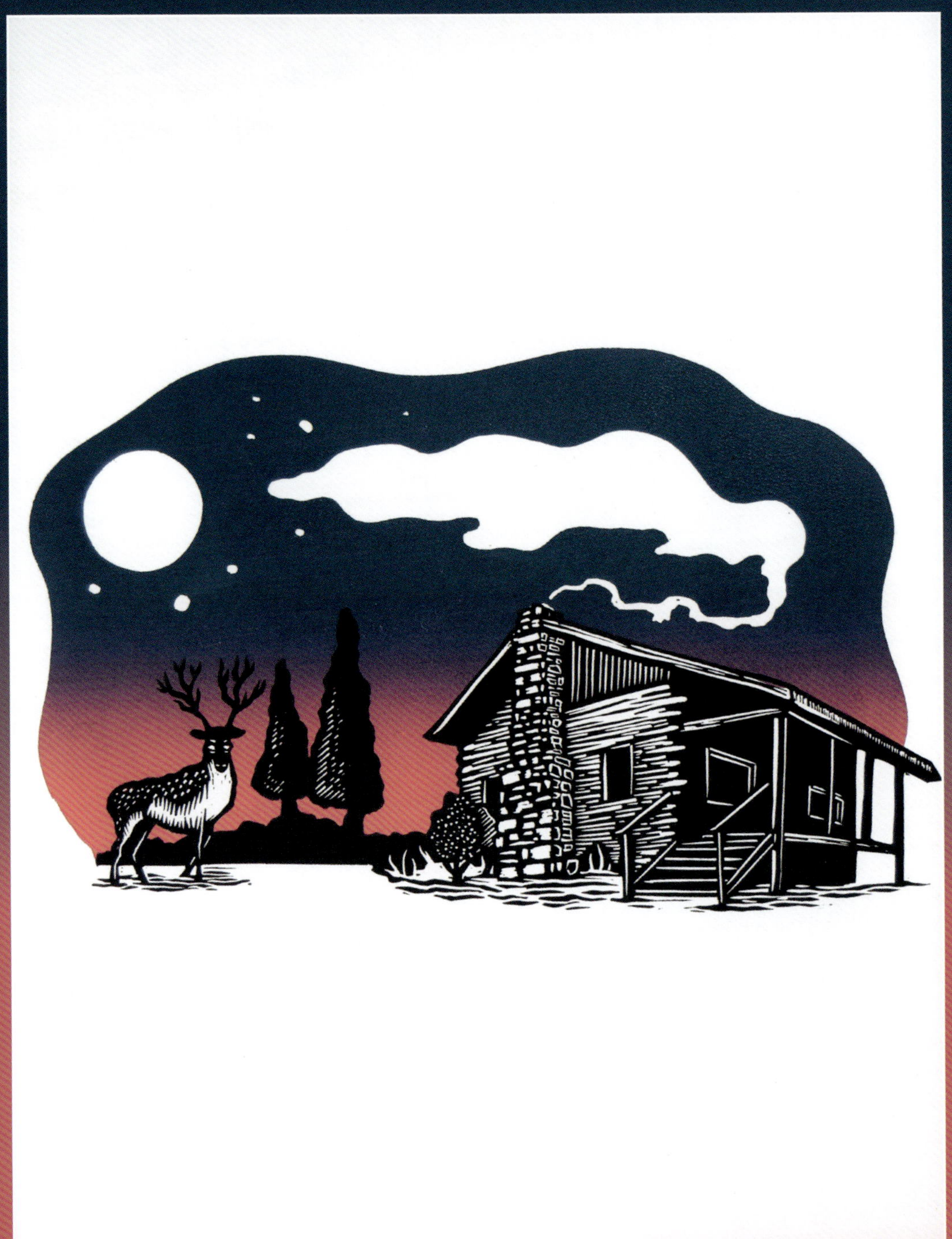

CREATING A GRADIENT EFFECT

A NIGHT AT THE CABIN

BY GARETH BARNES (SPINDLE PRINTER)

A gradient is created when two or more inks of a different colour or value are partially mixed when rolled alongside each other. This produces a beautiful effect as the colours softly blend together, creating a range of subtly different shades in between. Guaranteed to enhance any print, a colourful gradient can be used on background layers, detailed foreground layers, or even single-layer prints. In this tutorial, a gradient effect will be used on the background layer to create a sense of depth and a touch of magic. A second layer, printed on top of this, will contain the main details of the design.

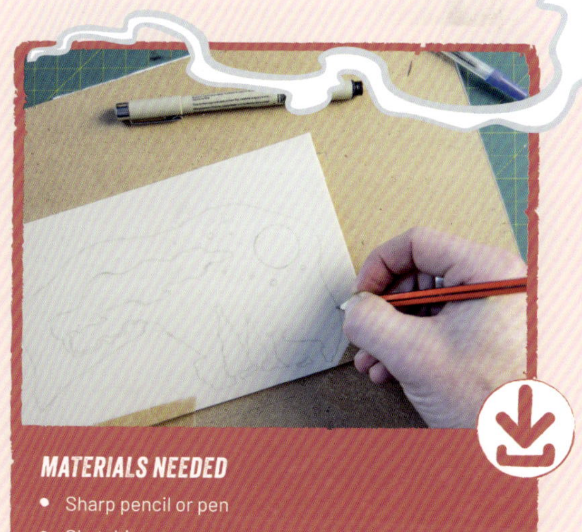

MATERIALS NEEDED

- Sharp pencil or pen
- Sketching paper
- Tracing paper, graphite paper, or carbon paper
- Masking tape
- Two lino blocks (one hessian-backed and one SoftCut)
- Carving tools
- Registration tabs and pins
- Inks and inking plate
- Rollers
- Spoon, baren, or press
- Print paper

01 PREPARE THE ARTWORK

Following the steps in the Processes chapter (page 42), draw a design and then reverse it. As this cabin illustration is drawn digitally, it can be reversed on-screen and then printed.

> The design printed at the exact size needed – additional details can be added later

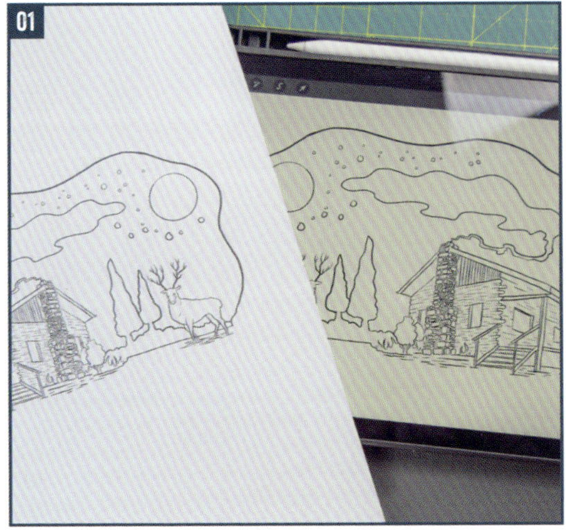

02 TRANSFER THE FOREGROUND LAYER

Two separate lino blocks are needed for this print: one for the foreground and one for the background. Traditional hessian-backed lino is perfect for the foreground layer, as it's better suited for more detailed carving. Prepare the lino by lightly coating it with either acrylic marker or ink. Once it's dry, use graphite paper (or your preferred transfer method) to transfer the design to the first lino block. Peel back the paper to check if the image has transferred fully.

< Checking the line work has transferred clearly onto the hessian-backed lino

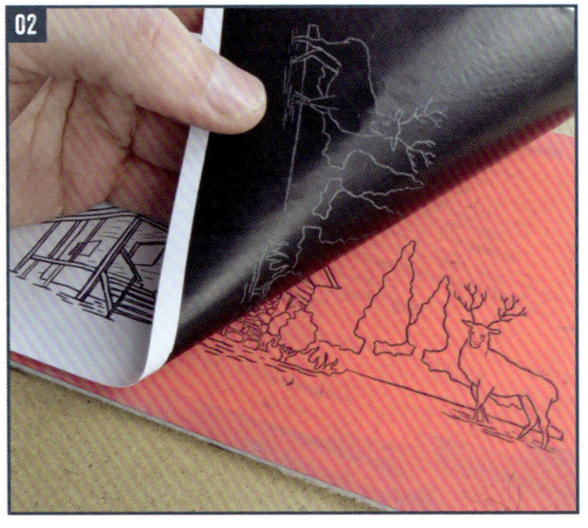

LINE UP THE TWO LAYERS

Ensuring the lino blocks line up with each other correctly is crucial when creating a multi-layered print. Position the first lino block and mark around it using pen or tape. Lay the paper on top of the lino, tape down one edge of the paper to ensure it doesn't move, and transfer the design to the lino. You can then use the same marks to position the second lino block and transfer the second layer design. As the paper can't move, and both lino blocks are positioned in the same place, the two layers will match and align perfectly for the final print.

03 TRANSFER THE BACKGROUND LAYER

Transfer the outline of the background layer onto the second lino block. Try using SoftCut lino, as it's especially good for large, flatter areas of colour without much detail – like this gradient background layer. The line work may not transfer as well, so go over it a few times with a pen or pencil.

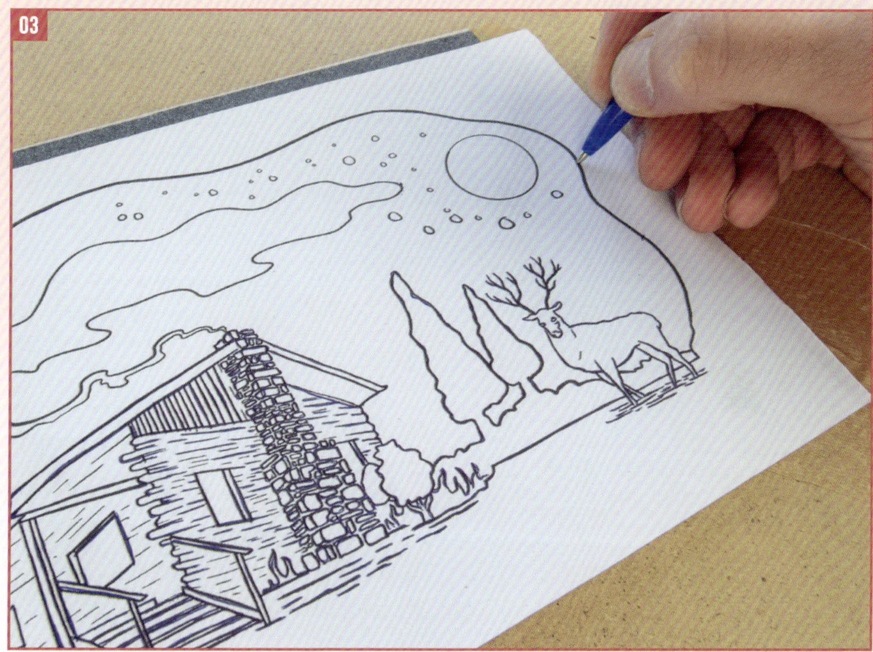

> A sharp pencil or ballpoint pen is ideal for pressing through the paper layers to transfer the image

04 CARVE THE FOREGROUND LAYER

Use a small V-shaped tool to carve the outline and details of the cabin design, then a wider, flatter U-shaped tool to carve away the space surrounding it. As you're only carving details from the lower part of this lino block, the upper part can be left uncarved. A mask will be used to cover the uncarved section when printing (see step 11). This spare lino can then be used for a later project, so nothing is wasted

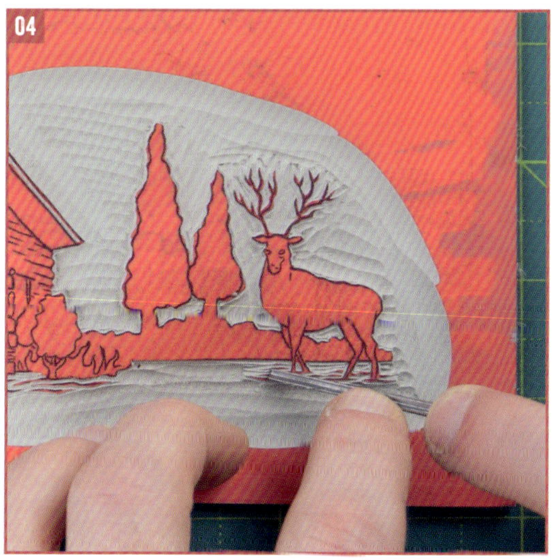

< Using a small V-shaped tool to carve the finer details

05 CARVE THE BACKGROUND LAYER

Use a small V-shaped tool to carve the outline of the background first, followed by broader, flatter tools to carve away the large areas in between. Carving the simple graphic shape of the sky is relatively easy. It's less about detailed mark-marking and more about cleanly removing big areas.

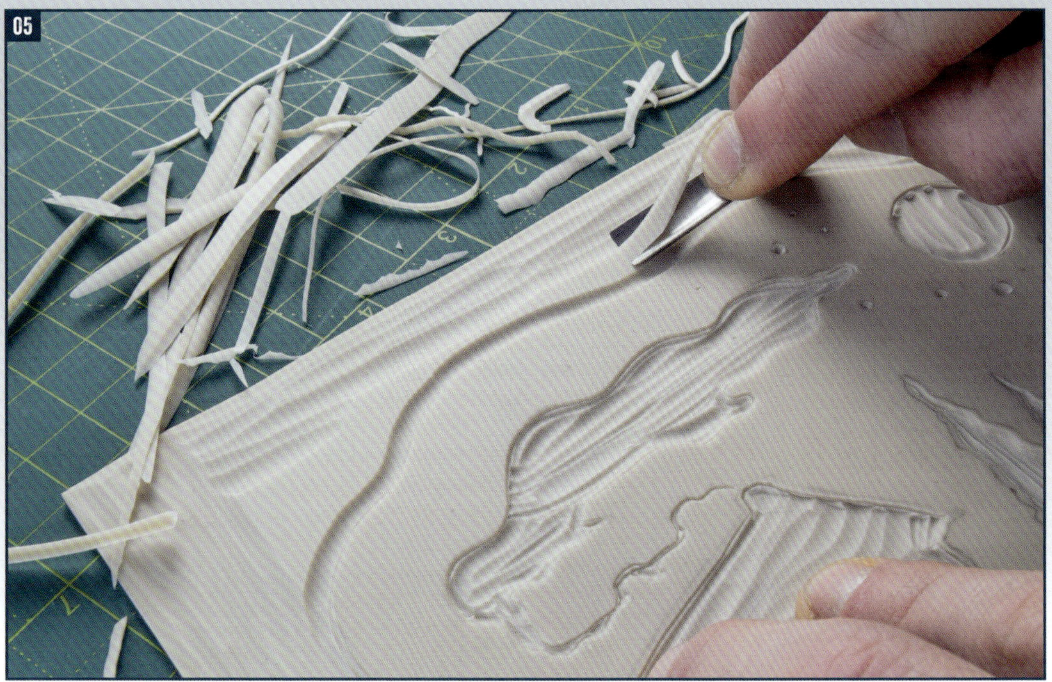

∧ Wider, flatter tools are ideal for neatly clearing away larger areas

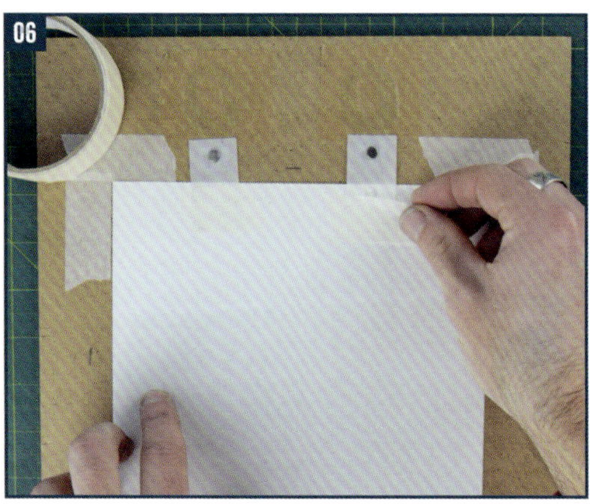

06 PREPARE THE PAPER

Prepare your chosen paper by cutting it to the correct size, adding tabs, and marking its position on your board. This bright-white 90 gsm Japanese Hosho paper is perfect for relief printmaking, as the striking contrast between paper and ink will make the image stand out.

< Using registration tabs and pins to position the paper

07 PREPARE THE INKS FOR THE BACKGROUND LAYER

Choose the colours for the gradient, then add a similar-sized splodge of each next to each other on the ink-mixing surface. Try to match this to the width of your roller, so each ink will cover half of the roller when rolled. If there's too much space between them, the ink thickness won't be even when rolled together, resulting in the ink being too thin in the blended section of the gradient.

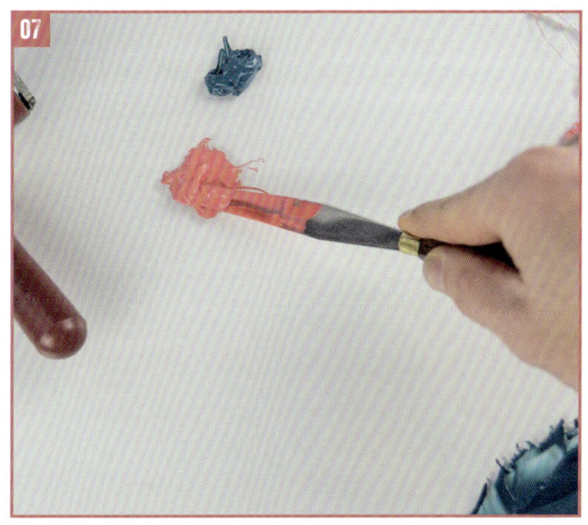

> To create the look of a sunset, use warm pink for the sky closest to the horizon and dark teal for the night sky above

08 MIX THE INKS

To create a gradient effect, choose a roller that is wide enough to cover the whole lino block. Roll in a straight line over the inks, continuing in the same direction until the inks have blended smoothly. It's easy to end up with too much ink on the roller. If you need to get rid of some ink, roll in the same straight motion somewhere else on your mixing surface, until the amount of ink on the roller looks correct.

< Rolling in a straight motion will ensure the two inks blend evenly

> Though there is too much ink on this roller, notice how the two colours have blended to create subtle variations

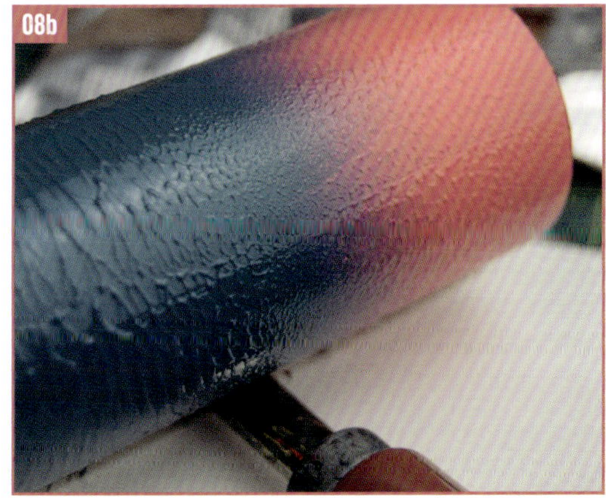

09 INK THE BACKGROUND LAYER

Secure the lino onto your board using strong tape. Carefully place the roller so it covers the full width of the lino block, then roll the ink across in a straight line. Only roll in one direction, either forwards or backwards, as rolling back over the lino in a different direction will mess up the gradient. When the lino is fully inked, check if the ink has applied evenly. If there are any stray ridges with ink on them, clean and carve these away before printing.

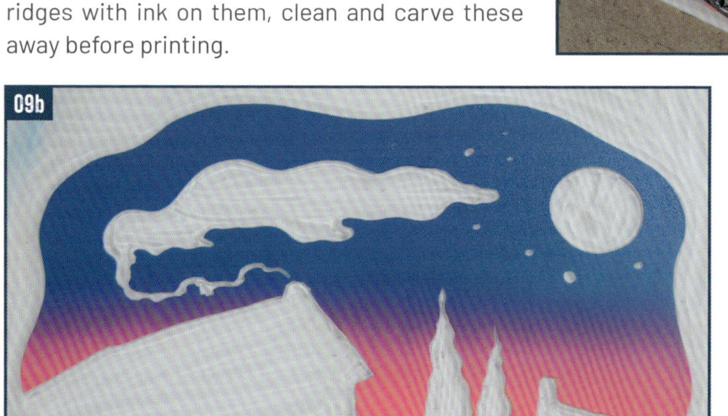

∧ The roller is just the right size to cover the width of the inking area

< The fully inked gradient background layer

10 PRESS THE BACKGROUND LAYER

Place your prepared paper over the inked lino block, then press it. If using a baren or spoon, go steady and take your time. Unevenly printed areas will stand out on larger, flatter areas of colour.

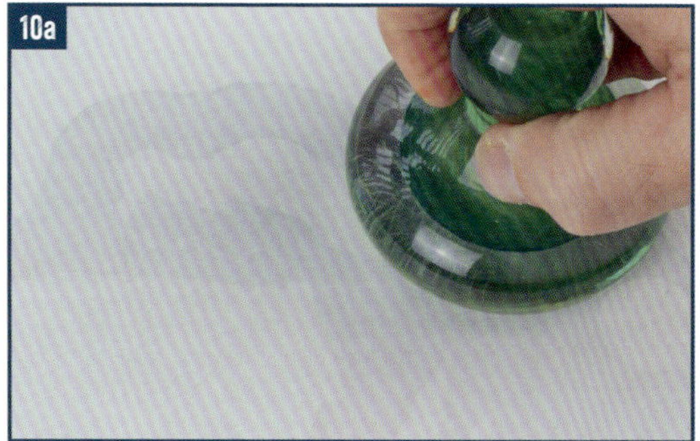

∧ Firmly guide the baren across the paper's surface

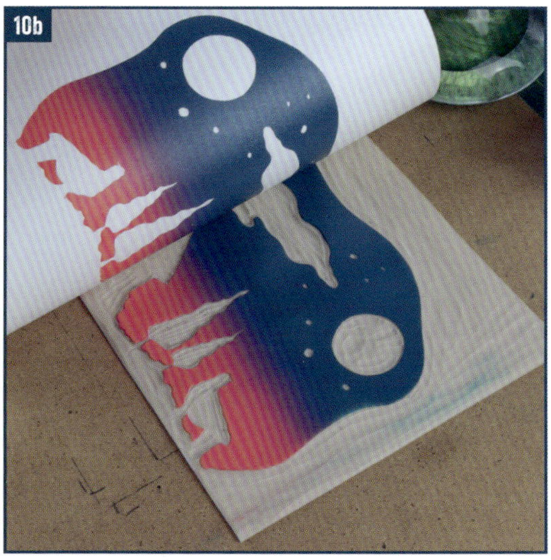

∧ Peeling back the paper to check the ink has transferred

DRYING TIME

If the layers of your print are going to overlap, make sure the first layer is completely dry before printing the next. You risk the second layer printing unevenly if the first layer is even slightly wet or tacky. Plus, the second lino block can sometimes pick up ink from the first layer, leaving blotchy ink coverage. Be patient and let each layer dry fully, no matter how excited you are to keep printing.

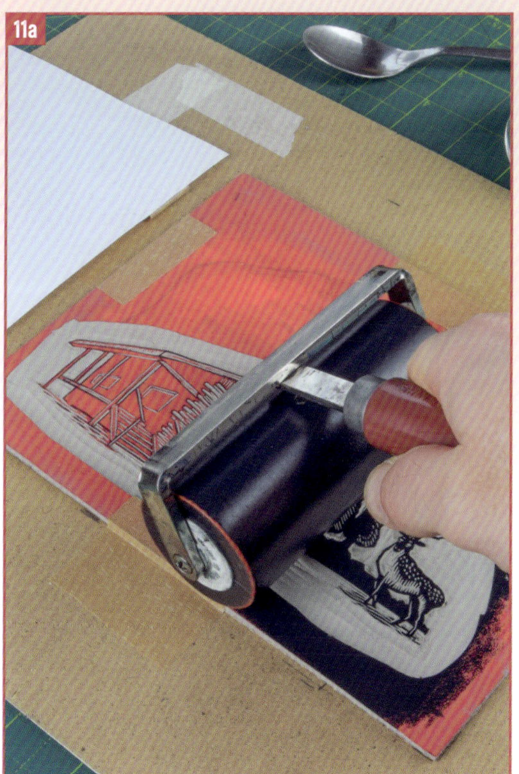

⋀ A few pieces of strong masking tape or strips of card taped against the edges will keep it in place

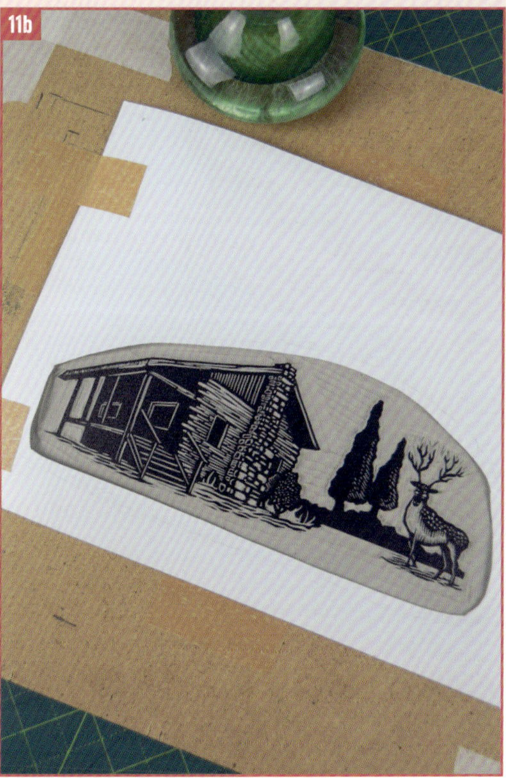

⋀ The fully inked design with a paper mask overlaying the uncarved lino that isn't to be printed

11 INK THE FOREGROUND LAYER

Wait until the background layer has fully dried before inking and printing the second layer. Remove the background-carved lino block from your board and replace it with the foreground block you carved earlier. Tape it in place to prevent it from moving. Apply black ink to the roller and roll it across the design.

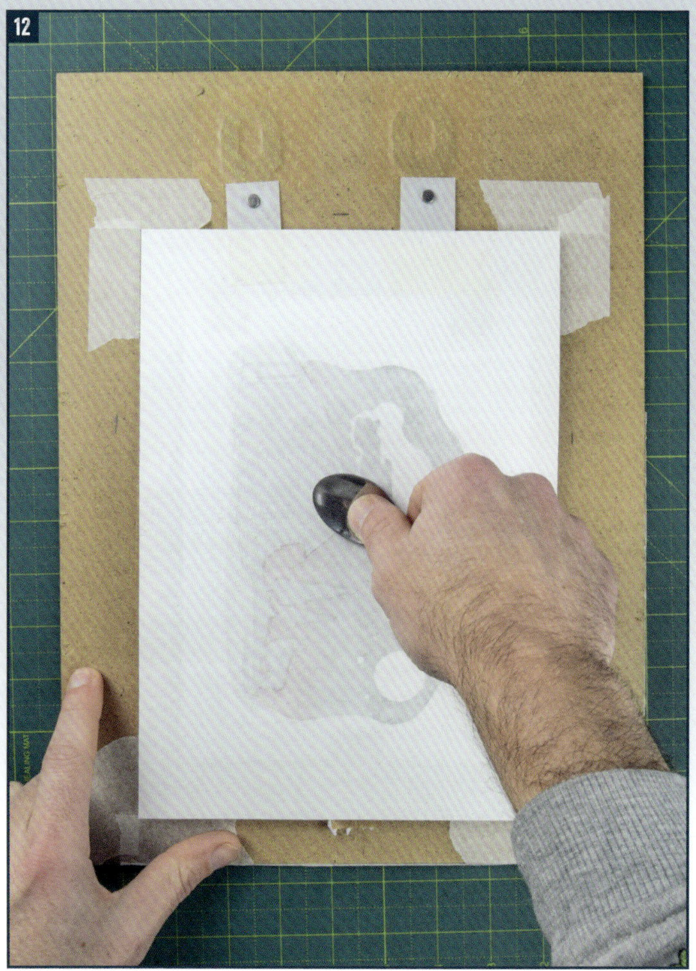

12 PRESS THE FOREGROUND LAYER

Take your fully dried print of the background layer and carefully place it over the lino block, face down, securing it in place with the registration tabs. Press it firmly and evenly to print the foreground layer. As this paper is fairly lightweight, a spoon or baren will work well.

< Firmly and carefully moving a metal spoon across the paper to press the foreground layer

EXPERIMENT WITH COLOUR

The gradient area doesn't have to be limited to just two colours. You could use three, or more! In the cabin scene, dark ink makes the foreground stand out against the sky, partially silhouetted. Experiment with various colour combinations, different directions of rolling the ink, and how the gradient looks alongside the other layers.

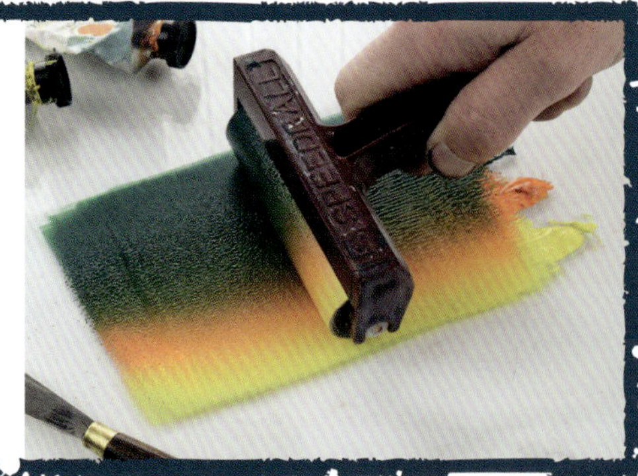

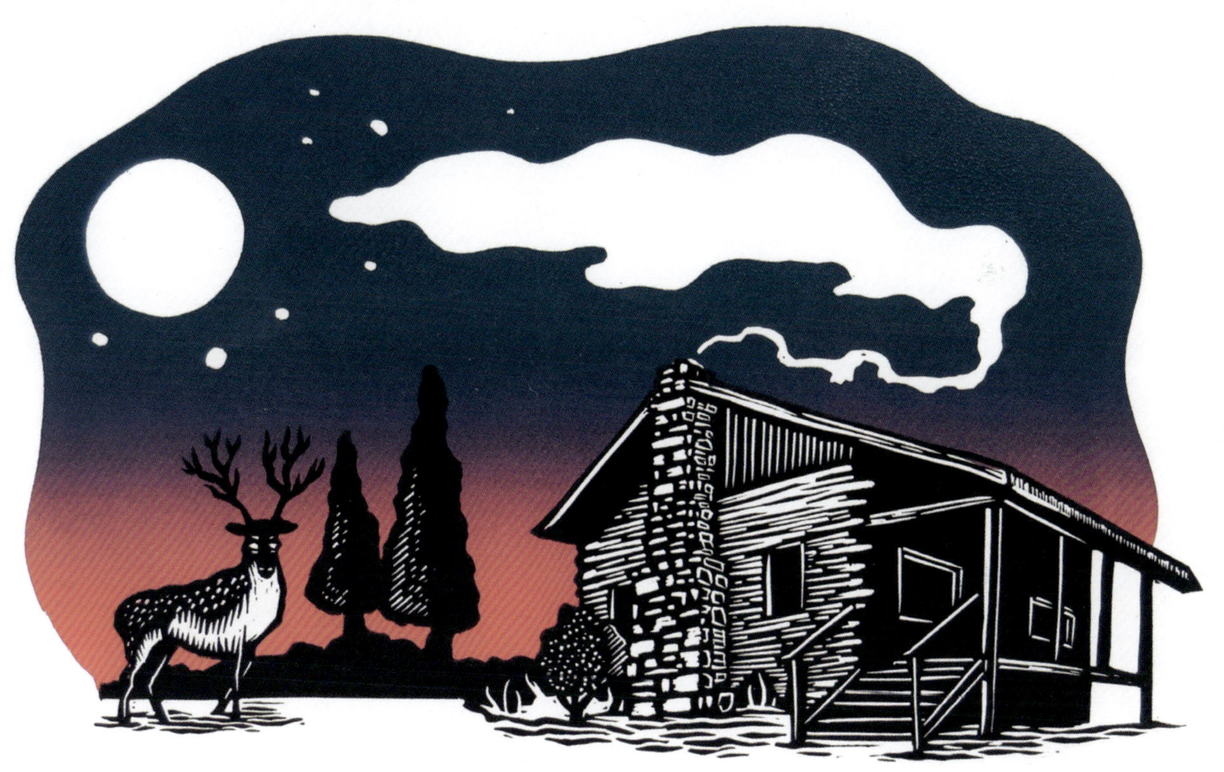

A Night at the Cabin | The vibrant gradient elevates the design, creating an interesting feeling of depth and quality of light

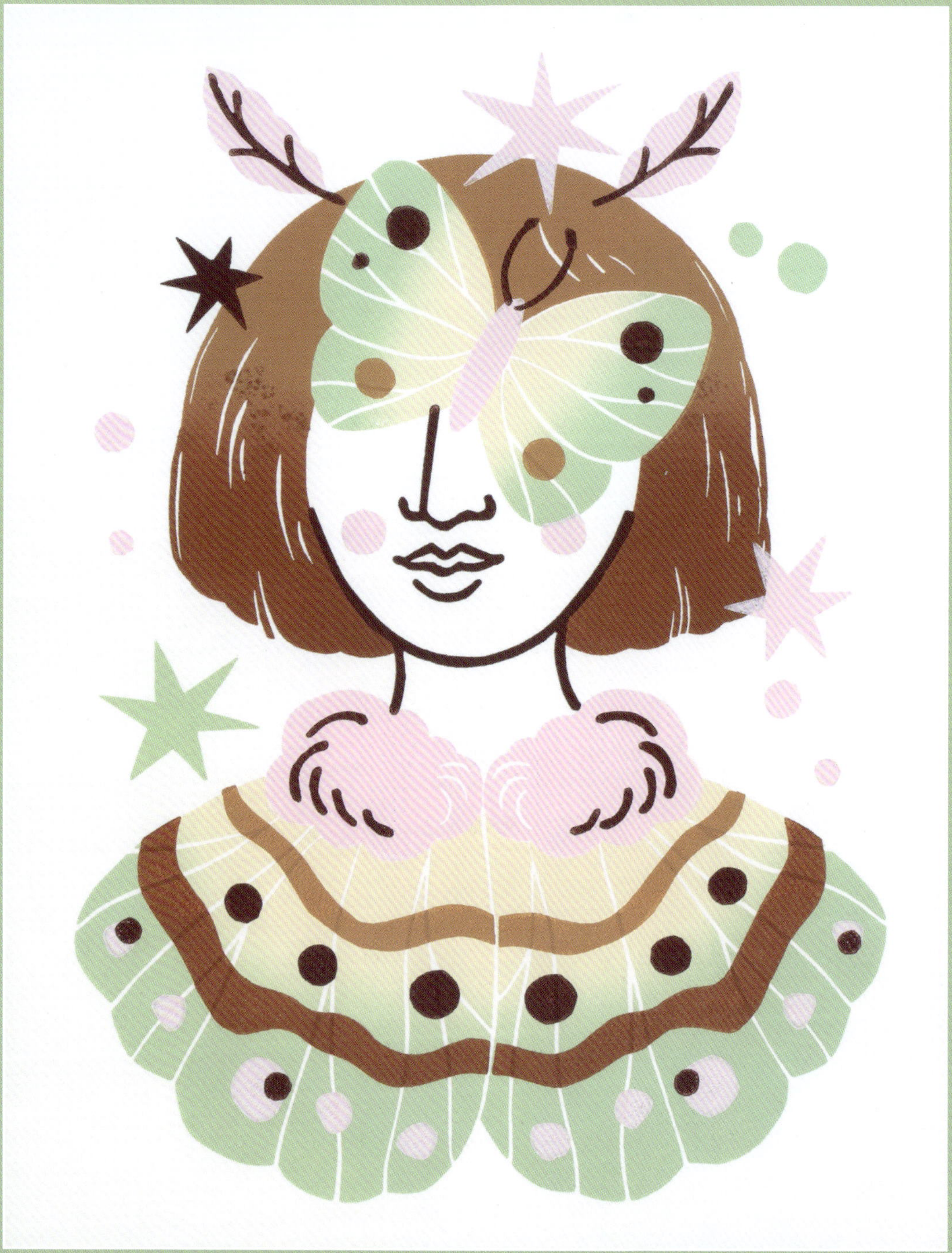

ADVANCED MULTI-BLOCK PRINT

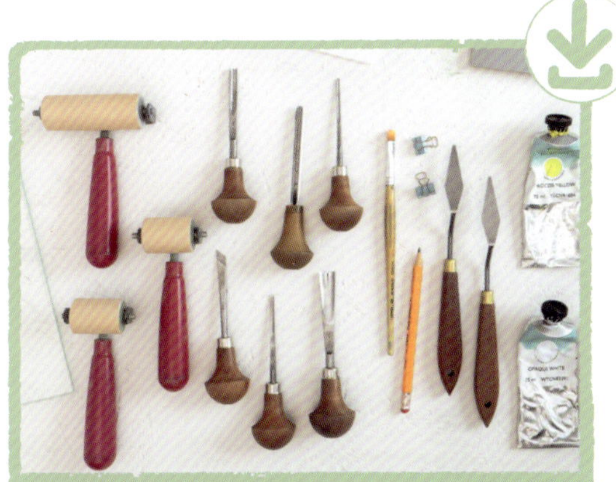

LADY MOTH

BY ANNA HERMSDORF

This tutorial will demonstrate how to create an impressive multi-block linocut print using four traditional hessian-backed lino blocks and six colours. As with the tutorial for *Lady Night Sky* (page 88), this *Lady Moth* design will come together by layering different colours on top of each other. This more advanced project requires accuracy at all stages, as any misalignment will show immediately. A table-top press is used to print this image, but it can be printed with a baren or spoon, too.

MATERIALS NEEDED

- Pencil, eraser, and sketch paper
- Carbon paper
- Architect clamps
- Four lino blocks (21 cm × 29.7 cm)
- Carving tools of various sizes
- Small brush
- Coloured tape and double-sided tape
- Inks (black, white, cyan, magenta, process yellow)
- Glass or acrylic plate
- Two palette knives
- Three rollers (two narrow and one wide)
- Coarse sponge
- Print paper (30 cm × 40 cm)
- Printing press (or baren or spoon)

01 ROUGH SKETCH

Start by creating a few small drawings on paper to explore ideas and establish a rough composition. Avoid getting lost in detail or over-polishing the artwork – the focus is on testing the arrangement of elements and proportions rather than creating a masterpiece.

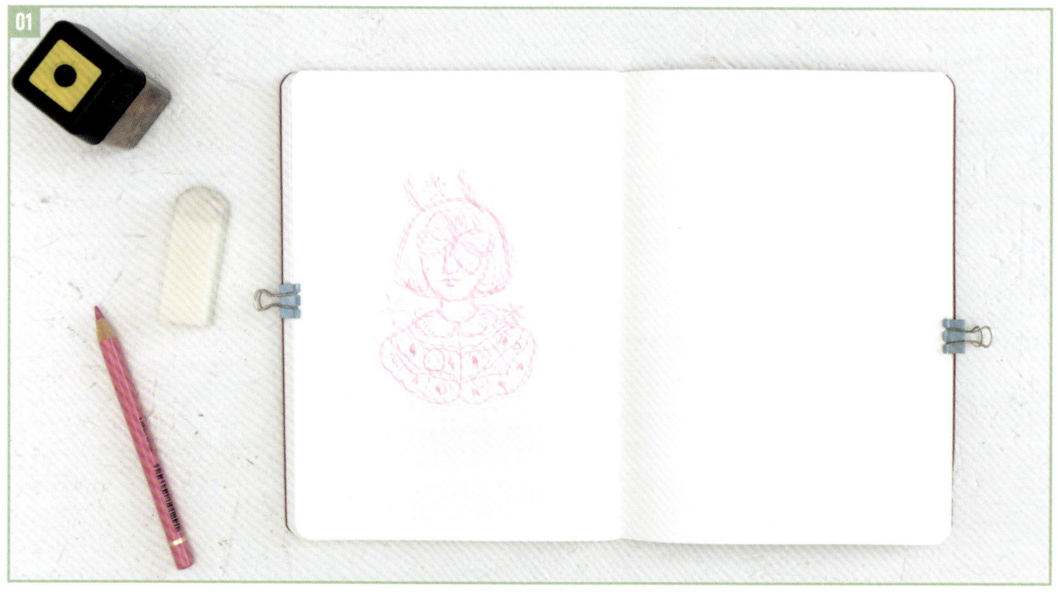

∧ Testing out composition and developing ideas

02 DIGITAL DRAWING

Redraw your favourite sketch in a digital drawing software, such as Procreate, and decide which elements will be on which layers. Test out various colours to create a harmonious, contrasting result. View the final design in greyscale to check it has a good balance of light, medium, and dark tones.

> Experiment until you find a harmonious colour palette

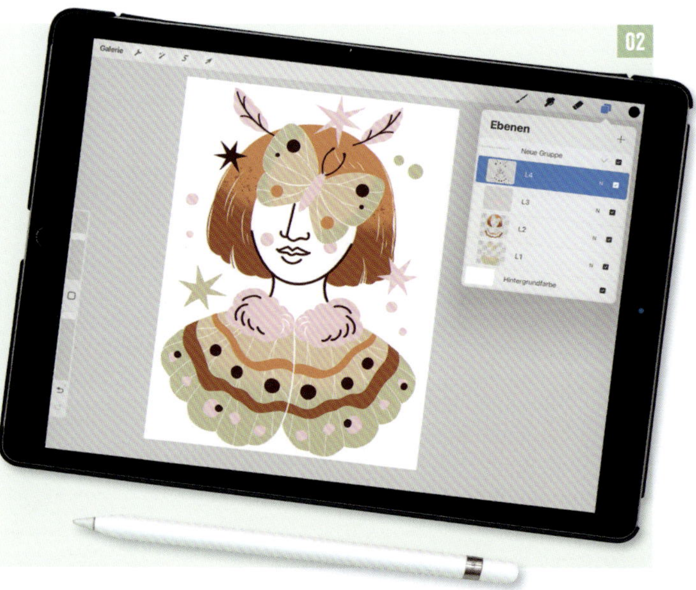

03 PRINT OUT LAYERS

Lady Moth is made up of four layers, each featuring a different colour or a two-colour gradient. Print out each layer on paper that's the exact same size as the lino blocks. This will make alignment much easier. Check the four layers are correctly aligned on your printouts by arranging them one on top of the other and holding them up to the light.

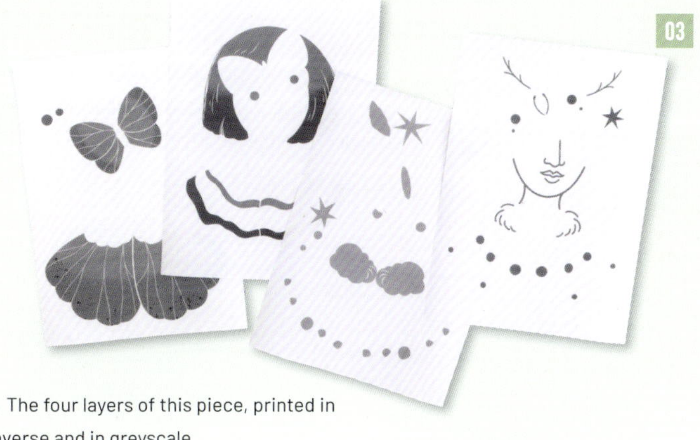

⋏ The four layers of this piece, printed in reverse and in greyscale

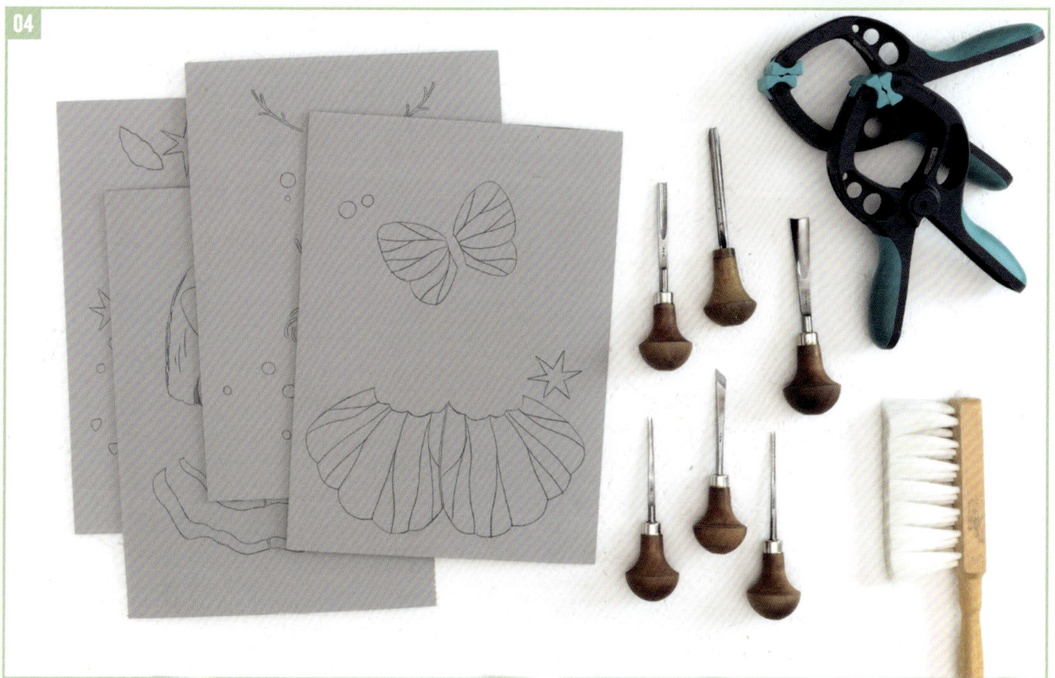

⋏ The prepared lino blocks, carving tools, clamps, and hand sweeper brush

04 PREPARE THE LINO & TOOLS

Use carbon paper to transfer each layer of the design onto a separate lino block. As this design is fairly complex and detailed, you will need a variety of different carving tool sizes. (Pfeil tool sizes L12/4, B7/14, and L9/5 are mainly used here.) Use large clamps to hold the lino block on the table as you carve, plus a hand sweeper to quickly remove carving residue.

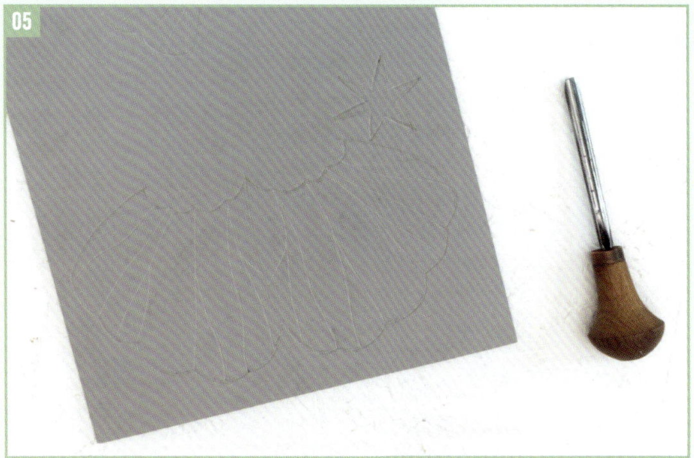

05 CARVE THE FIRST LAYER

Use a small V-shaped blade, such as Pfeil L12/4, to carve a thin, even line along all of the contours. Next, use the same blade, but with more pressure, to widen the outside lines only – this forms a protective space around the design.

< Use the smallest blade to carve the outlines of the moth-wing clothing

06 ENLARGE THE OUTLINE

Use a larger U-shaped blade, such as Pfeil L9/5, to further widen the outer lines. This will make the next step, carving the background with a bigger blade, easier and faster.

> Enlarge the outer lines even more with a U-shaped blade

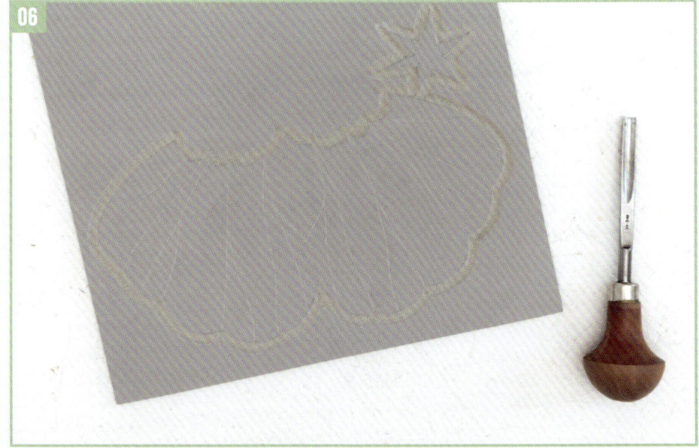

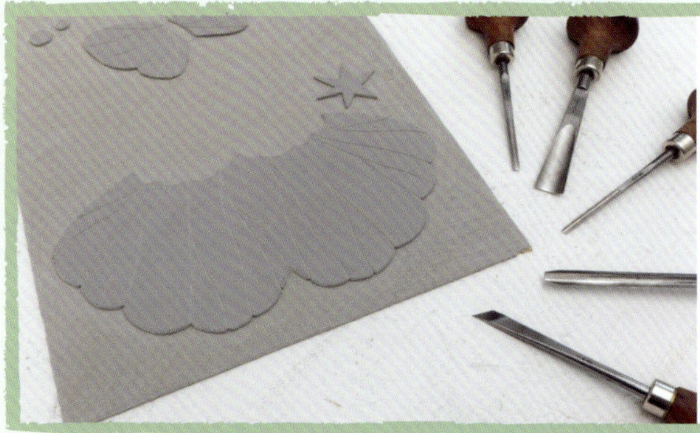

ADDITIONAL CARVING TOOL SIZES

In addition to the three basic carving tool sizes, a few others can be helpful. A scalpel-shaped tool, known as a chisel, will allow you to cut straight corners, such as those within the star. A small U-shaped tool is useful for creating small curves.

07 CARVE THE BACKGROUND

Carve the background next. Thanks to your preparatory work, you can carve safely away from the main design using a larger blade. It's important to hold the tool correctly for safe use: your index finger should rest on the top of the blade, while your other fingers grip the handle. You can also use your other hand to guide the blade, and always carve away from your body.

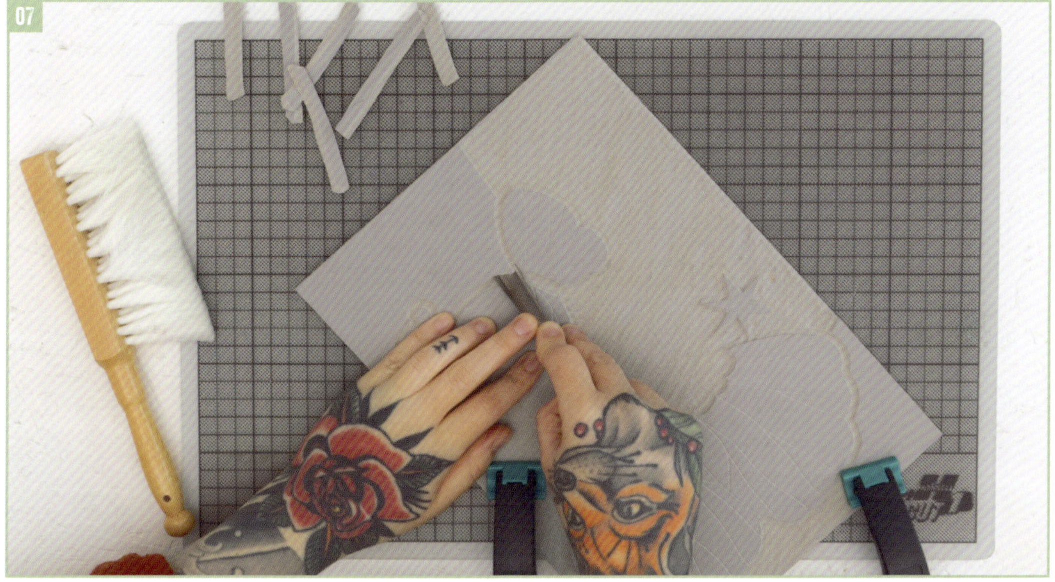

∧ Carving the background using a wide U-shaped tool

08 REGISTRATION TEMPLATE

Create a registration template to make sure you place each lino block and print paper in the same position each time. To do this, take a large blank sheet of paper (the same size as your print paper), place one of the lino blocks where you want your design to print, then mark the outline of it with tape. You can then place this template on the press bed.

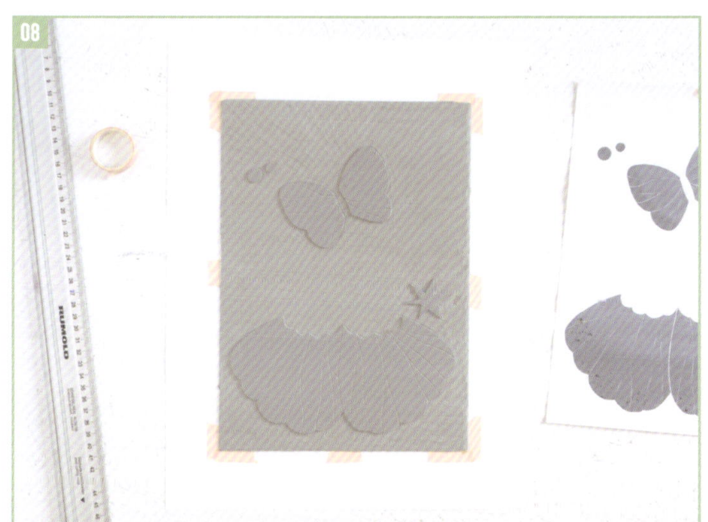

< Marking out the size of the lino blocks on a large sheet of plain paper

09 ALIGN THE BLOCK

Place the first lino block carefully within the taped frame on your registration template. Use the lower-left corner as your absolute reference point to ensure you place each block in the exact same spot, then use double-sided tape to keep the block in place. The more precise you are, the greater the likelihood of creating a perfectly aligned print on top.

> Reference points can help ensure completely accurate block alignment

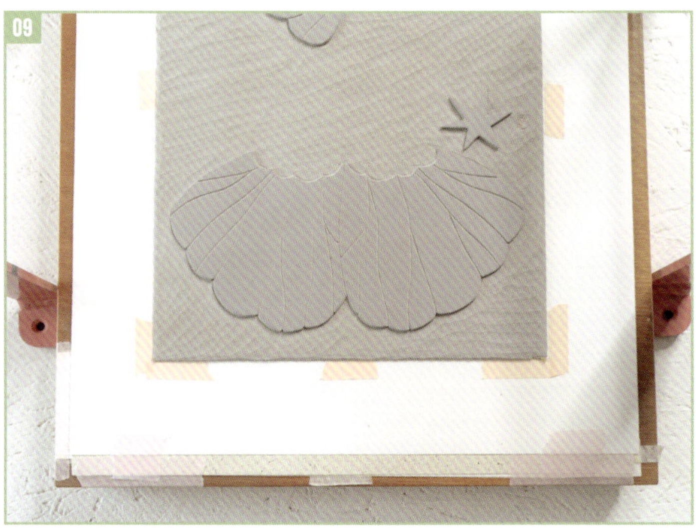

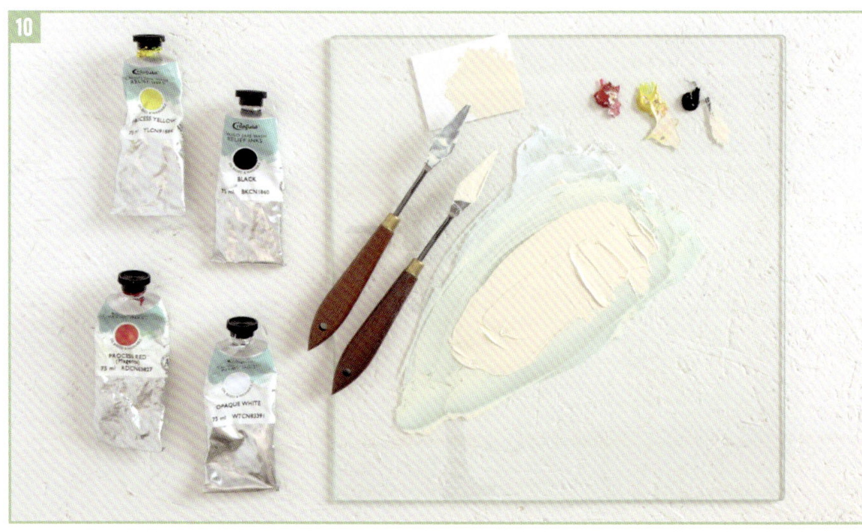

< Mixing colours from the five inks, starting with white as a base (the fifth colour is not needed for this shade of beige)

10 COLOUR MIXING

All of the colours required can be created from five inks: black, white, cyan, magenta, and process yellow. To make light beige, mix plenty of white with a little yellow and even less magenta, adding a tiny amount of black if needed. For light green, mix plenty of white, some yellow, and a small amount of cyan. White makes a good base, as it is opaque. Start with a small amount of ink and slowly add more, especially when mixing light colours. Oil-based inks, such as the Caligo Safe Wash Relief Ink used here, can be stored out of the tube, wrapped in tracing paper, for many weeks, which is useful if you end up with too much of a mixed colour.

11 PREPARING THE INK

Use small rollers to roll out the beige and green inks next to each other, but separately, on a mixing plate. Next, use a wide roller and roll it in the same direction along the line where the two colours meet. You will end up with one colour merging into the other along your roller, creating an attractive gradient.

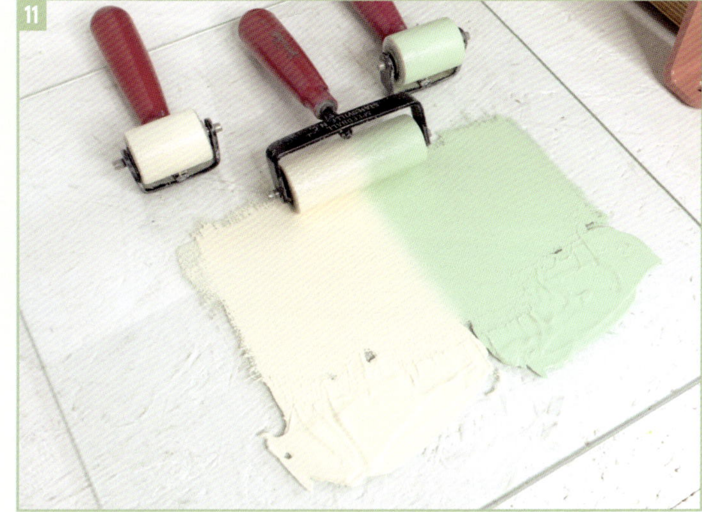

> Using a wide roller to combine the two colours to produce a smooth gradient

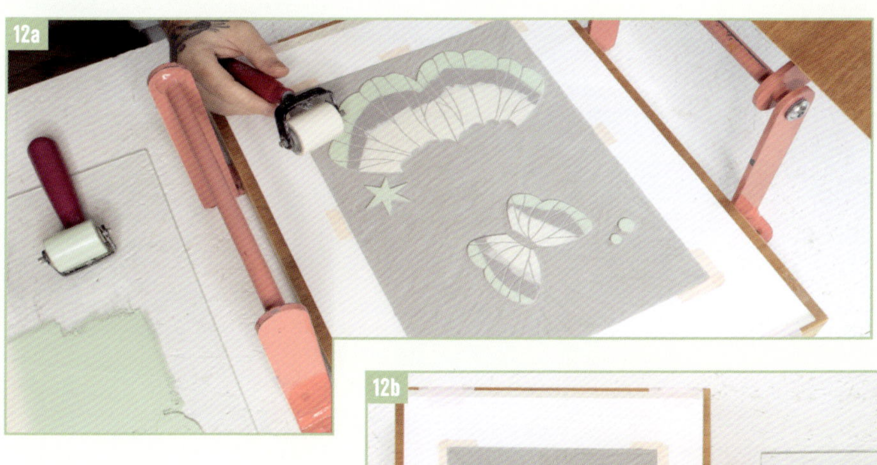

12 INKING THE FIRST LAYER

Use a small roller for areas that will be only beige, and another for those that will be only green. Next, use the wider roller that holds the gradient ink to connect the two areas, creating a smooth transition from beige to green.

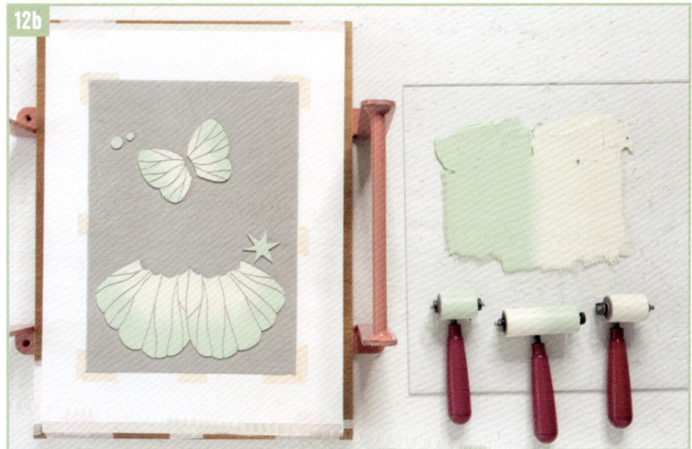

> The lino block for the first layer is inked

13 PAPER PLACEMENT

Now place your print paper over the inked lino block. (Smooth 130–180 gsm drawing paper is used here.) Make sure to align it perfectly with the corners of the paper used for the registration template.

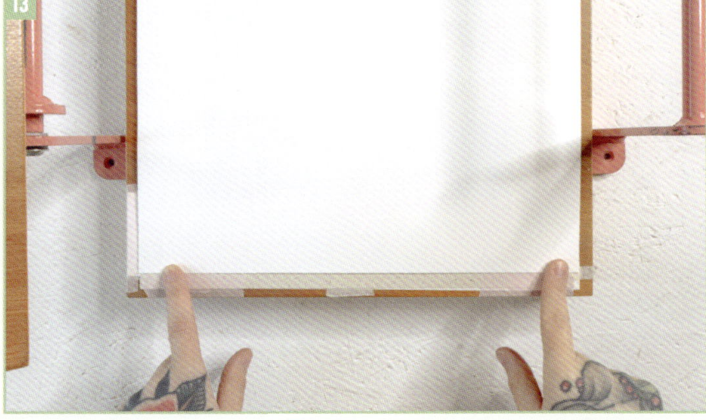

> Ensuring precise paper placement on the registration template

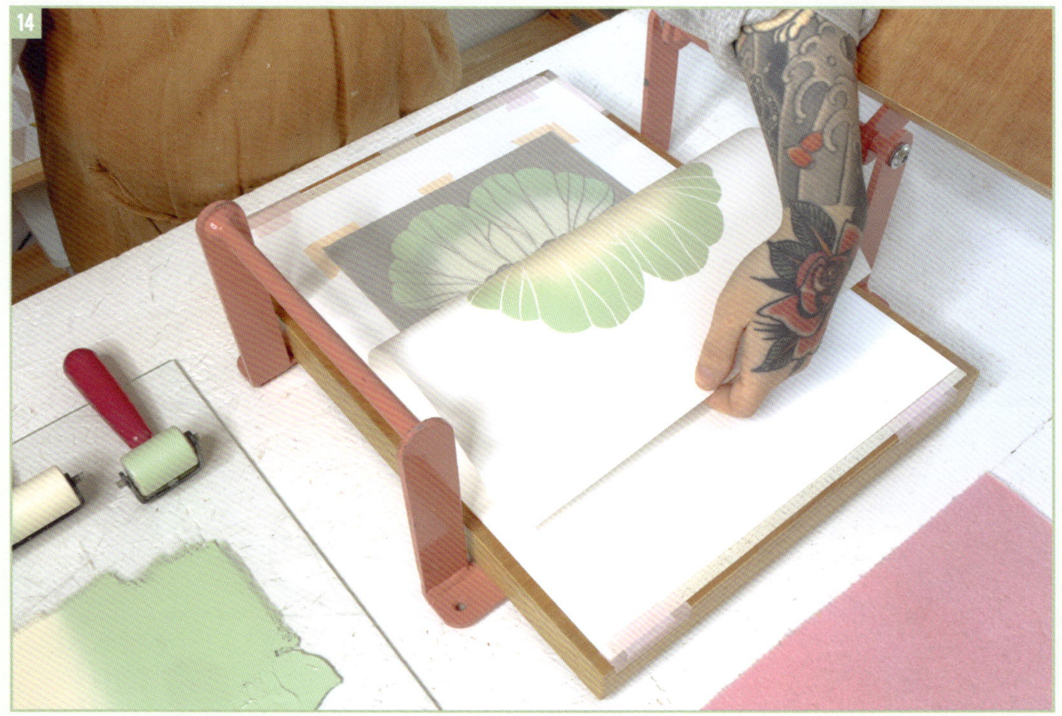

∧ Checking the print

14 INK CHECK

Before removing the paper completely, check the result by partially lifting up each side in turn. If the ink hasn't fully transferred, reapply pressure to that area using a baren. If you feel you didn't apply enough ink in the first place, roll on some more ink and again apply pressure.

15 FINISHING THE FIRST LAYER

Review the print of the first layer, fixing small blemishes by gently dabbing with a dry brush and the appropriate ink – this isn't usually noticeable when dried. Leave the first layer to dry for two to three days before inking the second layer.

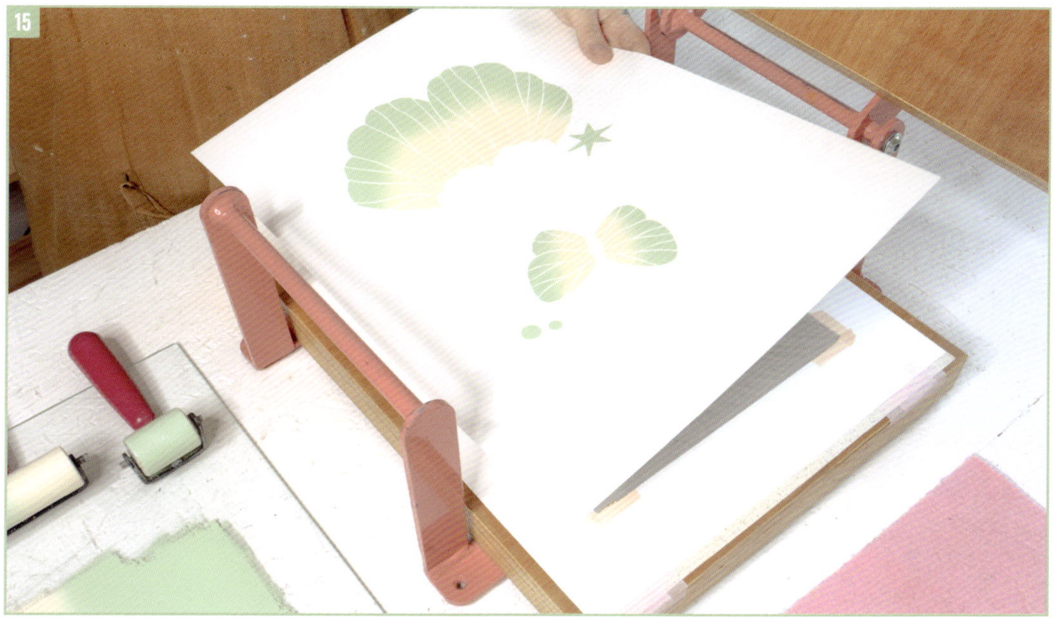

∧ Remove from the press and leave to dry

16 CARVE & INK THE SECOND LAYER

Carve the second layer using the same method as the first. Colour-wise, this layer will consist of two shades of brown. To mix dark brown, combine plenty of magenta with some yellow, black, and white, adding black gradually. Make a larger batch and split it: use two-thirds for the dark brown and mix the remaining third with white for a lighter shade. Next, create a gradient and apply the ink following the process in steps 11 and 12. To create an interesting visual effect, use a coarse sponge to dab some of the dark brown ink onto the gradient area. This will produce irregularly sized dots on the print.

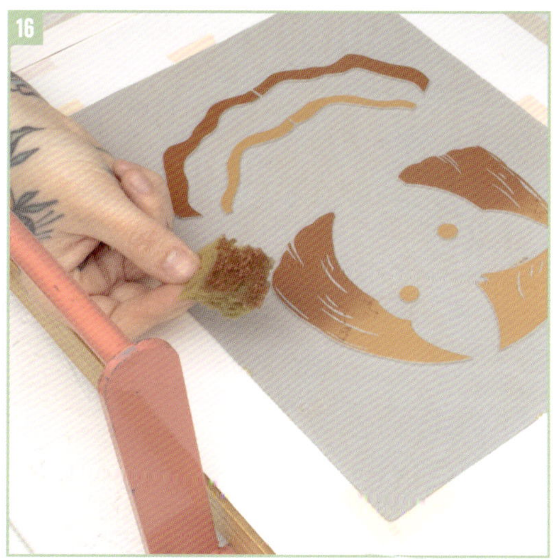

< A coarse sponge can be used to add speckled dots

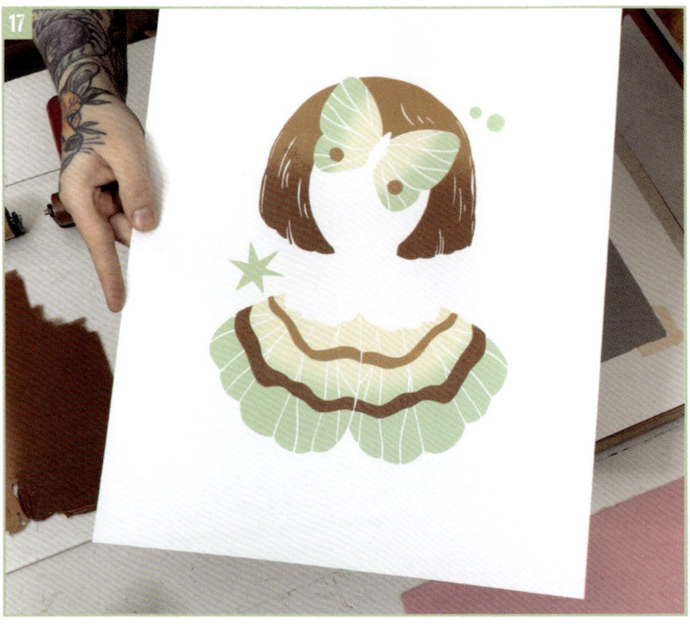

17 PRINT THE SECOND LAYER

Print the second layer on top of the first, then review the result. If you align the paper exactly, layers one and two should line up neatly. But remember, although it's good to aim for perfect alignment, small shifts are only human and will add to the handmade nature of the print.

< Layers one and two are printed

18 CARVE & INK THE THIRD LAYER

Carve the third layer, then create a light, cool pink ink by combining white, magenta, and a little cyan (for the coolness). Roll the pink onto the lino block.

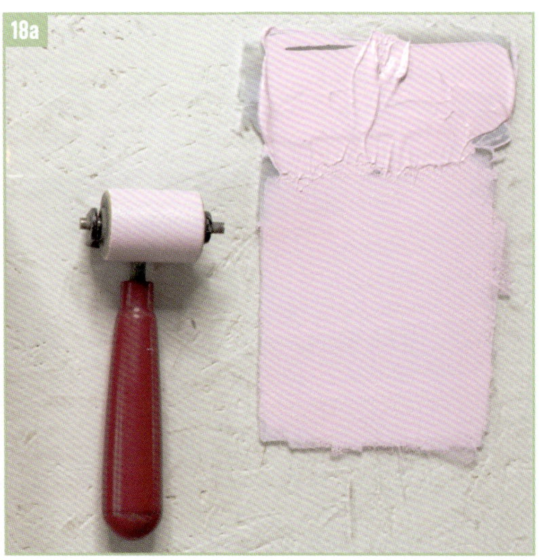

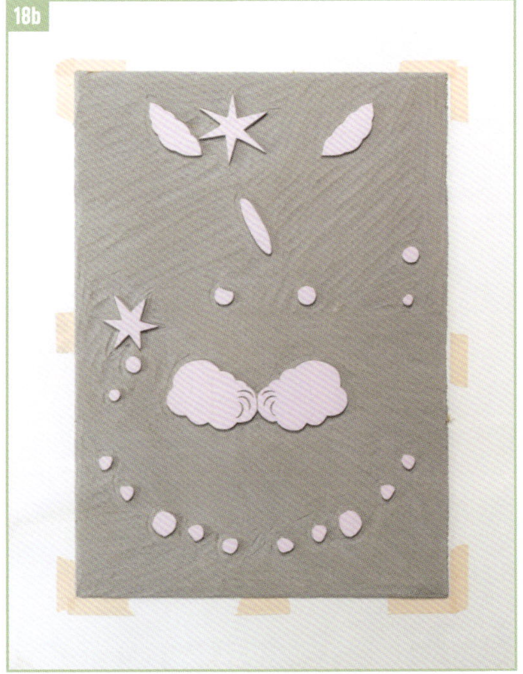

< Mixing a pastel pink ink

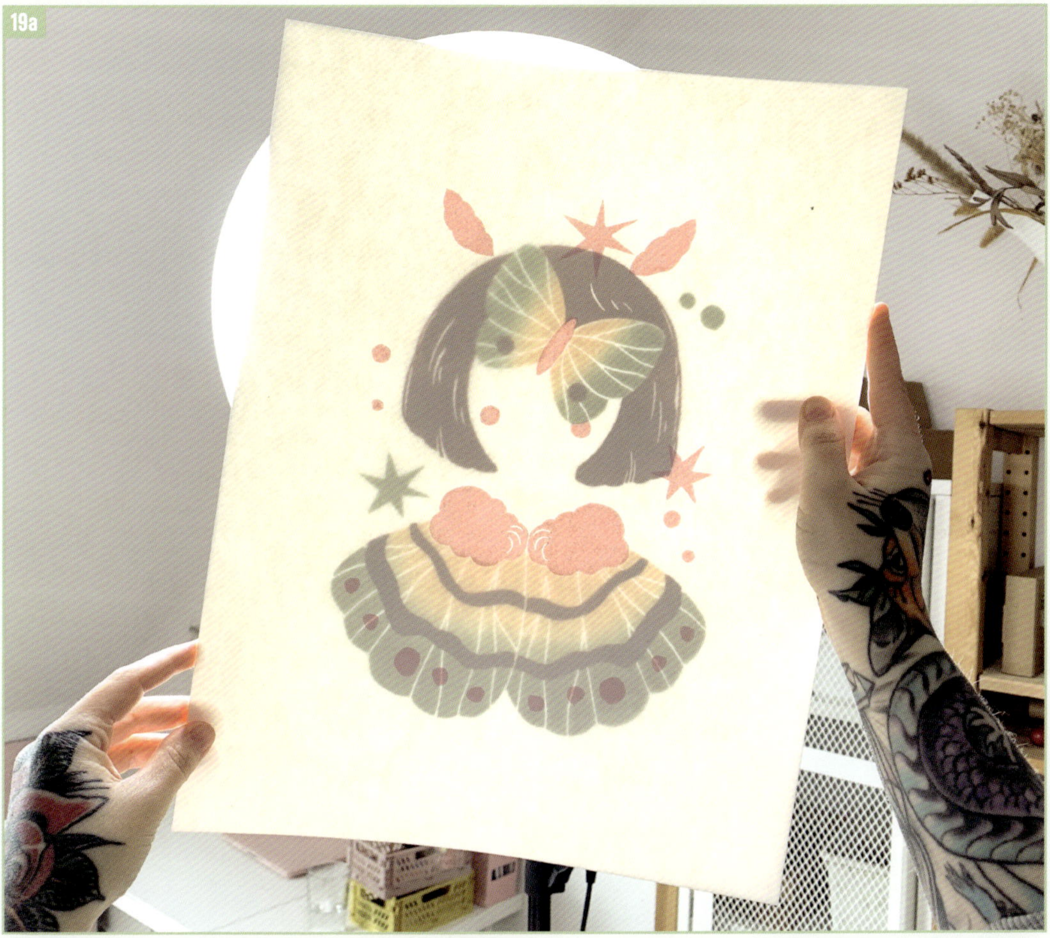

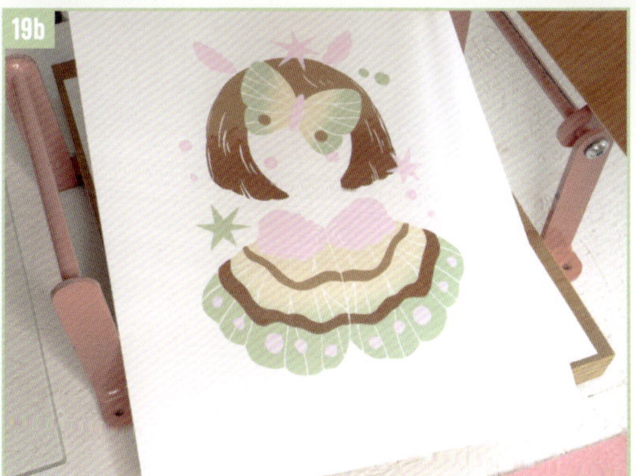

The third-layer test print held over the existing two-layer print

Layers one, two, and three are now printed

19 TEST & PRINT THE THIRD LAYER

Before printing any layer, you can check the placement of the lino block by pressing a test print on a separate piece of paper. Hold this over your existing print and put them up to the light. If they align successfully, you can carry on with confidence and print the third layer.

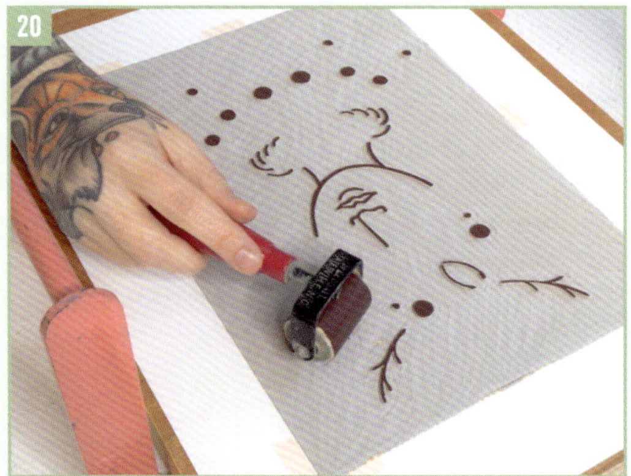

20 CARVE & INK THE FINAL LAYER

The more colours used in a print, the more contrast is needed to ensure the design is easy to read. Carve the fourth and final layer of this piece to provide that contrast. Ink this layer with a dark red-brown colour, created by mixing white, black, magenta, and yellow inks (white is mainly used here for opacity). Since the previous layers contain light and medium tones, this darker shade will create contrast and depth.

< The fourth layer inked with a dark red-brown shade

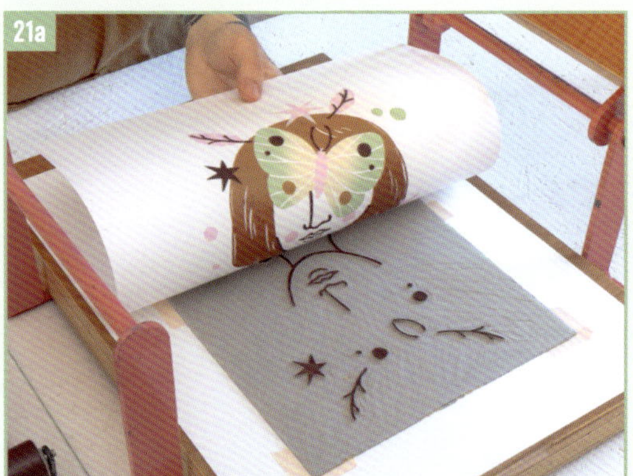

∧ Printing the final layer

21 PRINT THE FINAL LAYER

Watch the whole design come together as you print the final layer. As before, check all elements have printed with enough ink. Once happy, you can print this entire design as many times as you like!

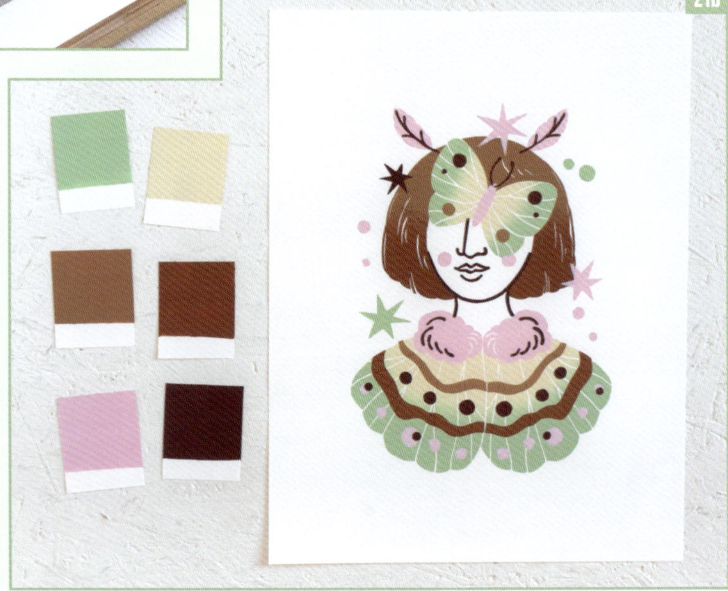

> Make colour swatches of each shade – this will help you to re-mix the inks when reprinting later

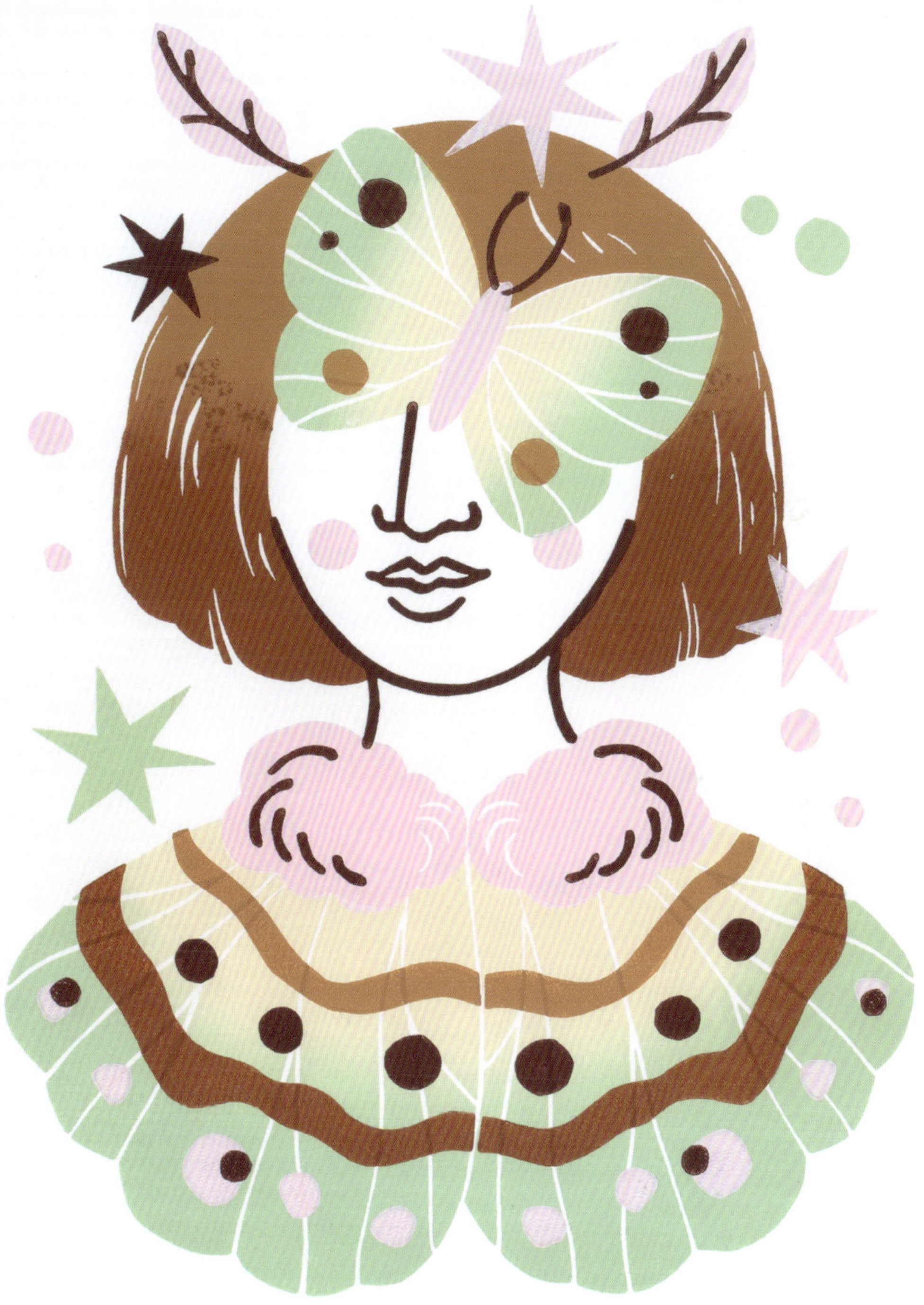

Lady Moth | This vibrant portrait is made up of six colours over four layers

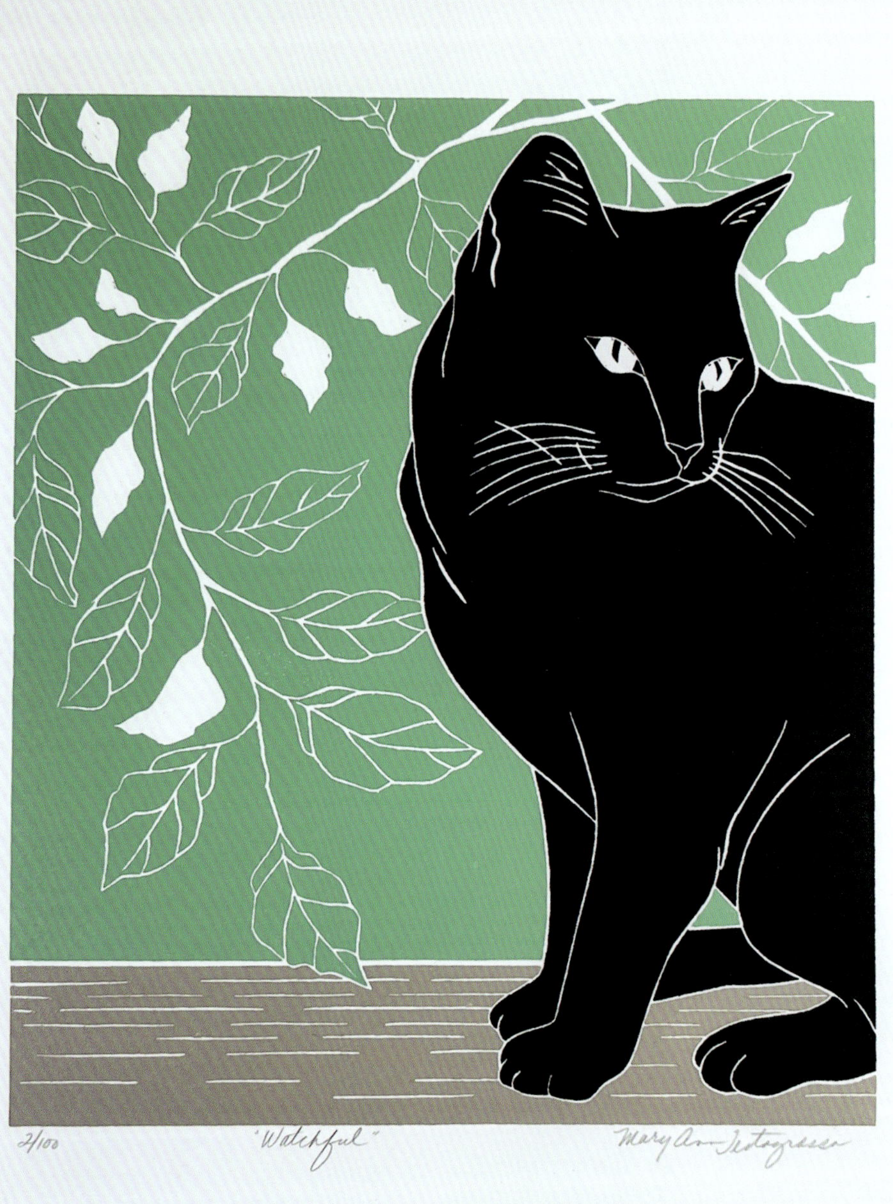
2/100
"Watchful"
Mary Ann Testagrossa

JIGSAW PRINT

WATCHFUL CAT

BY MARY ANN TESTAGROSSA

The jigsaw method is an impressive technique used to create a multicoloured print from just one lino block. After a design is carved into the block, it is then cut into separate pieces, each of which is inked with a different colour. The block is then reassembled like a jigsaw puzzle and printed. This method allows you to print all of the colours at the same time, without needing to wait for the ink to dry in between layers.

This tutorial will take you step by step through this method, creating an image of a classic black cat with green foliage in the background.

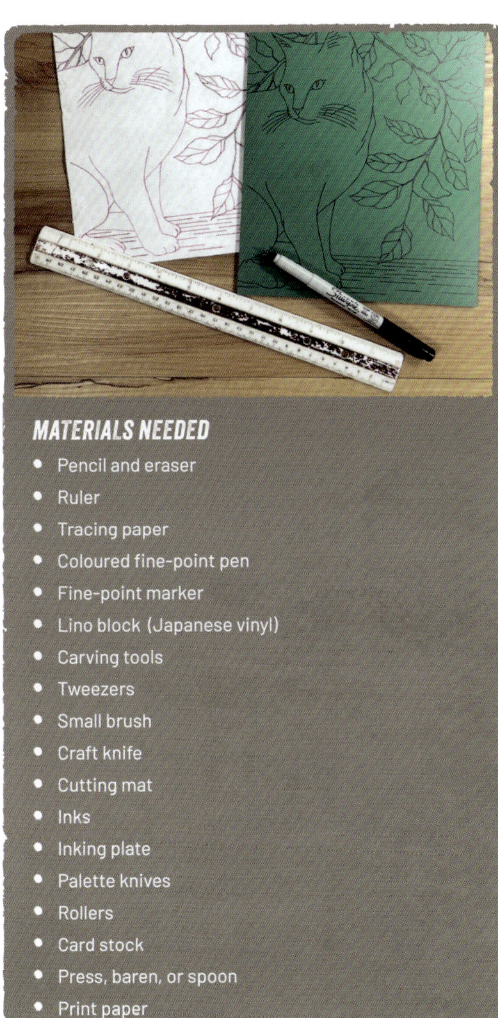

MATERIALS NEEDED

- Pencil and eraser
- Ruler
- Tracing paper
- Coloured fine-point pen
- Fine-point marker
- Lino block (Japanese vinyl)
- Carving tools
- Tweezers
- Small brush
- Craft knife
- Cutting mat
- Inks
- Inking plate
- Palette knives
- Rollers
- Card stock
- Press, baren, or spoon
- Print paper

01 DRAW THE DESIGN

It's a good idea to plan out your print using tracing paper, as this allows you to layer and move around the different elements of an image until you're happy. Once you have your final design, if you want to make it larger or smaller, scan it into photo-editing software and resize it. Next, reverse the design and print a copy the same size as your lino block.

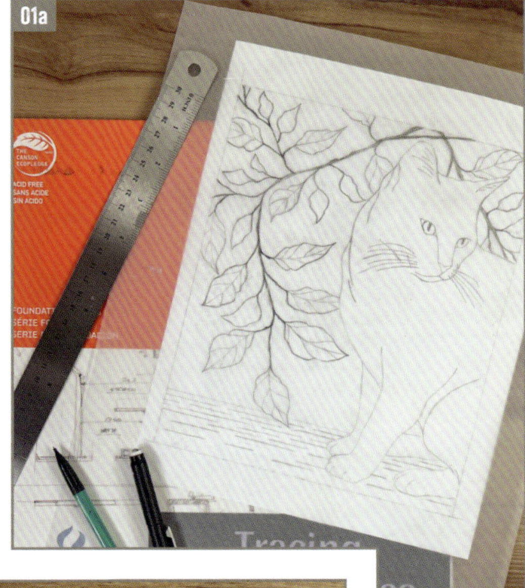

> Planning out the design on tracing paper

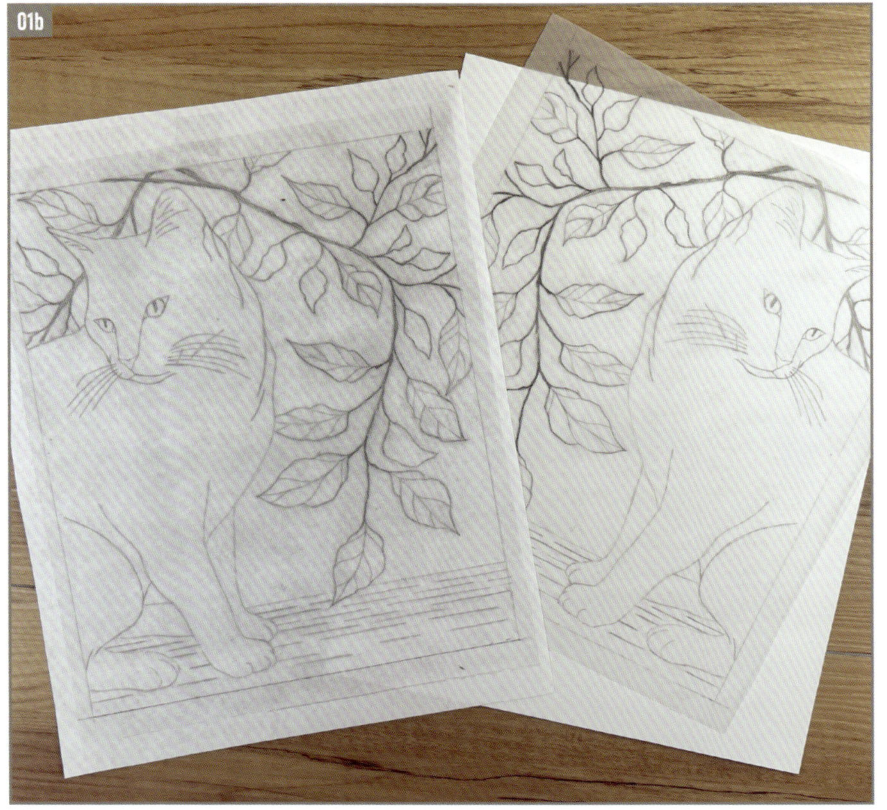

< Scan, resize, reverse, and print the design

02 TRANSFER TO LINO

If you don't have graphite paper, place the printed copy of the design face down and cover the back of the paper with graphite using a soft pencil (such as 4B–6B). Next, flip the printout right side up, position it on the lino block, and tape it in place. Use a coloured fine-point pen to draw over the lines of the design. The coloured ink will allow you to see where you have already drawn, and the pressure of the nib will transfer the design onto the lino in graphite.

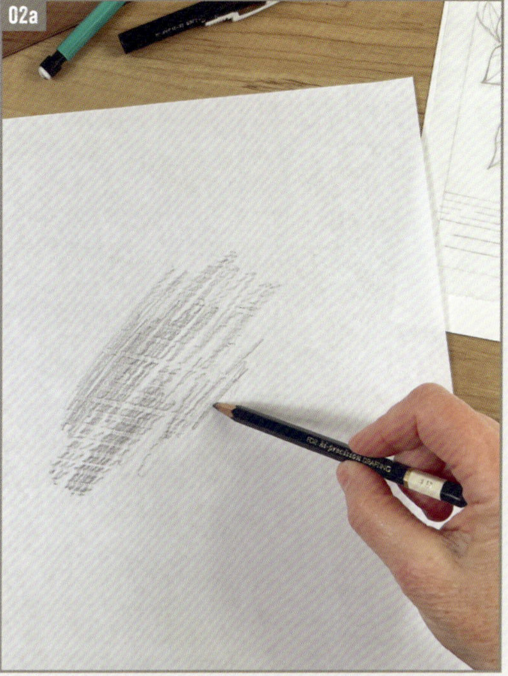

⋀ Cover the back of the printout with graphite using a soft pencil

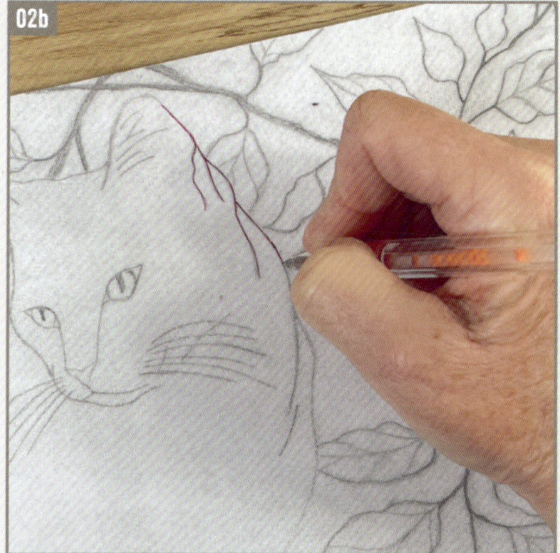

⋀ Using a coloured fine-point pen to draw over the lines

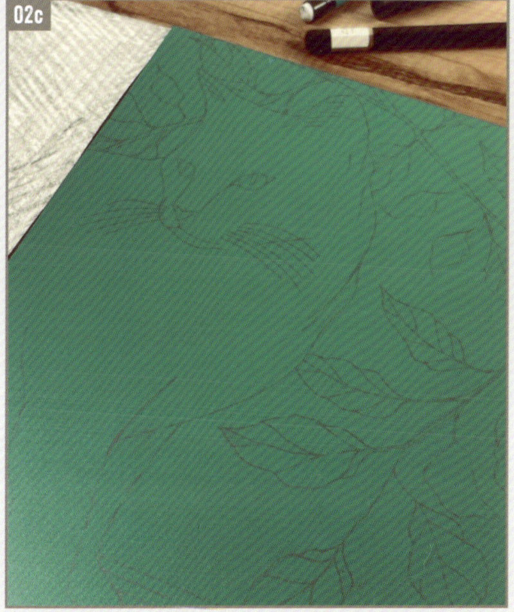

⋀ The design will transfer onto the lino

JAPANESE VINYL

Japanese vinyl (Gomuban) is double-sided and holds fine detail when put under pressure. It doesn't warp or bend, but stays flat, which is essential when creating a jigsaw print. It can be tough to cut through, so if you're new to linocutting, you may prefer to start with a softer lino instead.

03 FINE-POINT MARKER

This is an optional step, but a useful one. When using Japanese vinyl, it can be difficult to see the pencil lines on the dark green surface, so it can help to use a black fine-point marker to go over the lines. Just make sure the marker lines are completely dry before you carve or ink your lino, as you don't want the lines to smudge or mix with your printing inks.

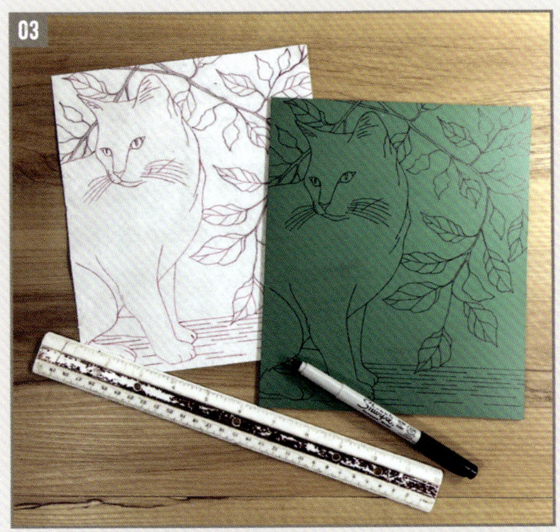

> The design is more visible after using the marker pen

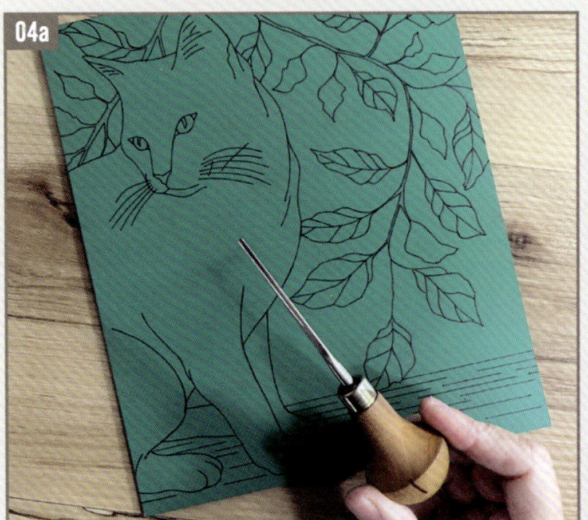

∧ The L 12/1 gouge by Pfeil carves a neat, fine line

04 CARVE THE DESIGN

Use a small V-shaped gouge to slowly and carefully carve the lines of the design. Next, carve away any of the leaves you want to remain white (unprinted). Experiment with varying sizes and shapes of carving tools to create different-shaped grooves.

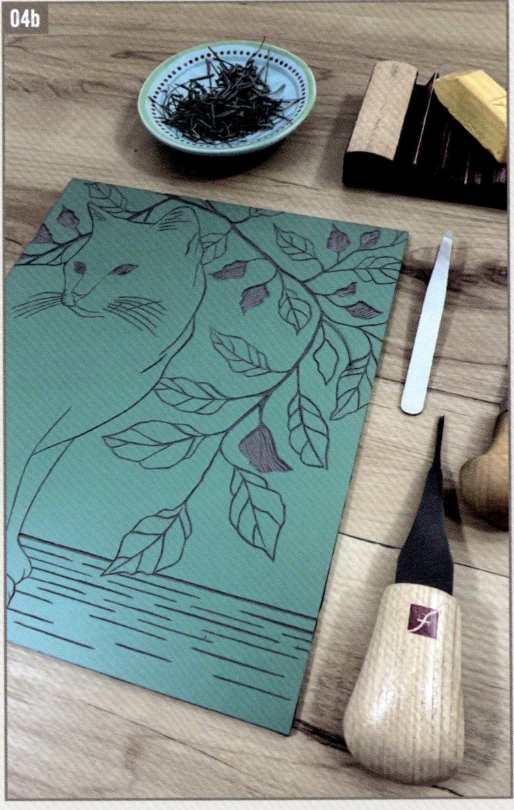

∧ Tweezers are useful for removing small pieces of lino

05 CUT UP THE BLOCK

With a mat board or self-healing cutting mat placed beneath the lino block, use a sharp craft knife to cut the lino into three pieces – the cat, the surface the cat is standing on, and the leafy background. Make multiple cuts in the same place, over and over, until you cut all the way through. Once the block is cut apart, carefully trim the edges. You want to be able to easily slot the pieces together and take them apart when inked.

> The X-ACTO knife #1 with the #11 blade or the #2 knife with the #2 blade are good knife options

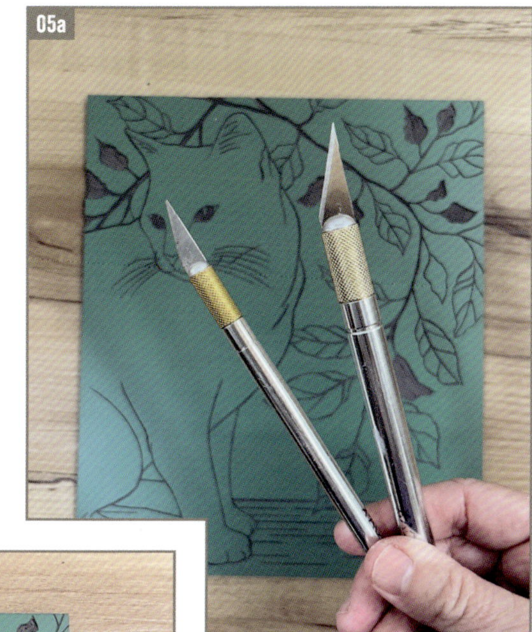

< This is where 'jigsaw printing' gets its name

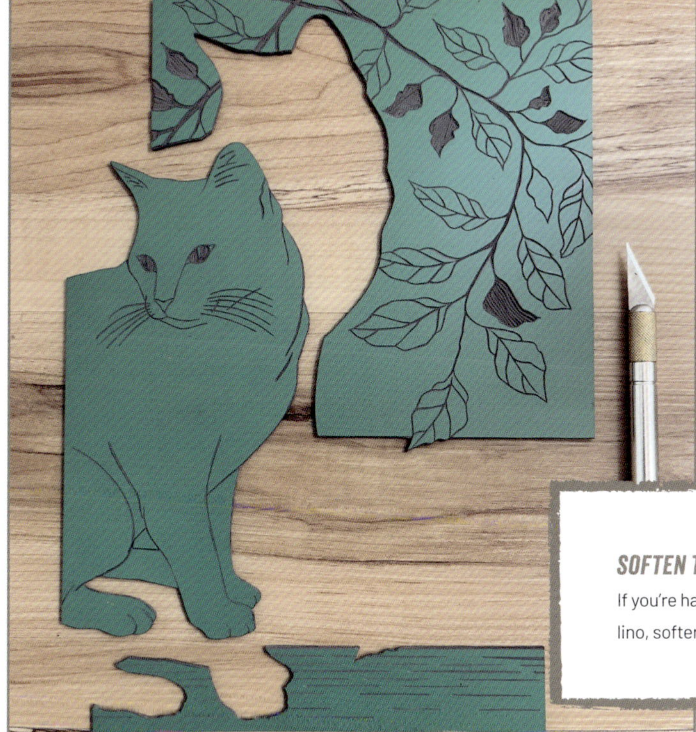

SOFTEN THE LINO

If you're having trouble cutting through the lino, soften it by warming it up with a hairdryer.

06 INK THE BLOCK

Decide on colours, then use a palette knife to mix your inks. Caligo Safewash Relief Inks are used here, as they are oil-based, water-soluble, and non-toxic. Roll out your inks on glass sheets, with the edges taped for safety. Roll three to four thin layers of ink on each jigsaw block.

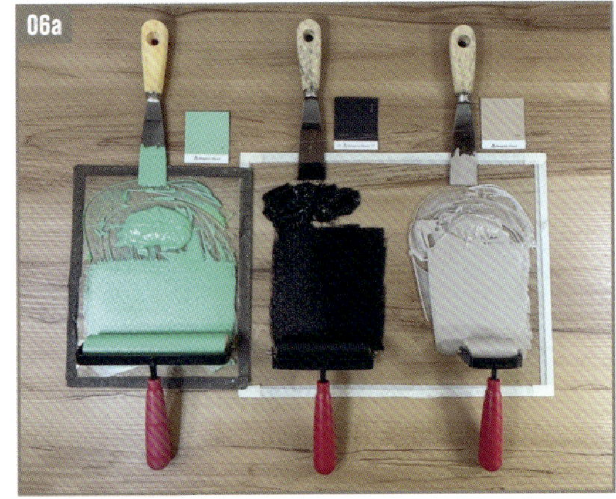

> Using Speedball's soft rubber brayers, in various sizes, to roll out the inks

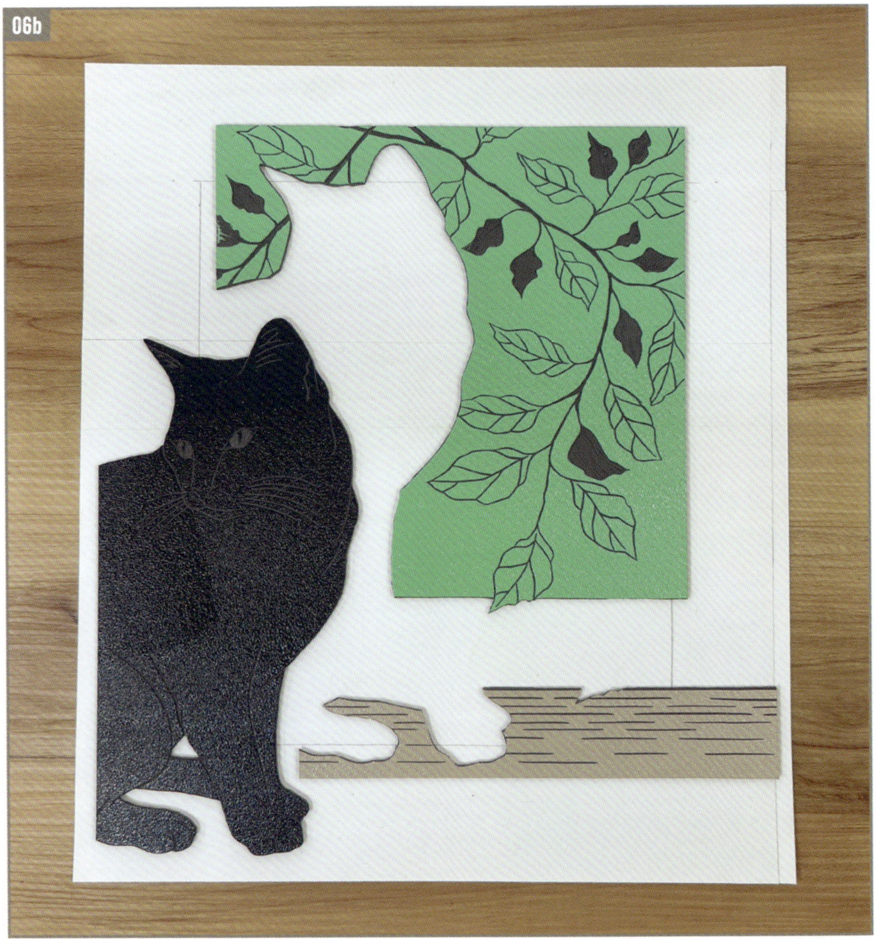

< Ink each jigsaw piece separately

07 CREATE A TEMPLATE

Before printing, create a registration template from card stock. The card template should be the same size as the paper you plan to print on. Position the lino block in the centre of the template, then draw around the block. You can now use this to ensure each print is positioned in the same place.

> A card registration template will ensure consistency in print placement

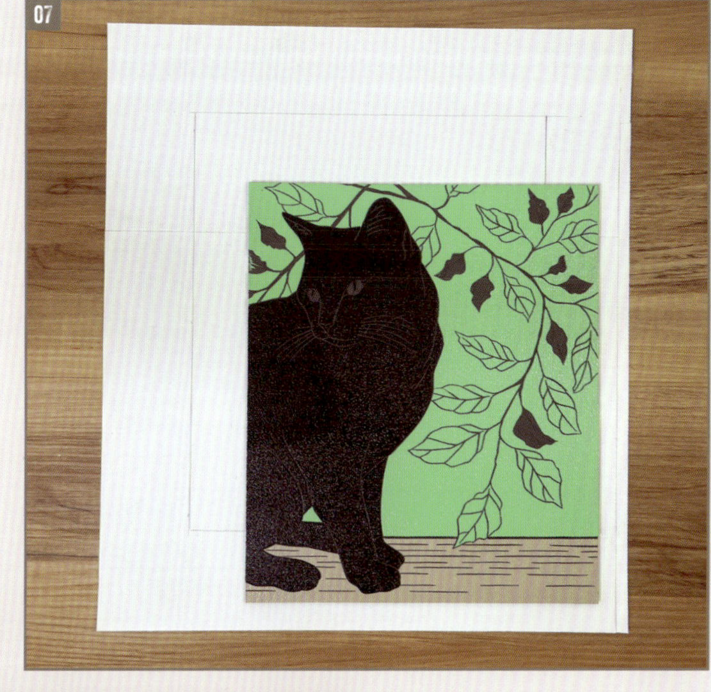

08 ALIGN THE PAPER

Place your template on a piece of mat board for stability, then carefully fit the three jigsaw blocks together and position them on the template. Align the edge of the printing paper with the edge of the template, then carefully lay the paper over the inked block. The paper used here is Stonehenge 250 gsm printing paper, which is a heavier paper and good for use in a press.

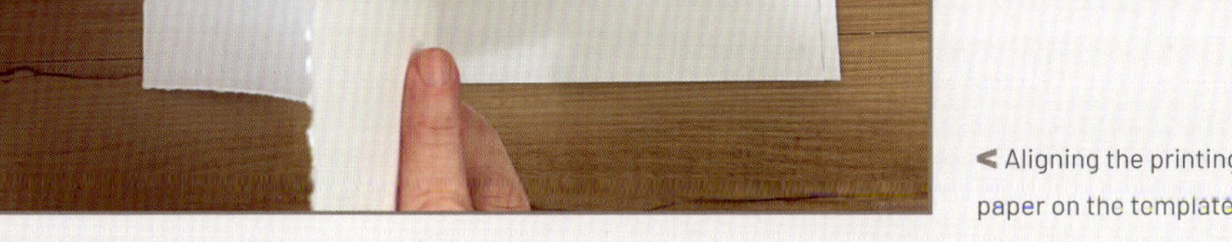

< Aligning the printing paper on the template

09 PRINT

If you're using a lever-style table-top press, as shown here, transfer the board, template, inked blocks, and paper to the press and use the lever to apply pressure. Alternatively, you can use a baren or spoon to print the design. Once printed, lift the paper to check how the ink has transferred. If you're happy with how it looks, leave the print to dry.

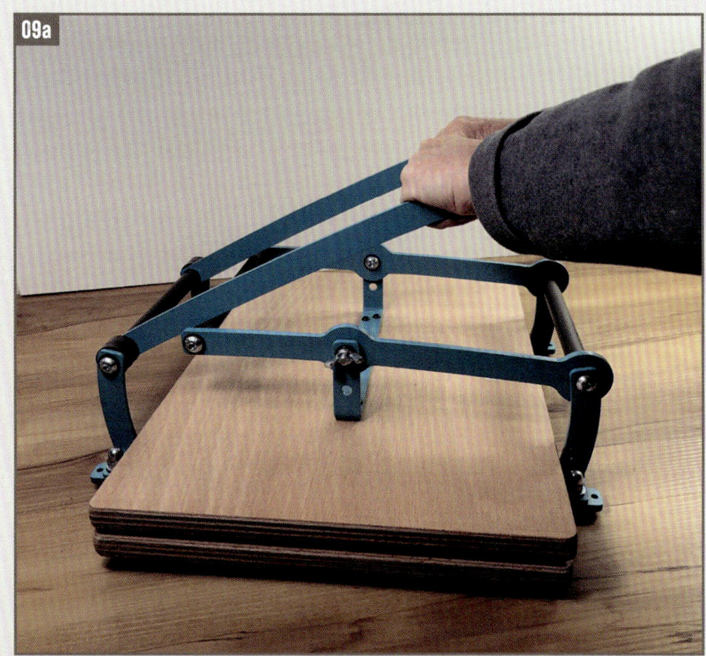

> The inked block and printing paper placed in the press

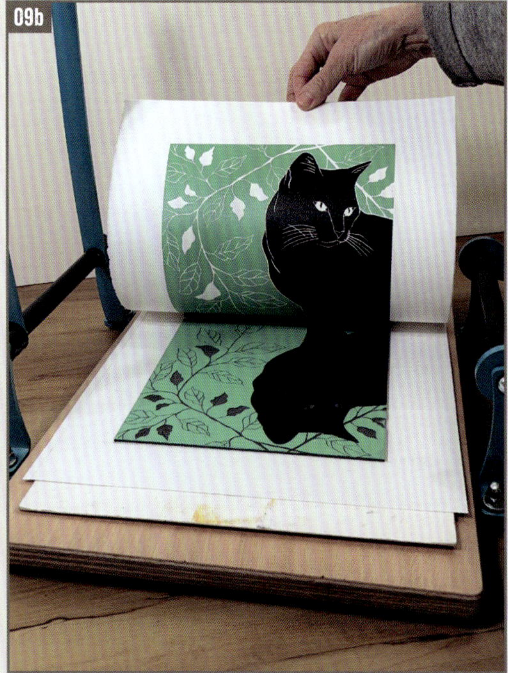

⋀ Checking how the ink has transferred

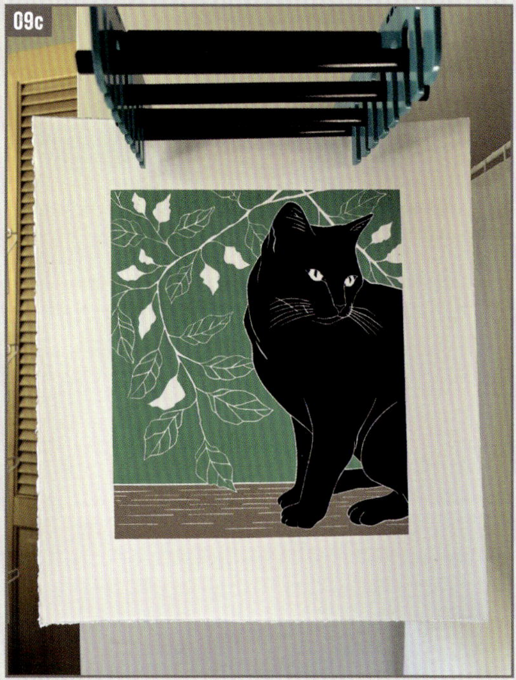

⋀ The finished print, hung to dry

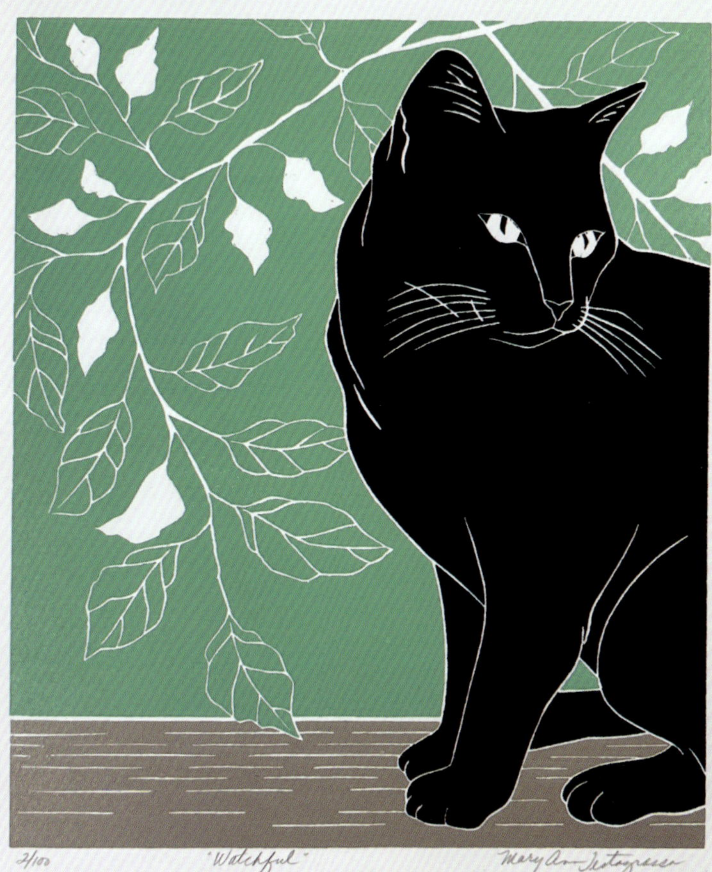

Watchful Cat | The three jigsaw blocks fit together beautifully to create an attractive three-colour print

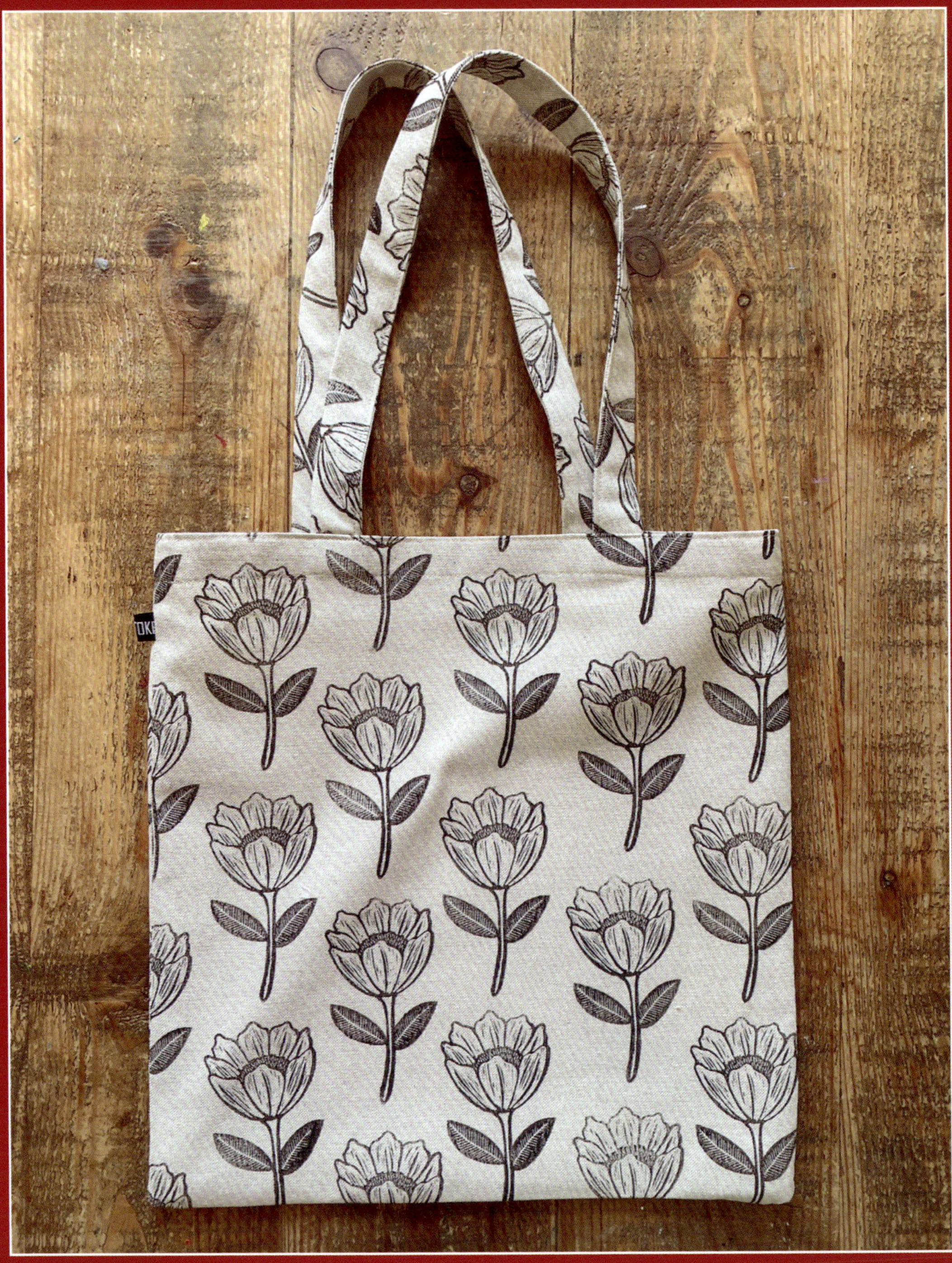

PATTERN PRINTING ON FABRIC

FLOWER POWER

BY ESTHER VAN DAM (STUDIO TOKEK)

Printing on fabric allows you to create truly unique projects. This tutorial will show you how to make a stamp from soft lino that can be used to create a variety of repeated-pattern designs. While you can also use this stamp on paper, this tutorial will share specific tips for fabric printing.

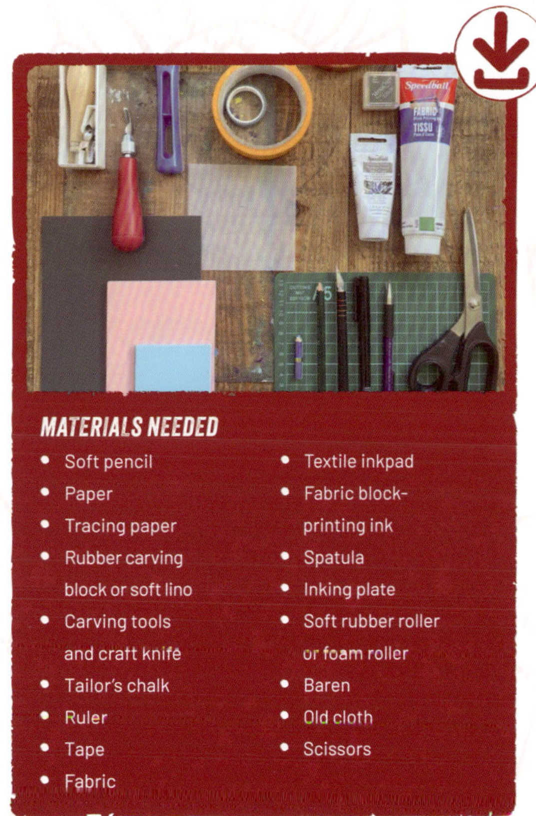

MATERIALS NEEDED

- Soft pencil
- Paper
- Tracing paper
- Rubber carving block or soft lino
- Carving tools and craft knife
- Tailor's chalk
- Ruler
- Tape
- Fabric
- Textile inkpad
- Fabric block-printing ink
- Spatula
- Inking plate
- Soft rubber roller or foam roller
- Baren
- Old cloth
- Scissors

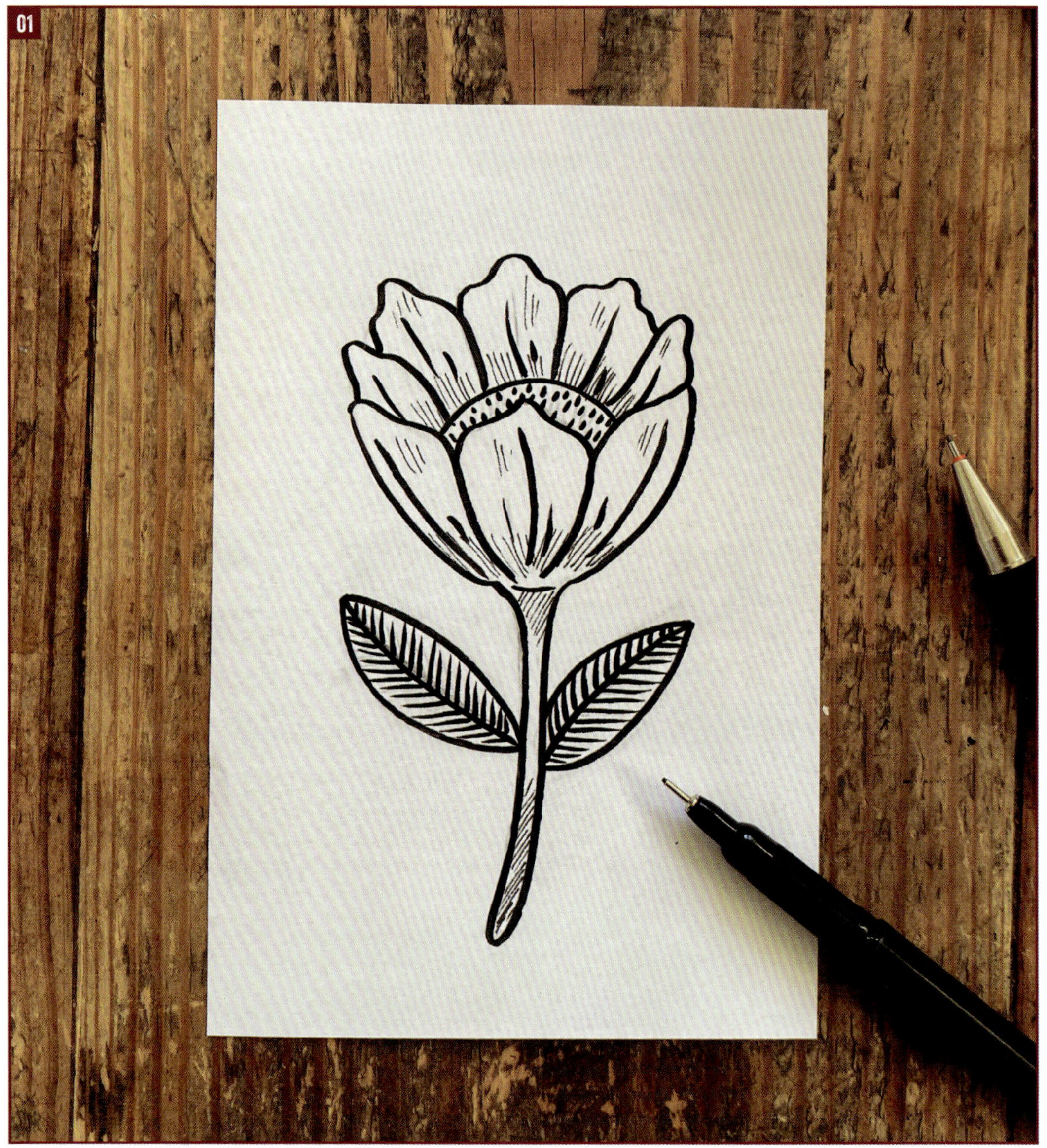

∧ A simple flower design

01 DRAW A DESIGN

Draw a simple design for your stamp, looking for inspiration in nature, books, or the internet. Don't overcomplicate it. A simple leaf or flower makes a beautiful print. Place your sketched design on the lino block to ensure it fits.

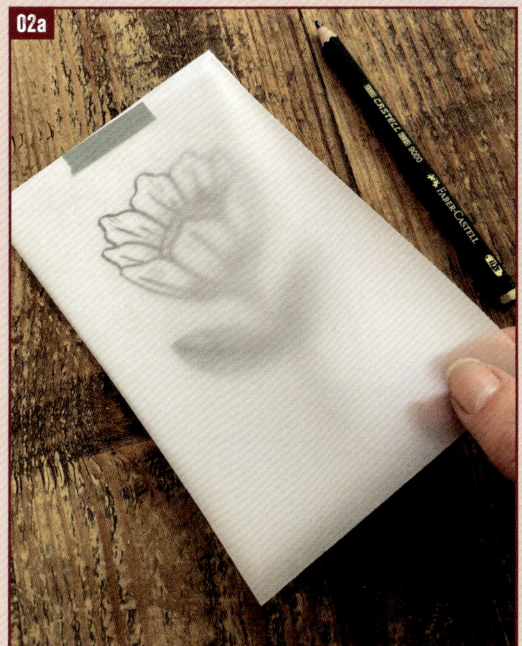

▲ Tracing paper taped over the drawing

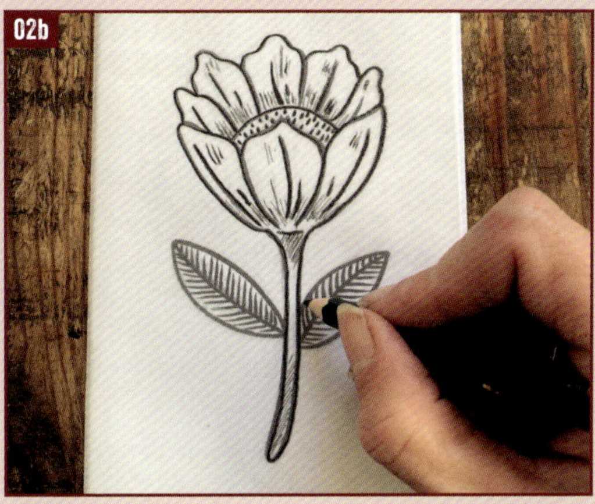

▲ Tracing the design using a soft pencil

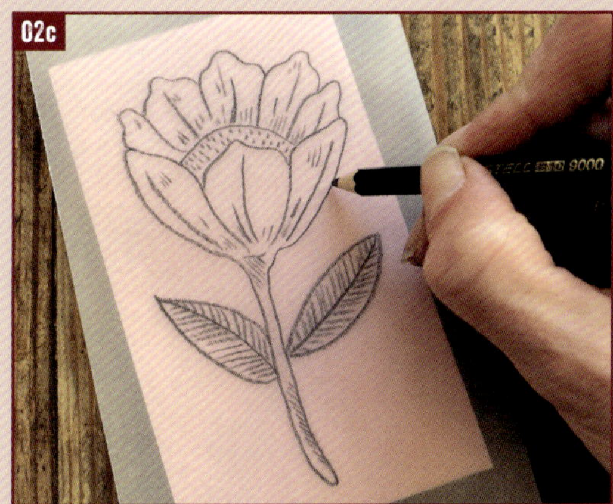

▲ Going over the design with pencil

02 TRANSFER TO LINO

Place a sheet of tracing paper over your design and tape in place. Use a soft grey pencil (8B is used here) to trace over the design. Next, place the tracing paper pencil-side down on the lino block. To transfer the design, go over the reverse side of the lines on the back of the tracing paper with a pencil. Be careful not to move the paper, otherwise the design transfer will be blurry. Carefully remove the tracing paper to see if the design has transferred successfully.

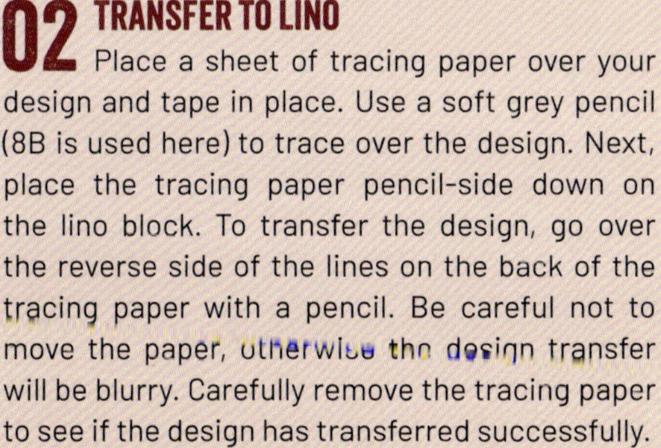

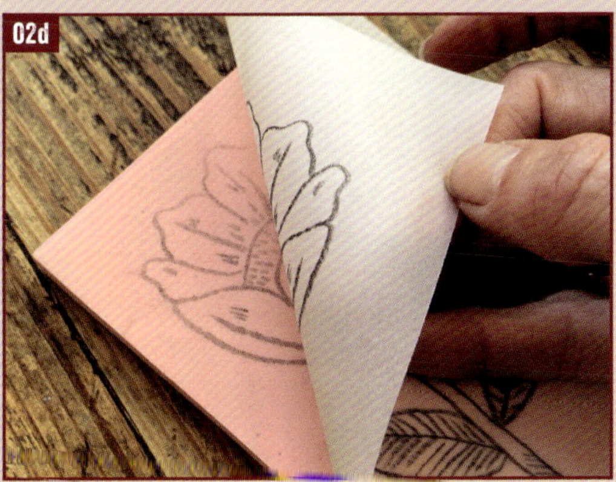

▲ Checking how the design has transferred

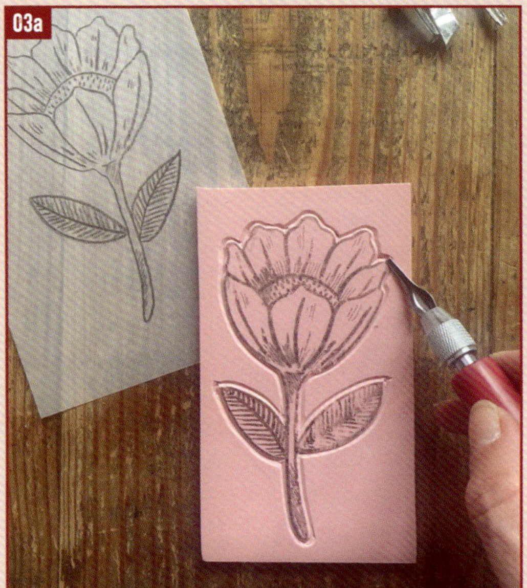

▲ Carving the outlines first

> Carving the details second

03 CARVE THE DETAILS

Start by carving the outlines using a V-shaped tool. Next, move on to the details, carving slowly and not too deep. You can make the lines a little deeper or wider later if necessary.

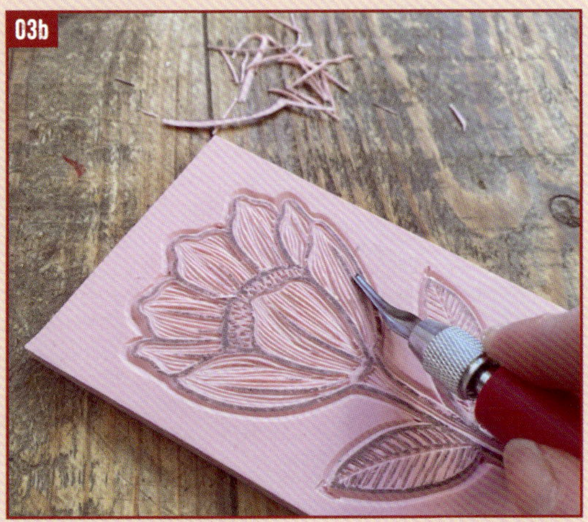

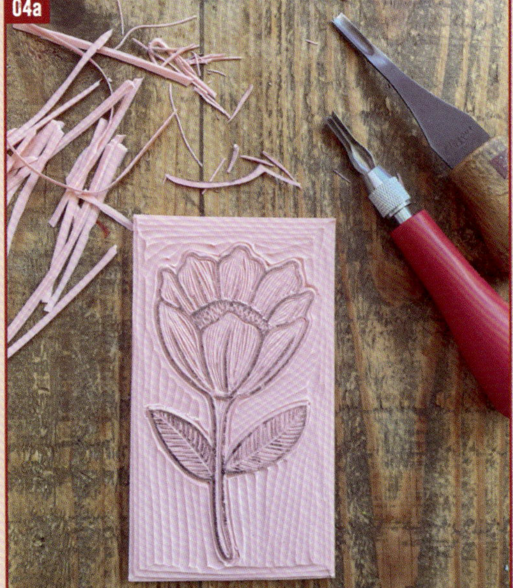

▲ Option one: noisy, textured background

04 CARVE THE BACKGROUND

Clear the background around the design using one of two methods. Option one: roughly carve away the background to create a dynamic look. Option two: carve away the background then cut around the design with a craft knife – this will create a cleaner print.

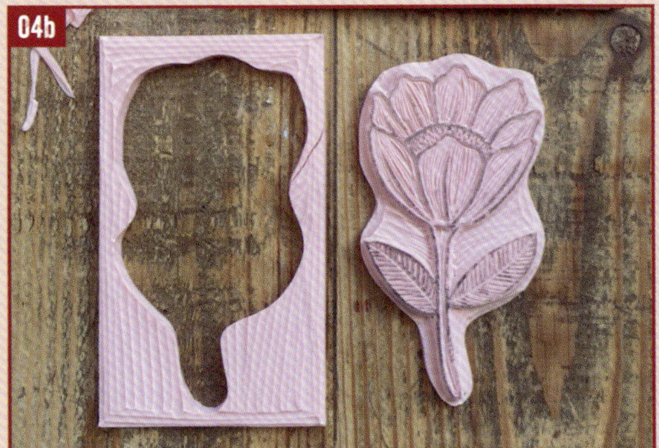

▲ Option two: cut-out stamp

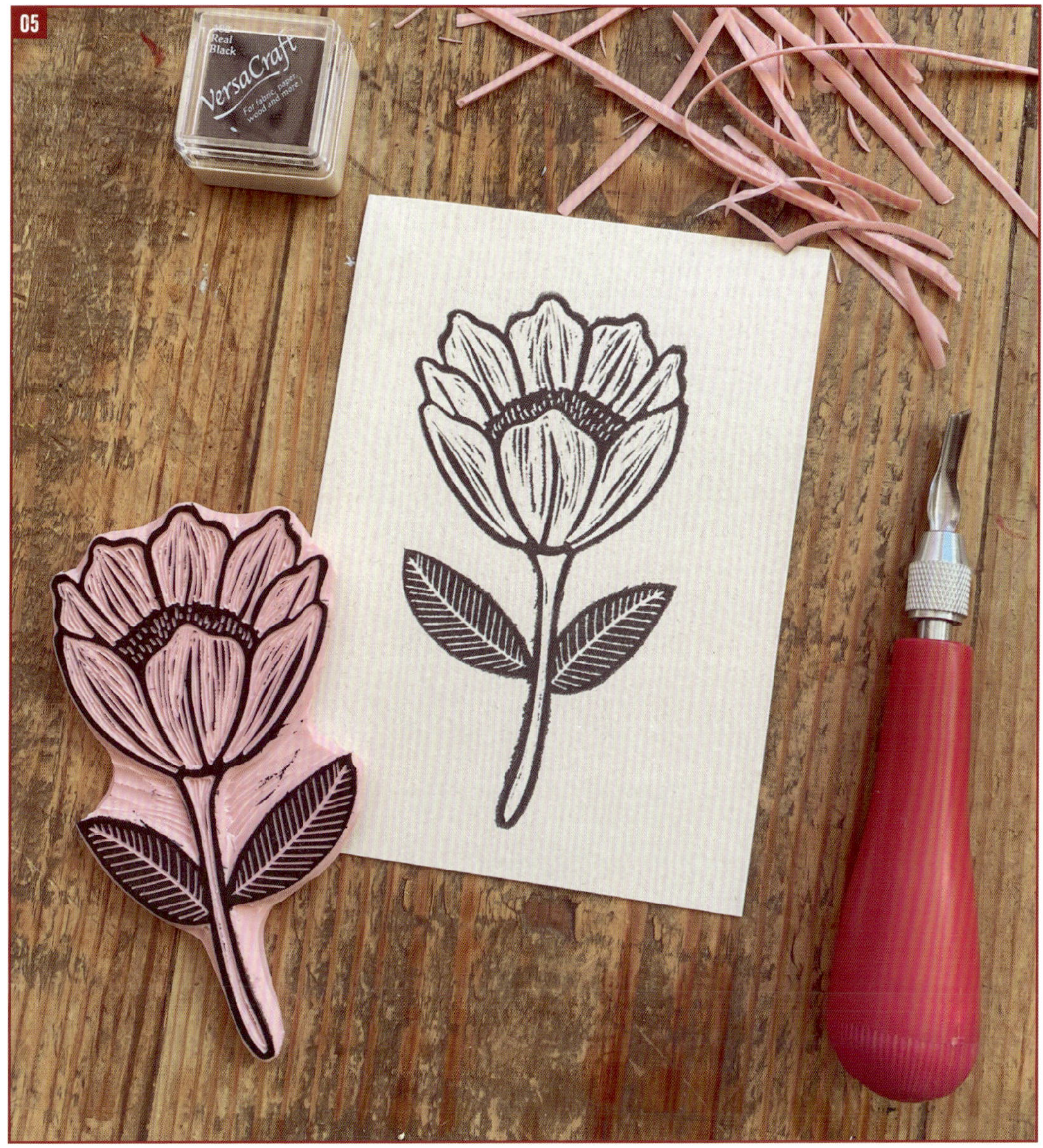

∧ A test print will show the design more clearly

05 TEST PRINT

It can be hard to know if the stamp is finished until you make a test print with it. Apply some ink from a simple textile inkpad and print the stamp on paper, then review the result.

If there are any stray lines or ridges you wish to remove, simply wash the stamp and then carve them away. You now have a stamp block that can be used on paper and fabric.

CHOOSING FABRIC

Selecting a fabric is an aesthetic as well as a practical choice. Natural fibres – such as cotton, silk, and linen – work best with fabric inks. The weave and texture of the fabric is also important.

The easiest type of fabric to print on is a plain, smooth weave. Experiment with different fabrics and explore what works best. And make sure to wash your chosen fabric before printing onto it.

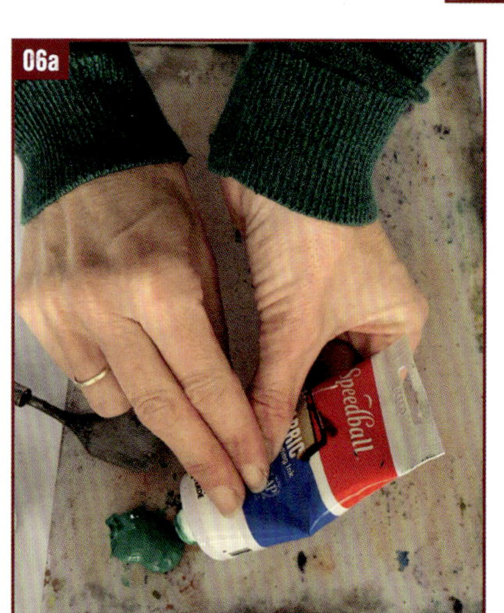

▲ Adding ink to the plate

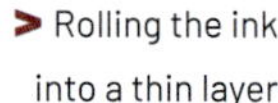

❯ Rolling the ink into a thin layer

06 PREPARE THE INK

Once you've chosen your fabric, it's time to start printing. Place a dot of high-quality block-printing fabric ink in the corner of an inking plate, then roll a small amount into the centre. Continue to roll the ink until both plate and roller have a thin coating. The ink should make a sticky sound. Avoid using too much ink, as this will flood the details in the stamp and result in an unclear print. If you can't see the texture of your roller under the ink, you're using too much ink.

07 INK THE STAMP

Lay an old cloth down to protect your workspace and provide a soft surface on which to work. Gently roll the ink onto the stamp until it's evenly covered. Don't use pressure, as this risks forcing ink into areas you want to remain clear.

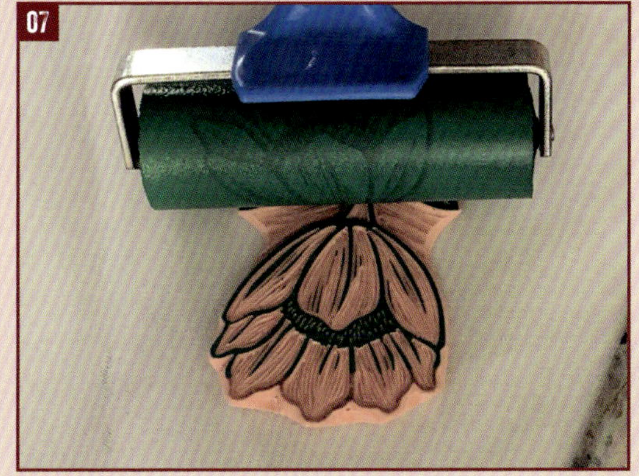

> Carefully rolling ink onto the stamp

08 TEST PRINT ON FABRIC

Always make a test print on small piece of fabric before starting your main project. Place the inked stamp on your test fabric and use your hands or a baren to apply pressure evenly to all parts of the block. Gently lift a corner of the stamp to check how the ink has transferred. You may need to experiment with the amount of ink or pressure used.

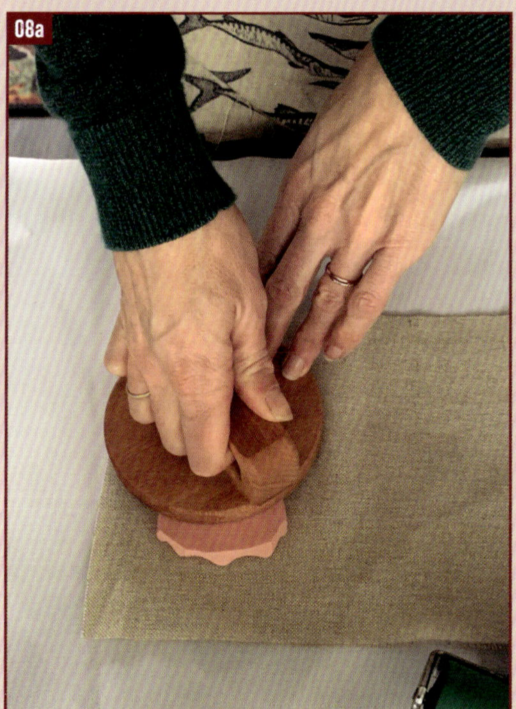

∧ Using a baren to apply pressure to the stamp

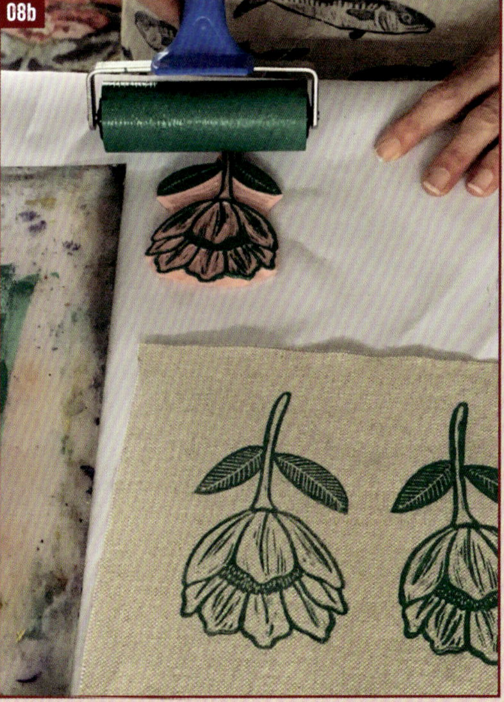

∧ Applying fresh ink to the stamp for every print

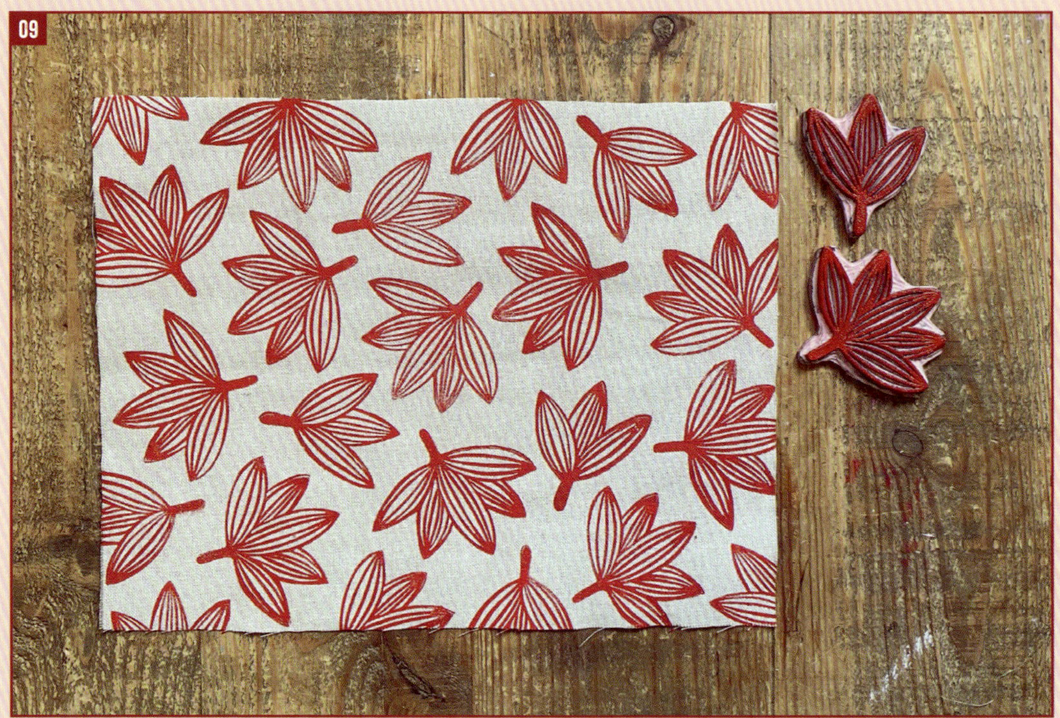

▲ Random repeat pattern

09 CHOOSE A PATTERN TYPE

Different pattern types will create different looks. Experiment to see what works best for your project.

RANDOM REPEAT PATTERN

This is the easiest print to start out with. You can make the first print at random in the middle of the fabric, then gradually print around it all the way to the corners. Rotate the stamp slightly with each print to create a dynamic final design.

STRAIGHT REPEAT PATTERN

A straight repeat pattern is simple but effective. Use a reference point, such as the corner of your fabric, and decide how much space to leave between each print. You can use tailor's chalk and a ruler to make small guiding marks. Start by printing a vertical or horizontal row, then repeat.

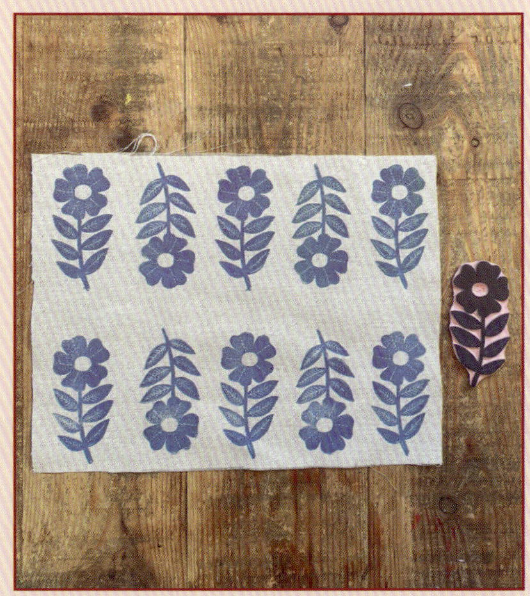

▲ Straight repeat pattern

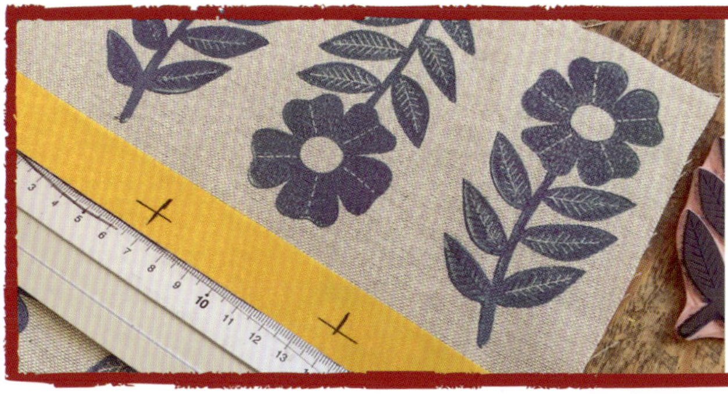

PAINTER'S TAPE

Use painter's tape to help with mapping out print placement. Stick the tape to the fabric and draw the reference point on the tape. Simply remove the tape after printing.

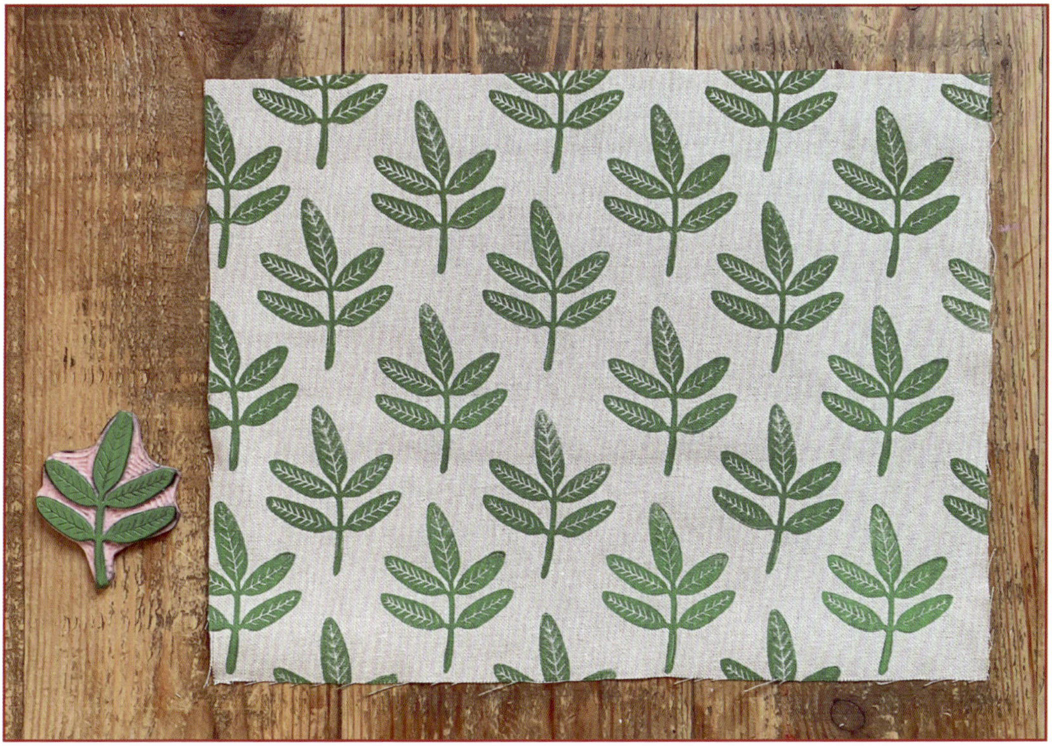

Λ Bricked repeat pattern

BRICKED REPEAT PATTERN

This design is laid out in a similar way to the pattern of brick walls. The first row of prints are made horizontally and evenly spaced. The prints in the second row sit above the gaps in the first row. The third row is then the same as the first row, and so on.

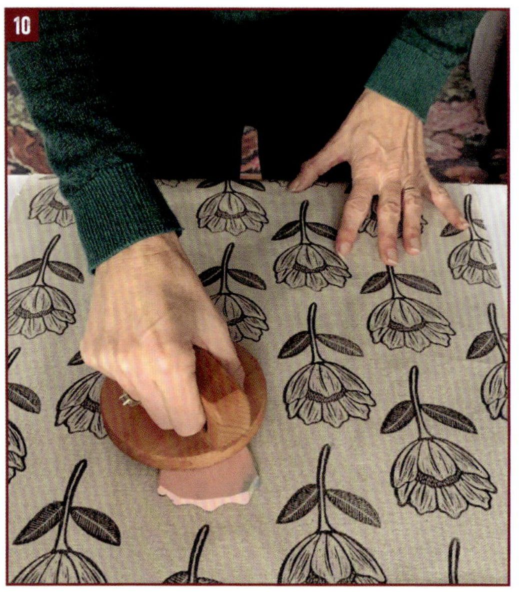

10 FINAL PRINT

Apply your chosen ink to the mixing plate, roll it out, and then ink the stamp. Print the inked stamp on the fabric using a baren to evenly apply pressure. Once finished, leave our printed fabric to dry. Some brands of ink need to be heated, by ironing them, while others can simply air-dry for a few days. Once completely dry, you can cut up the fabric and use it to sew into bags, clothes, or whatever you like!

◄ Printing the flower in a bricked repeat pattern

MULTICOLOUR PRINTS

Once you've mastered the art of basic fabric printing, you can experiment with using more than one colour in the design. For example, you could give the flower and stem different colours, or use a simple shape (such as a circle or square) as a second stamp behind the flower. You could even make a two-layer stamp to give the flower's petals extra colour.

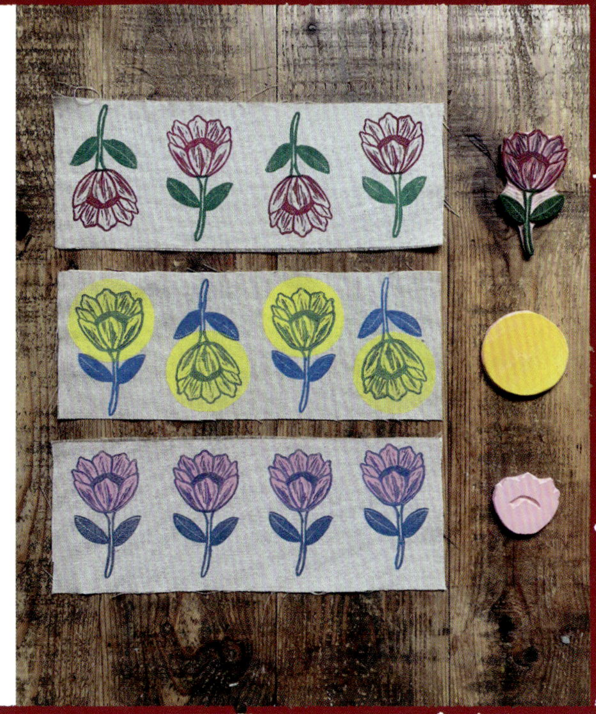

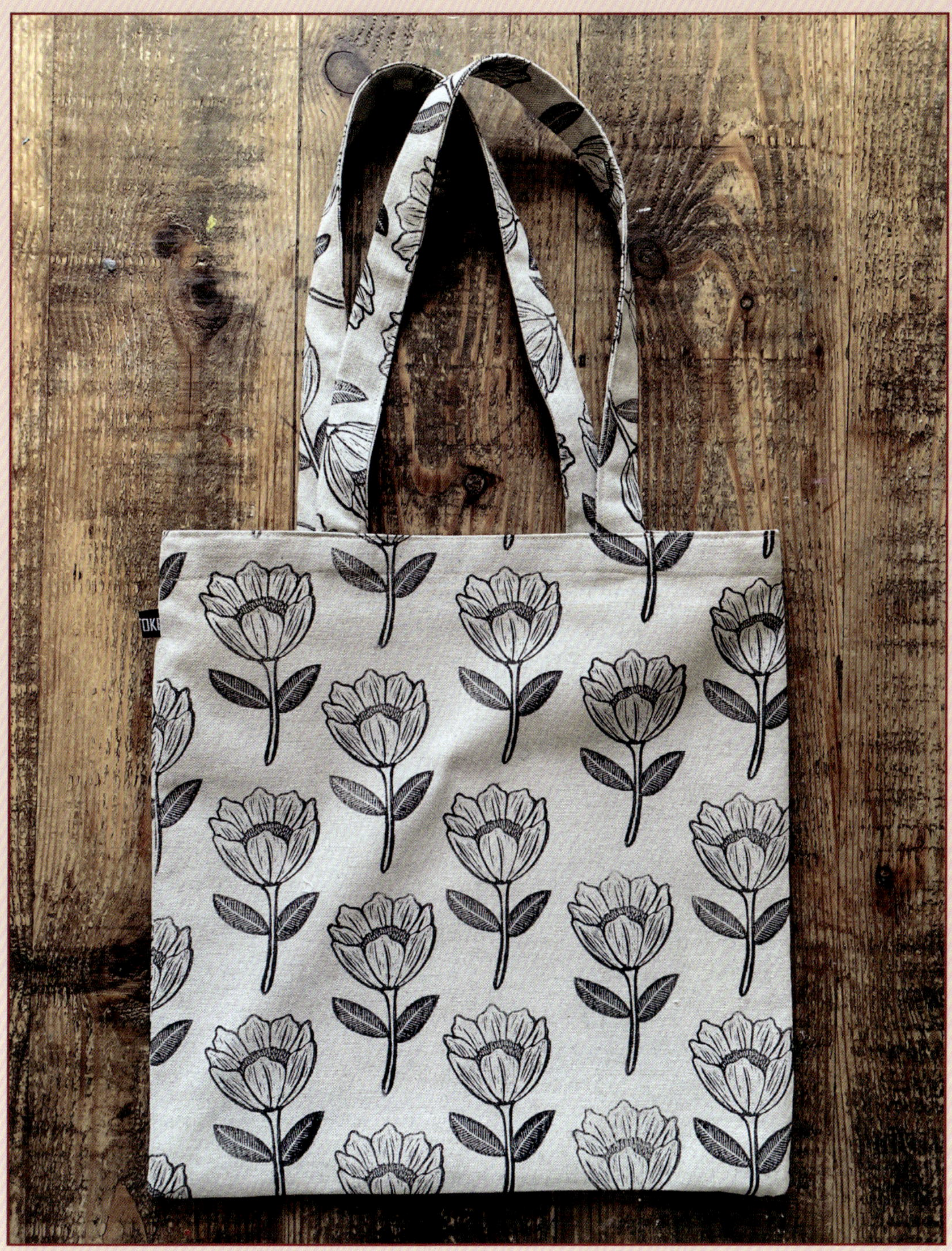

Flower Power | The final flower-pattern fabric print sewn into a tote bag

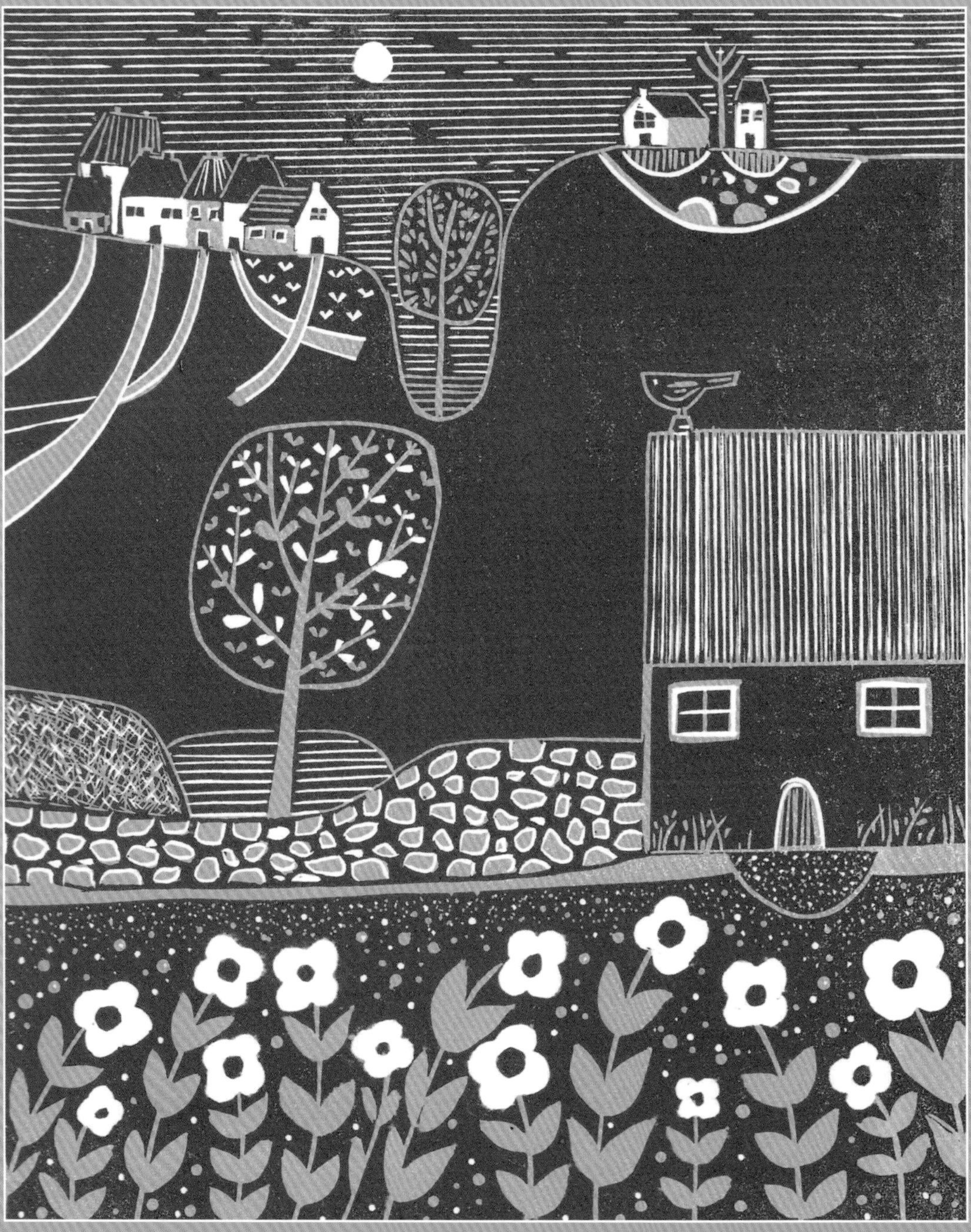

REDUCTION PRINT

GREEN GARDEN

BY LAYLA KHANI

Reduction linocut printing uses a single block of lino that is carved and printed in stages to create multi-layered images. Unlike the multi-block technique, in which numerous blocks are used with a different carving and colour on each, reduction prints build up colour and detail from a single block. This allows for a seamless alignment of colours, a dynamic interplay of layers, and an overall richness and depth. Each stage involves inking and printing the block, then carving away sections to preserve areas of the previous colour before moving on to the next shade. With each pass, new layers of colour add complexity and dimension. Reduction prints challenge you to plan each layer with precision, as the block cannot be reused or reprinted in the same way once carved further.

This tutorial will guide you through the process of creating a two-colour reduction linocut print. Once you have mastered the technique, a more advanced tutorial is available as a downloadable accompaniment to this book (see page 06).

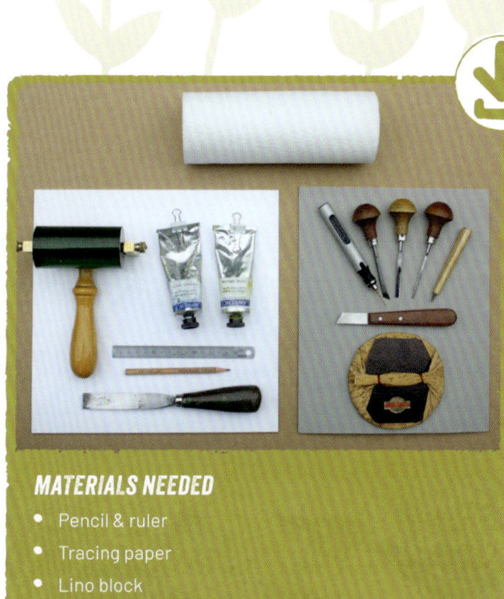

MATERIALS NEEDED

- Pencil & ruler
- Tracing paper
- Lino block
- Permanent marker
- Carving tools (a variety of gouges and blades)
- Cutting tools (such as knives or chisels)
- Bench hook or non-slip mat
- Registration board, pins, and tabs
- Ink (two colours)
- Palette knife
- Inking plate
- Roller
- Print paper
- Printing press, baren, or spoon

01 REGISTRATION

To ensure precise alignment, start by making a sturdy registration board from mount board or cardboard. Mark the position of the lino block then cut an aperture to hold it securely and prevent it from shifting during printing. Attach registration pins (Ternes Burton pins are used here) at the top of the board to make sure the paper remains in place. This setup will enable consistent, accurate registration throughout the printing process.

> The lino block sits snug in the aperture on the registration board, with pins to secure the printing paper

02 PREPARE THE PAPER

Cut each sheet of paper to the desired size, leaving a margin around the printed area for handling. Attach registration tabs to each sheet to align with the registration pins on the board. This preparation will ensure each sheet of paper sits in the same position with every print, reducing the risk of misalignment and ensuring consistency.

< Arches 88 300 gsm paper with the registration tabs attached

03 DRAWING

Create a sketch that will serve as the foundation for your linocut design. You can draw it on paper then transfer it to the lino block, or draw directly onto the block if you prefer, remembering that the final print will be a reverse image of what you draw.

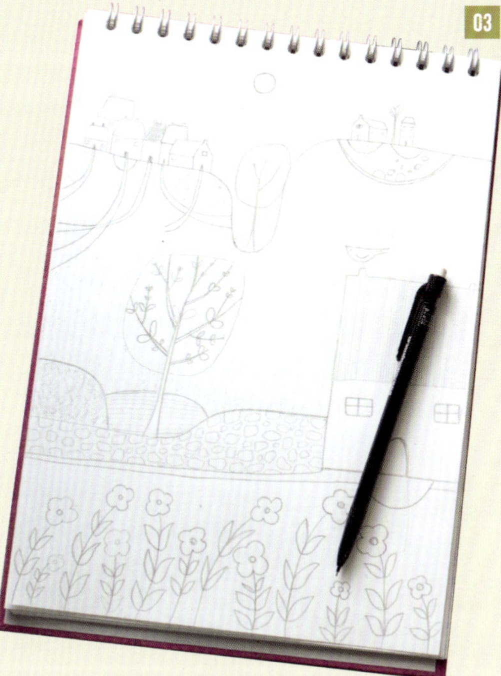

> Sketching out a clear design, using bold lines and simple shapes for maximum impact

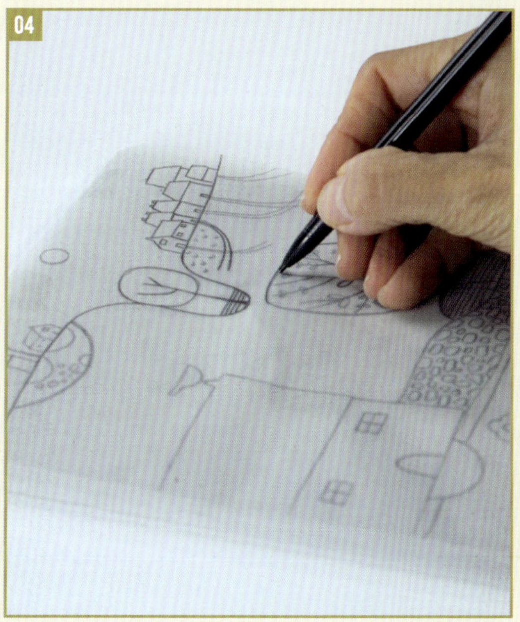

04 TRANSFER TO LINO

Lay tracing paper over the design and draw over the lines in soft pencil, then place it pencil-side down on the lino block. Using a pen or sharp pencil, retrace the lines on the back of the tracing paper to transfer the design to the lino. Next, use a permanent marker to go over the pencil lines on the lino block, then leave it to dry for twenty-four hours to prevent the marker from transferring to the paper during printing.

< Using tracing paper to transfer the design to lino

MAKE A PLAN BEFORE YOU CARVE

It's a good idea to photocopy your drawing to test out different colour variations. Decide on two colours before you start carving and create a clear plan for which areas to carve away and which to leave for each colour. Taking the time to plan will ensure greater precision and a more successful result.

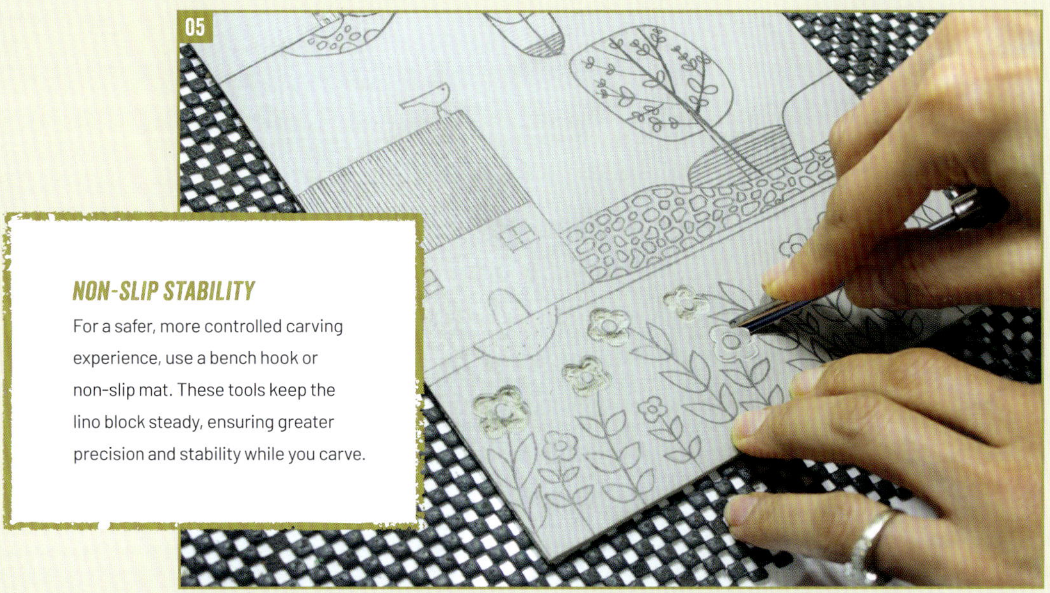

▲ Carving away areas that will remain white

05 CARVE THE FIRST LAYER

Carve away areas you wish to remain the paper's natural colour (in this case, white). Use a V-shaped gouge for fine lines, a U-shaped gouge for wider areas, and a knife for outline cuts. A small Dremel tool can be used to create perfect dots. Careful carving will provide a clean separation between white areas and colour layers in the final print.

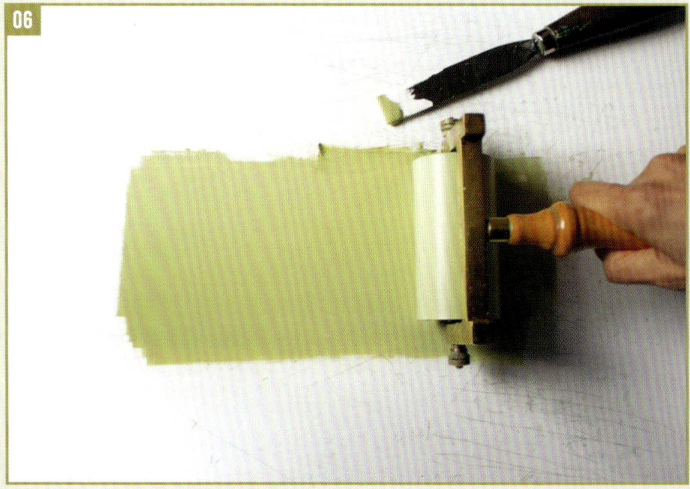

▲ Rolling out a thin layer of the lighter ink

06 INK THE FIRST LAYER

This print will feature just two colours, with the lighter colour used for the first layer. Here, a green linseed oil-based ink is mixed with white to achieve an olive green. After mixing and rolling on an inking plate, roll a thin, even layer onto the lino block. Make sure it is evenly applied and covers the entire surface. This will create a smooth foundation and consistent base for the second colour.

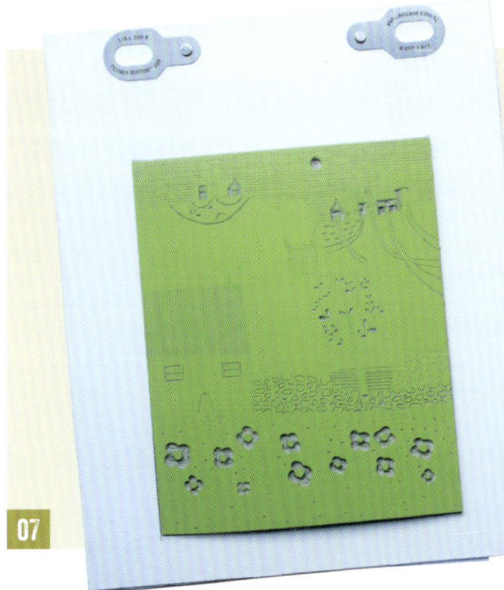

07 LINO REGISTRATION

Place the inked block into the aperture on the registration board. Position the paper on top, ensuring the punched holes in the paper tabs attach securely to the registration pins to achieve precise alignment.

< The inked lino block placed securely in the registration board aperture

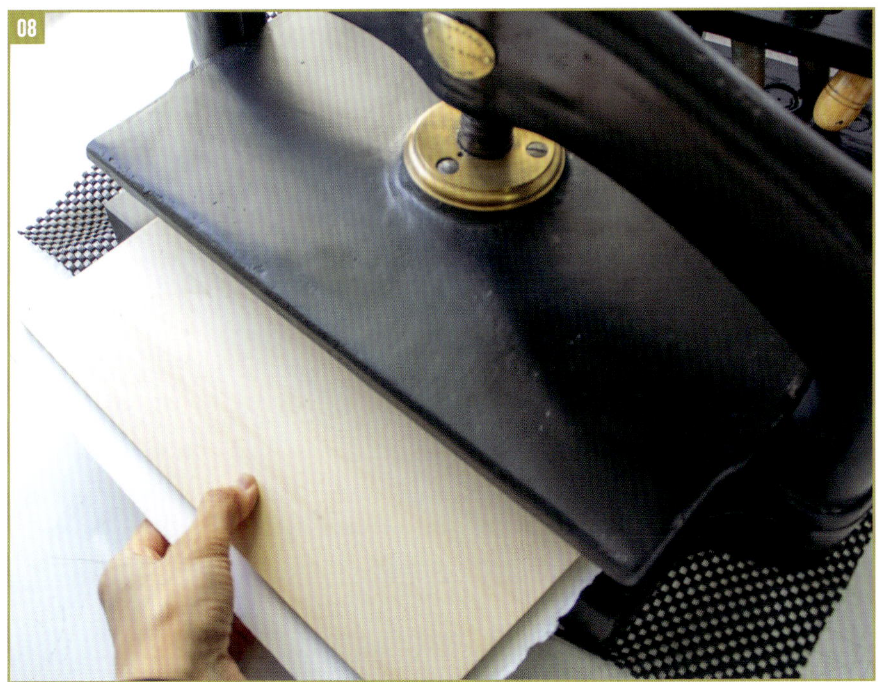

< A bookbinding press distributes pressure evenly when transferring the print

08 PRINT THE FIRST LAYER

If using a bookbinding press, as shown above, place the registration board, inked lino, and paper between the two thin pieces of wood in the press. Turn the handle to apply pressure, transferring the ink from lino to paper. The press ensures even pressure distribution across the surface, resulting in a clean, precise print. Alternatively, you can use a baren, spoon, or other type of press.

09 FIRST LAYER REVEAL

Open the press then carefully lift the paper to reveal the first layer. Examine it closely to check for even ink coverage, clean edges, and proper alignment. This step is crucial before progressing to the next. Once satisfied, set the print aside to dry.

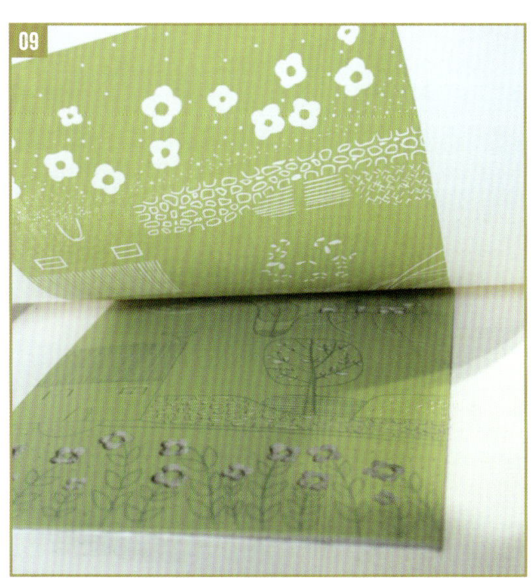

> The first layer of ink has transferred well

10 CONTINUE PRINTING

With reduction linocut, you must print the entire edition (set of prints) for the first layer before proceeding to the second, as you're now going to re-carve the same lino block for the next step. Determine the number of prints you wish to make, then add a few additional copies as backups. Ensure each print is aligned accurately using the registration board, then proceed to print the complete set of first-layer impressions.

KEEP GOING

Don't be discouraged if the first few prints aren't as crisp as expected. It often takes several impressions for the lino block to fully absorb the ink and transfer it evenly onto the paper. With each print, the block will improve, resulting in sharper and more consistent results.

⋀ Print the entire run of first layers, then leave to dry

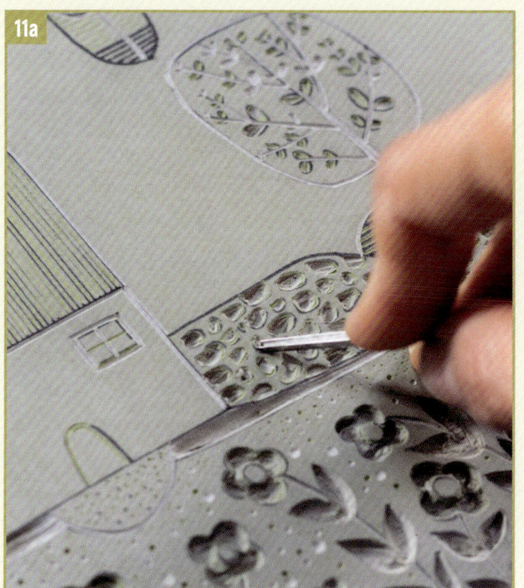

▲ Carving the second layer

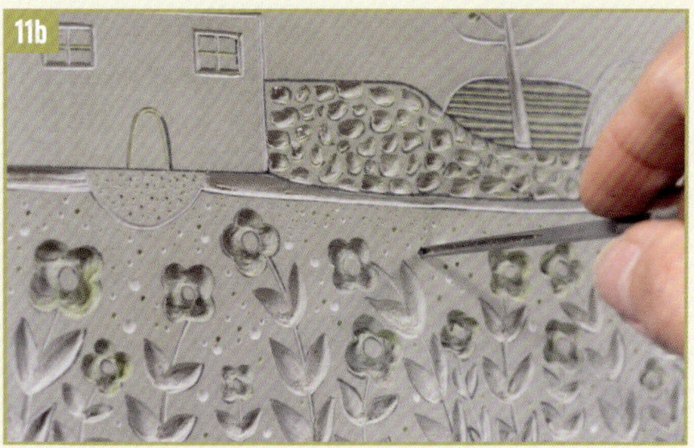

11 CARVE THE SECOND LAYER

Clean the lino block you used for the first layer, then carve away the areas that you want to remain olive green (the lighter colour). The areas that were already carved will still remain in white (unprinted) on the final image. Any uncarved areas will now hold the second, darker colour on the final print. Focus on precision for a crisp, clean result.

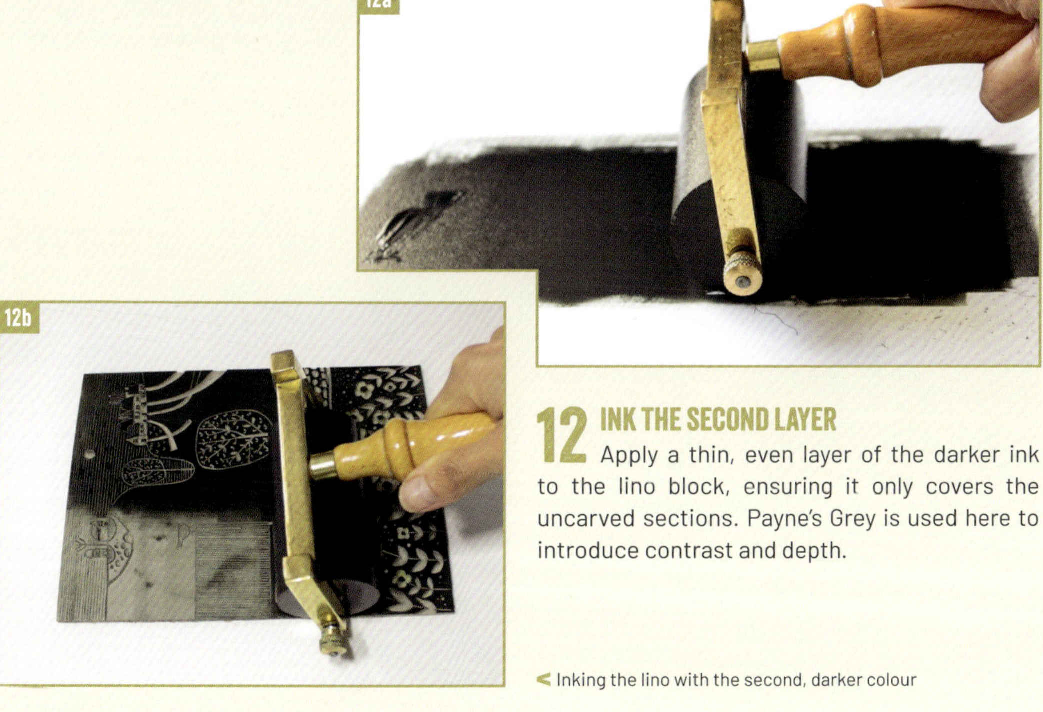

12 INK THE SECOND LAYER

Apply a thin, even layer of the darker ink to the lino block, ensuring it only covers the uncarved sections. Payne's Grey is used here to introduce contrast and depth.

◀ Inking the lino with the second, darker colour

13 PRINT THE SECOND LAYER

Place the re-inked block on the registration board. Lay the first-layer print face-down over the top, ensuring the tabs fit over the pins and it aligns correctly. Even minor misalignments can impact the final result. As you did in step 08, press the paper onto the inked block, then gently lift the paper to reveal the second layer.

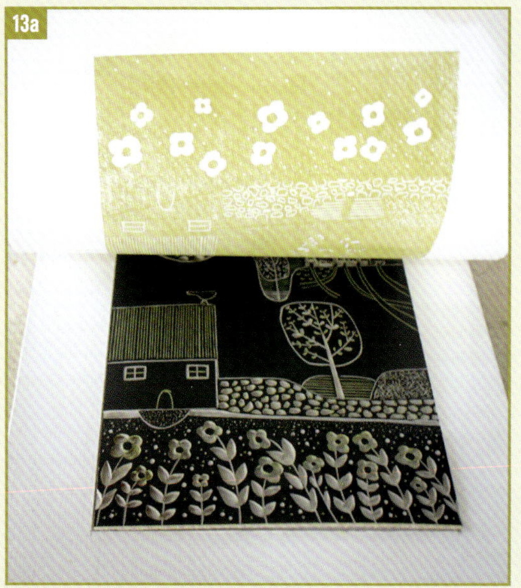

Aligning the punched tabs over the registration pins to guarantee accurate placement

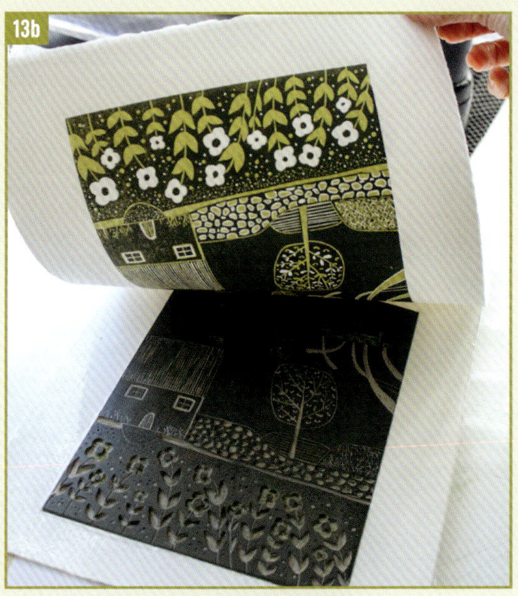

Revealing the second layer after printing

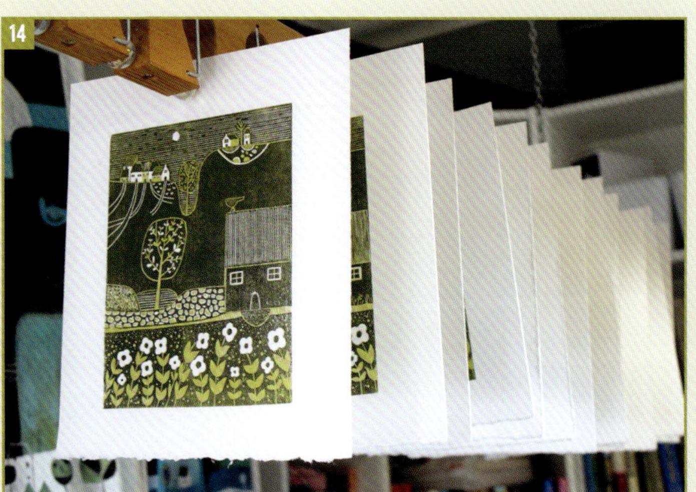

Drying the second-layer prints

14 COMPLETE THE PRINT RUN

If you're happy with the first print, go ahead and print the second layer on every copy. Once completely dry, you can sign and number each one. This certifies the authenticity of each print in the edition and ensures they are unique.

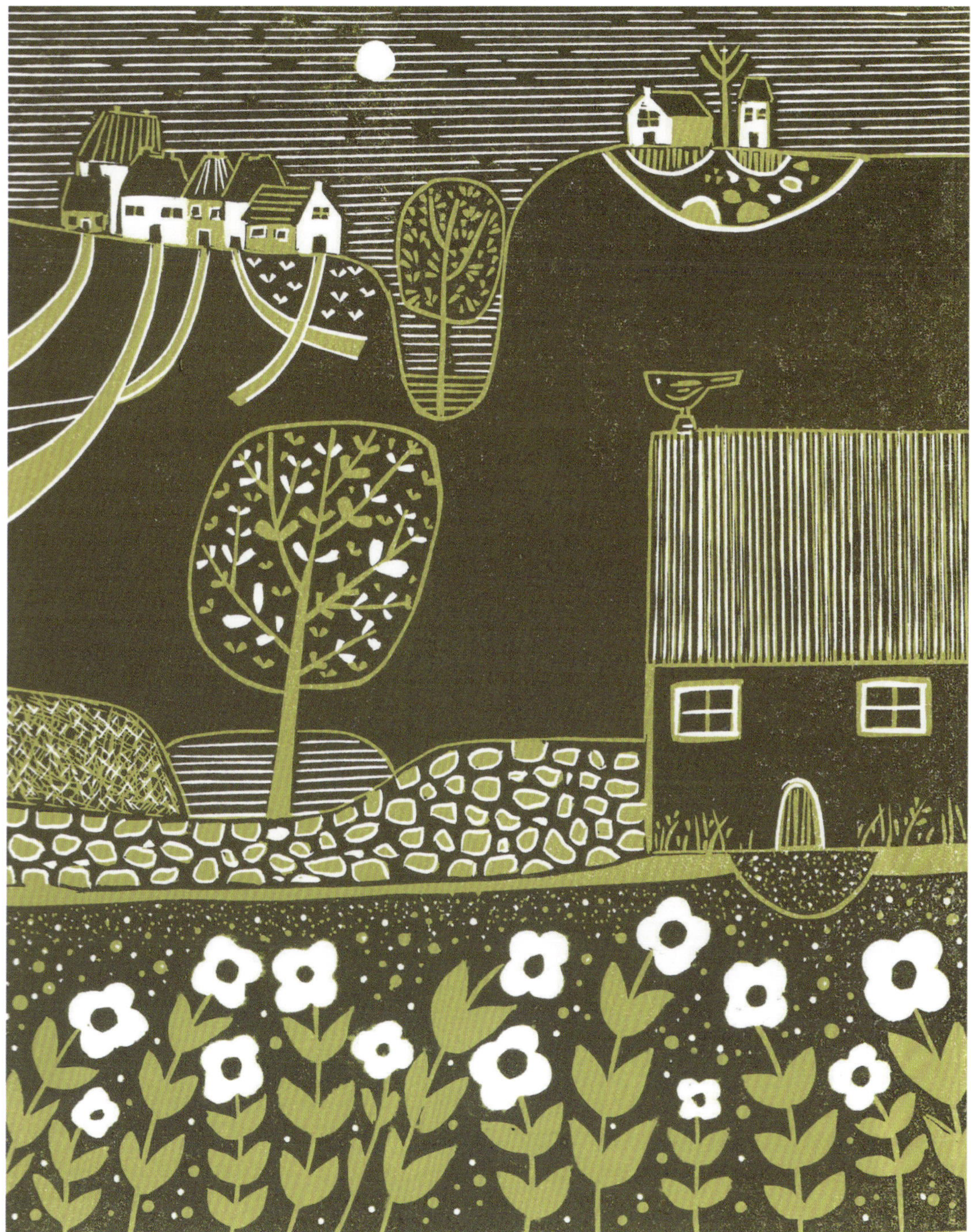

Green Garden | The olive green and dark grey create a vibrant final print with a perfect alignment of visually interesting details

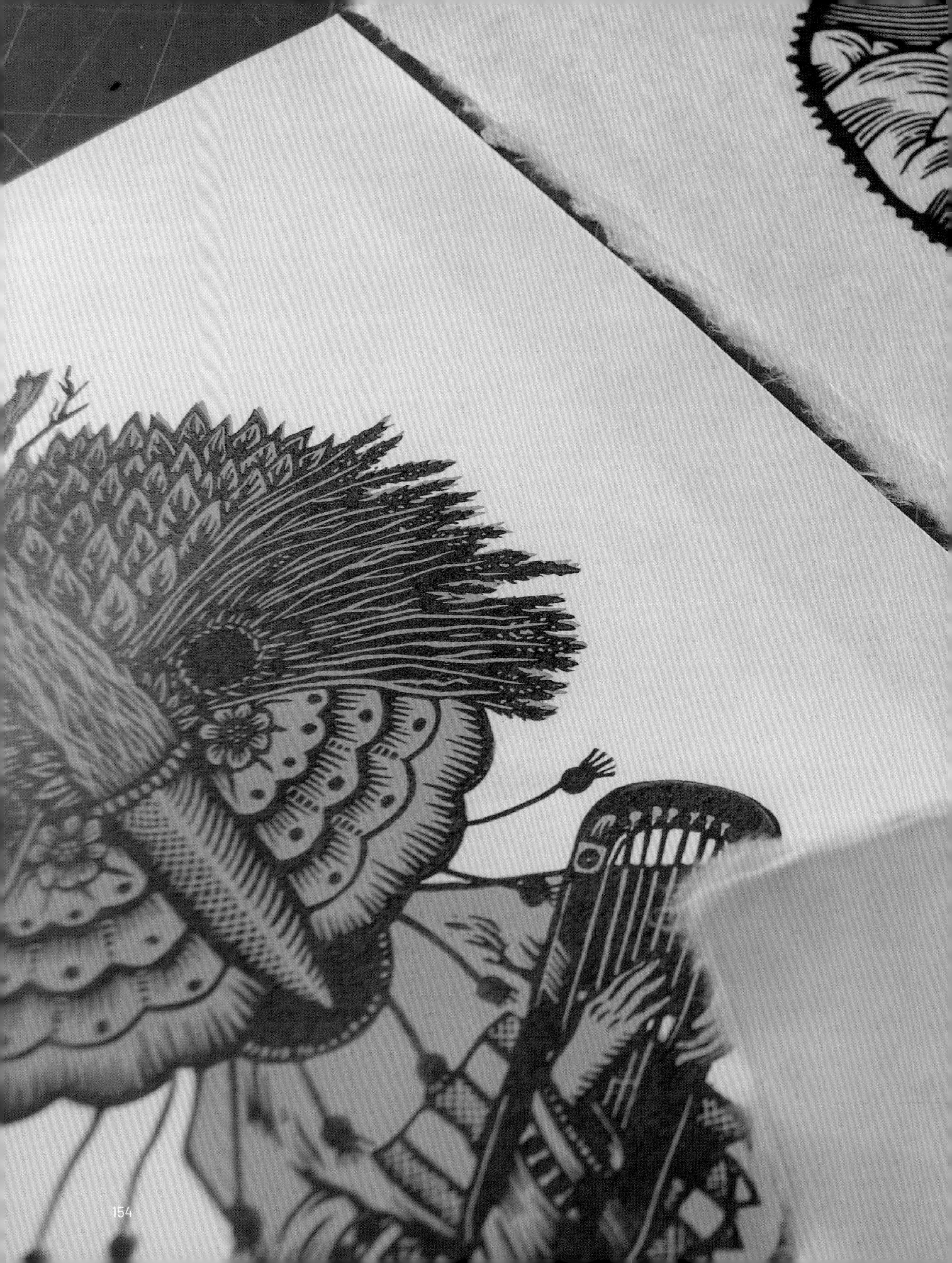

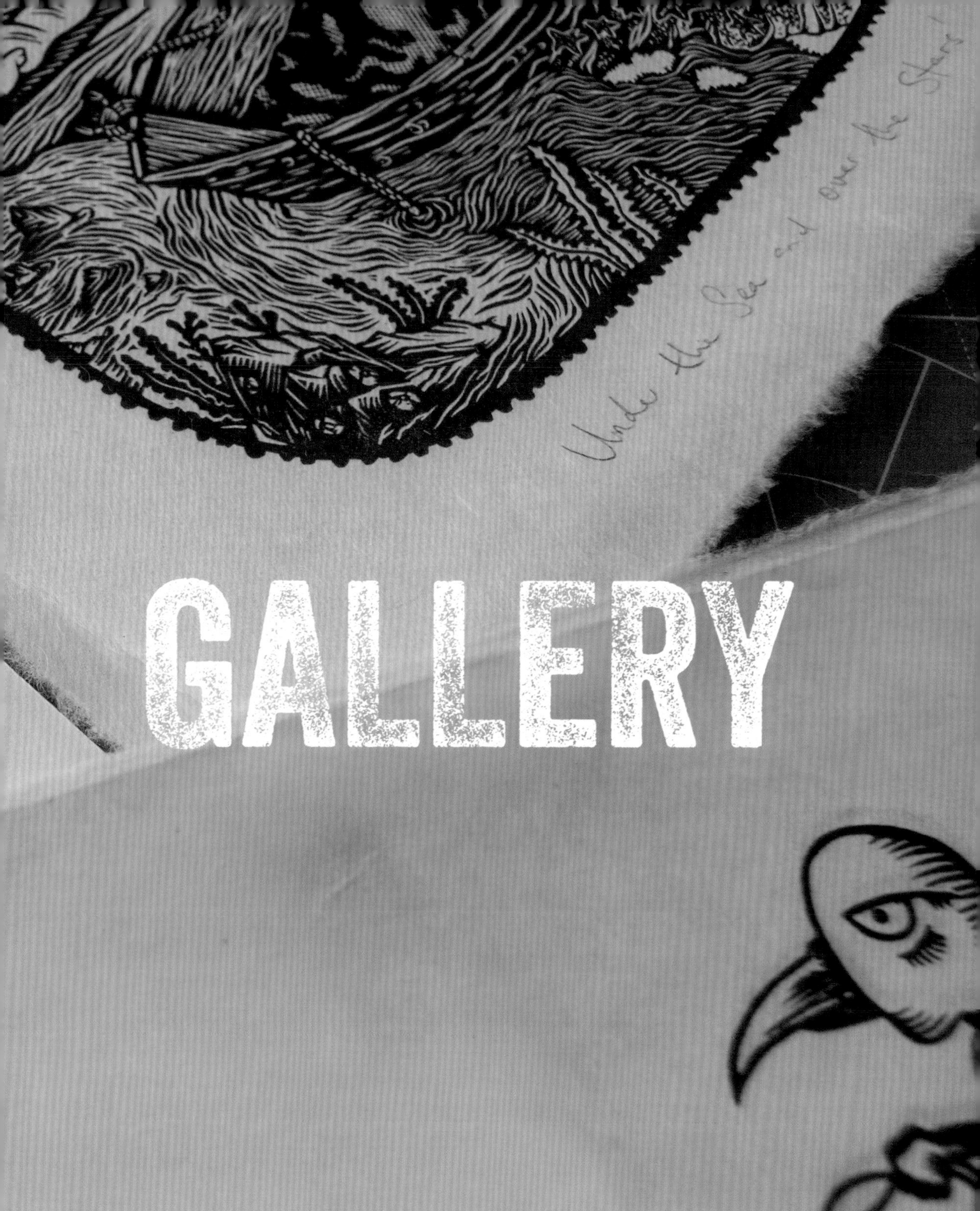

GALLERY

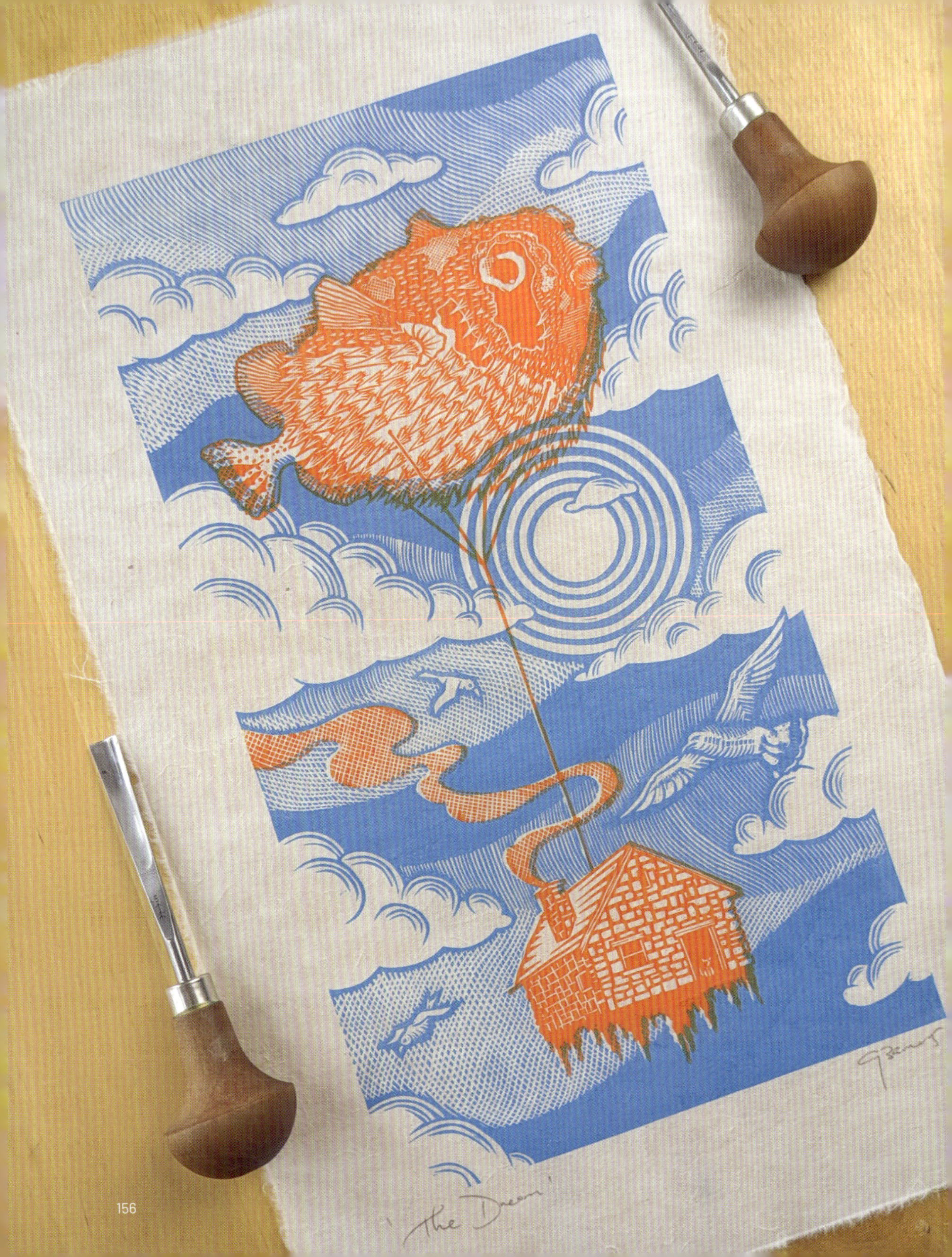
The Dream

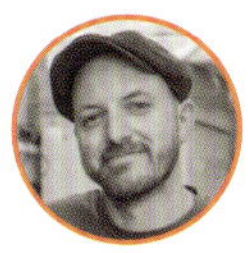

GARETH BARNES (SPINDLE PRINTER)

Printmaker | *spindleprinter.com*

Originally from New Zealand, Gareth Barnes works as a printmaker from his home studio in Leeds, UK. His work is inspired by folklore, the natural world, history, and vintage illustration. He can often be found selling his work at print fairs around the UK.

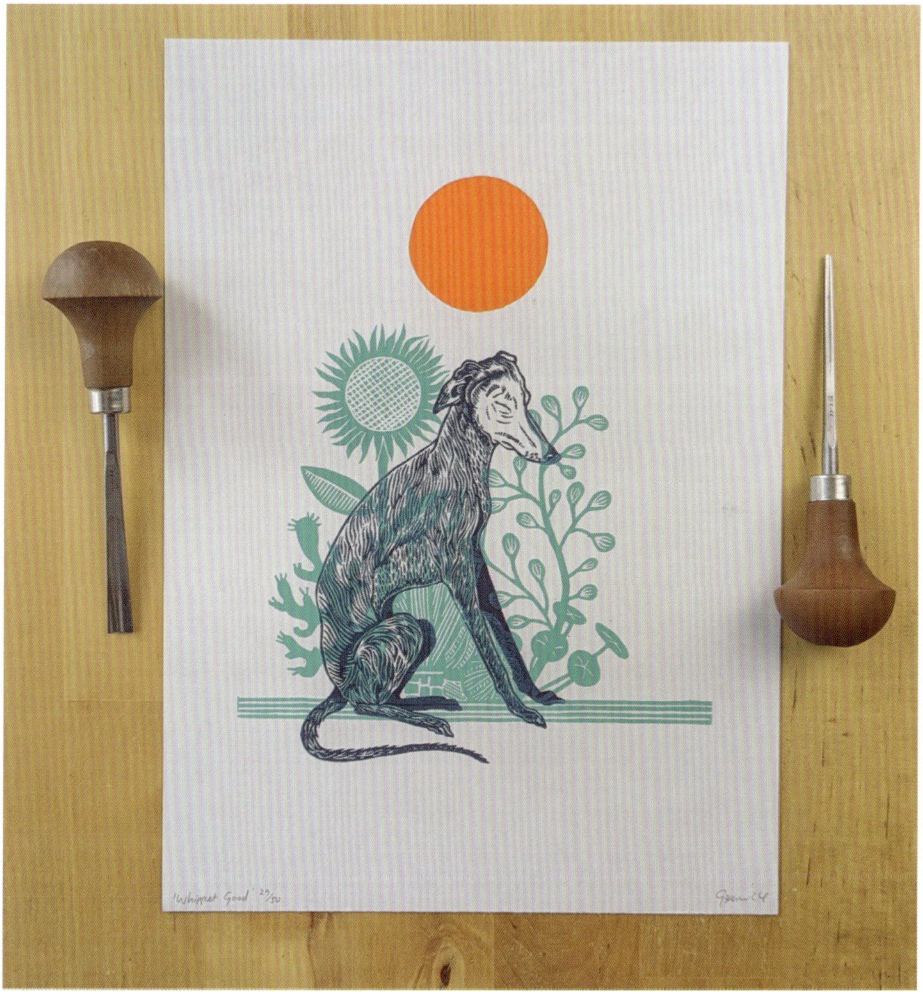

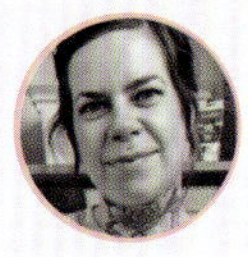

ANNA HERMSDORF

Printmaker & tattooist | *anna-hermsdorf.de*

Anna is a printmaker and tattoo artist based in Germany, where she works on her series of themed girl linocuts, custom tattoo work for clients, and her online course for beginners to linocut printmaking.

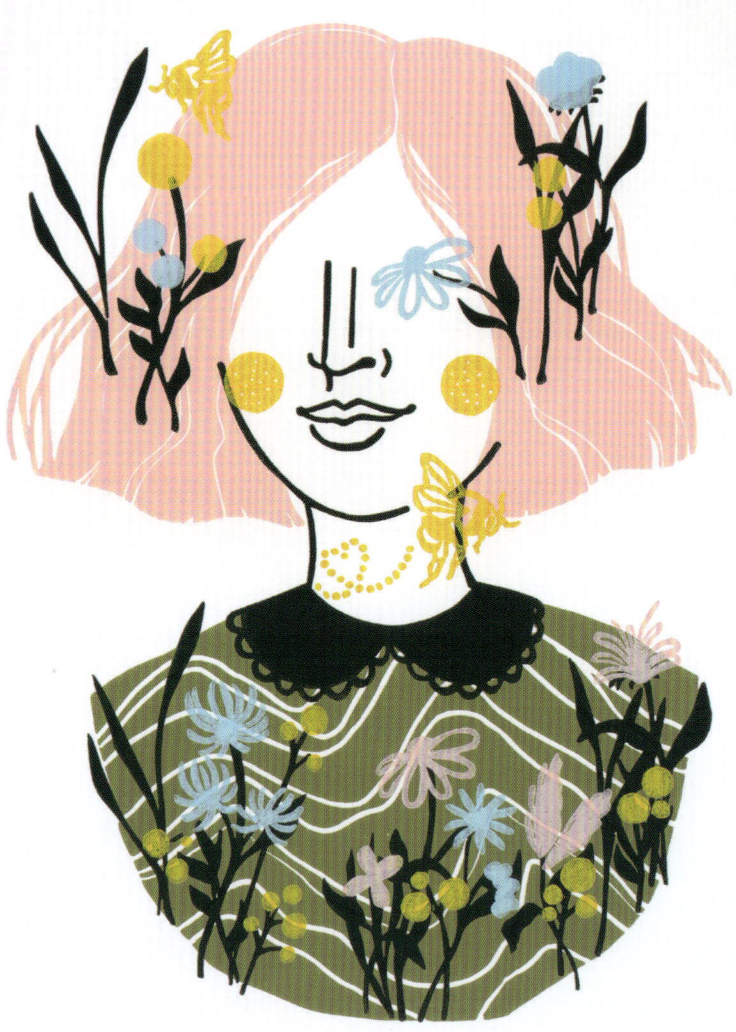

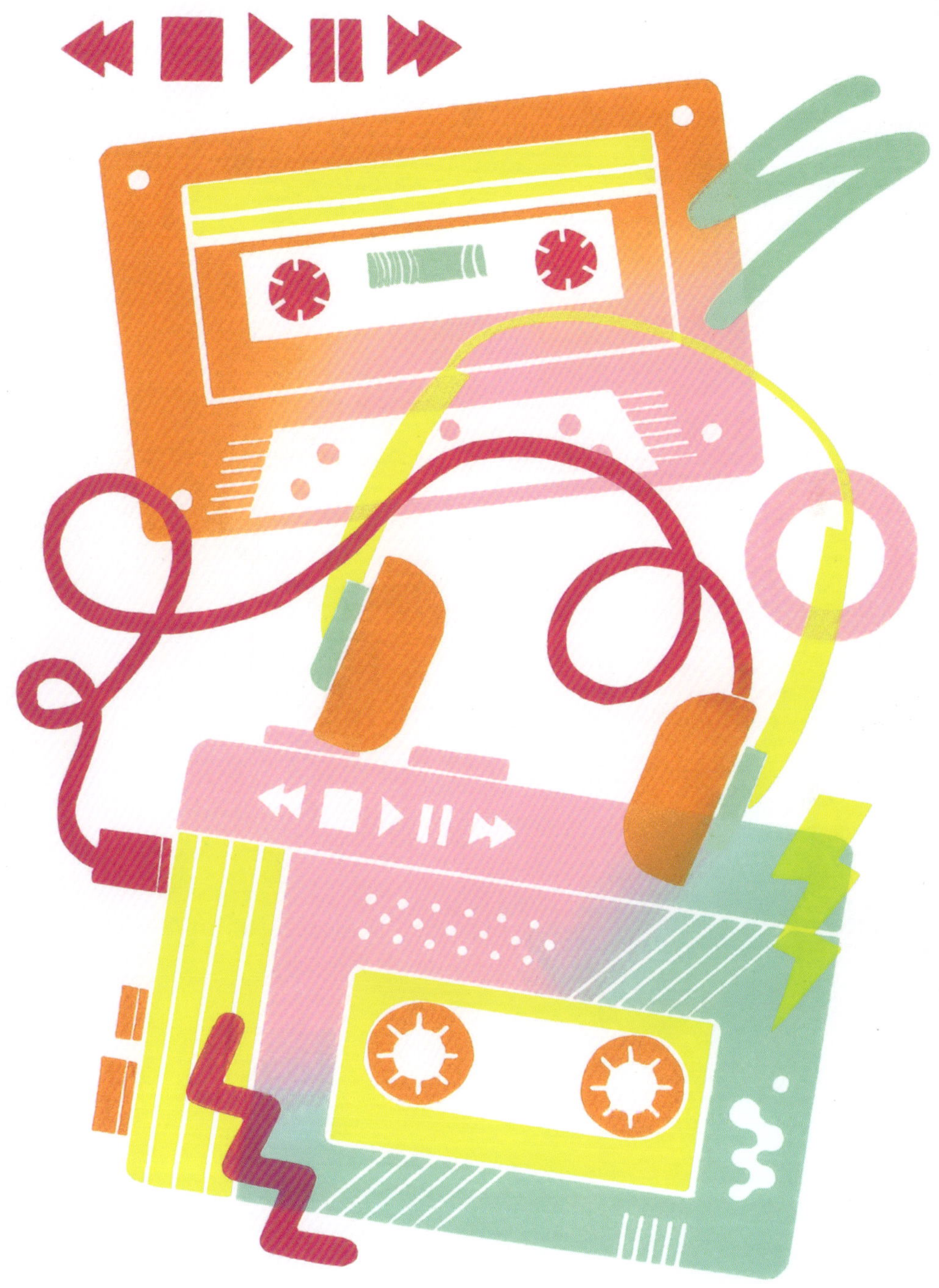

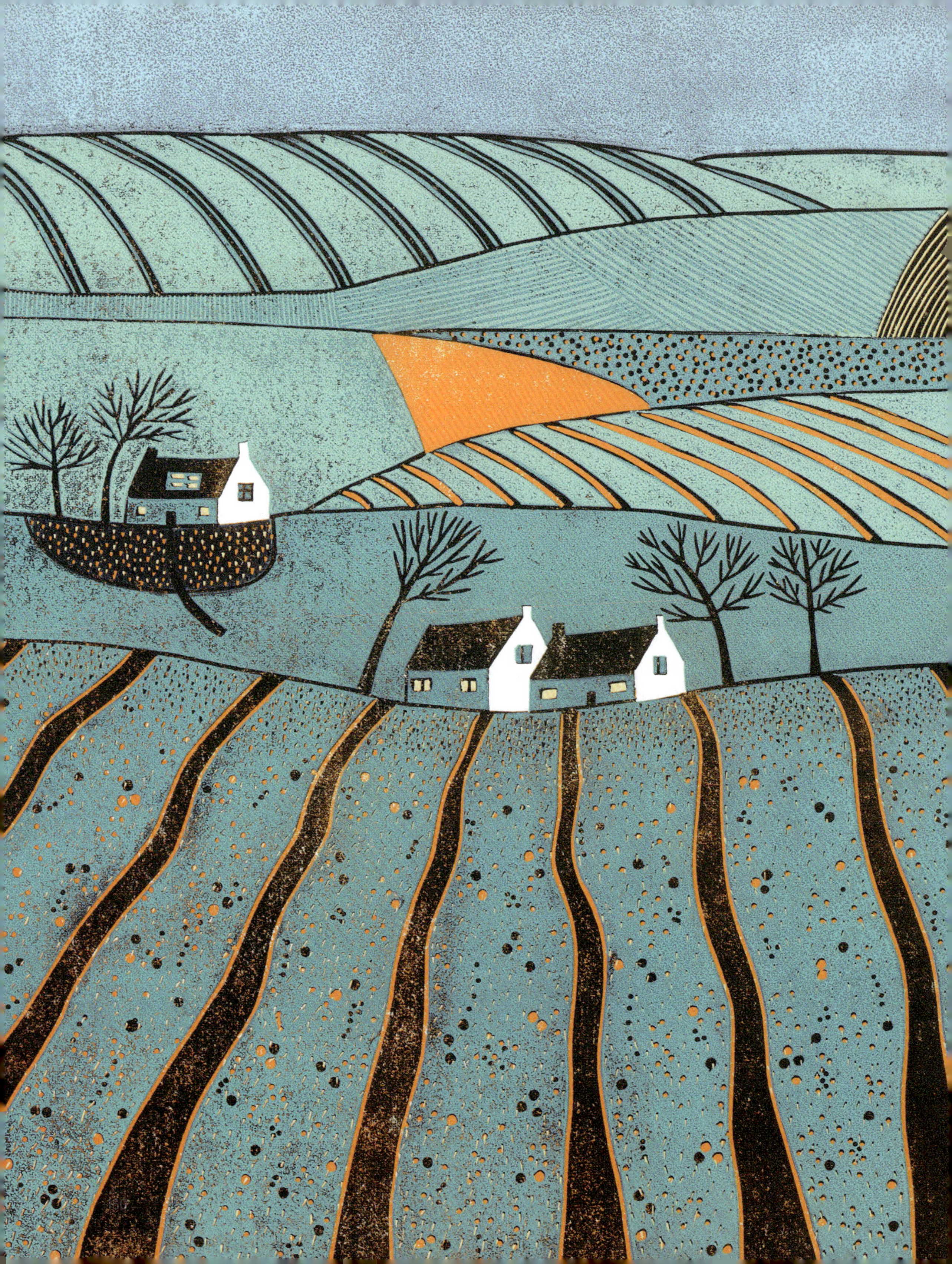

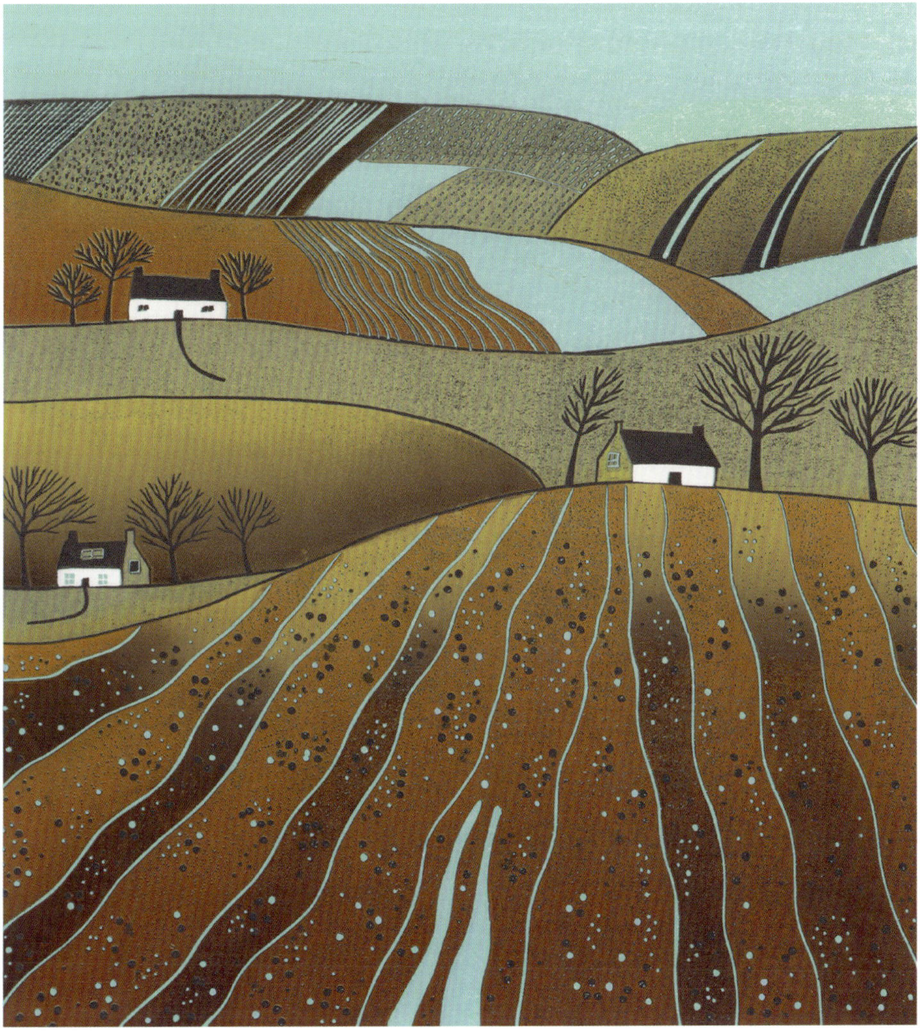

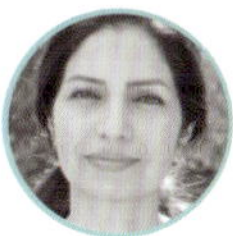

LAYLA KHANI

Artist & printmaker | *laylart.com*

Layla Khani is a UK-based artist and printmaker whose vibrant reduction linocut prints celebrate the breathtaking landscapes of the Malvern Hills and British countryside. Each piece offers a glimpse into nature's harmony and wonder.

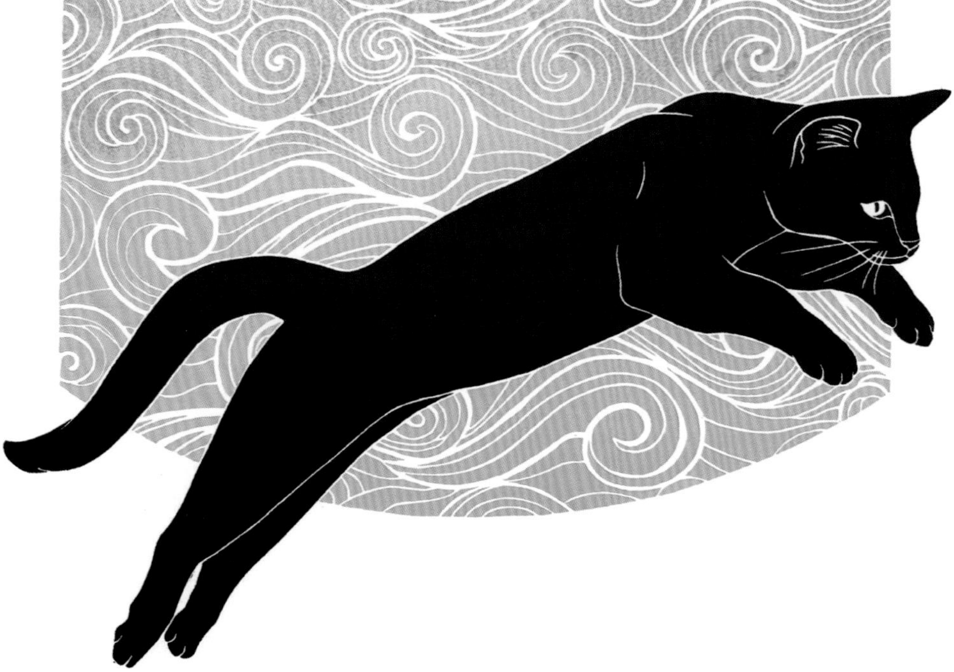

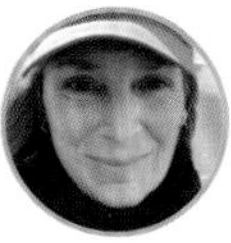

MARY ANN TESTAGROSSA

Artist & printmaker | *maryanntestagrossaart.com*

Mary Ann Testagrossa is an artist living in Northern California, USA. She specializes in printmaking, as well as painting and collage. Mary Ann is known for her black-cat artwork, with collectors and followers worldwide. She shares her print studio with her two cats, Hobbs and Oreo, who are the inspiration for much of her artwork.

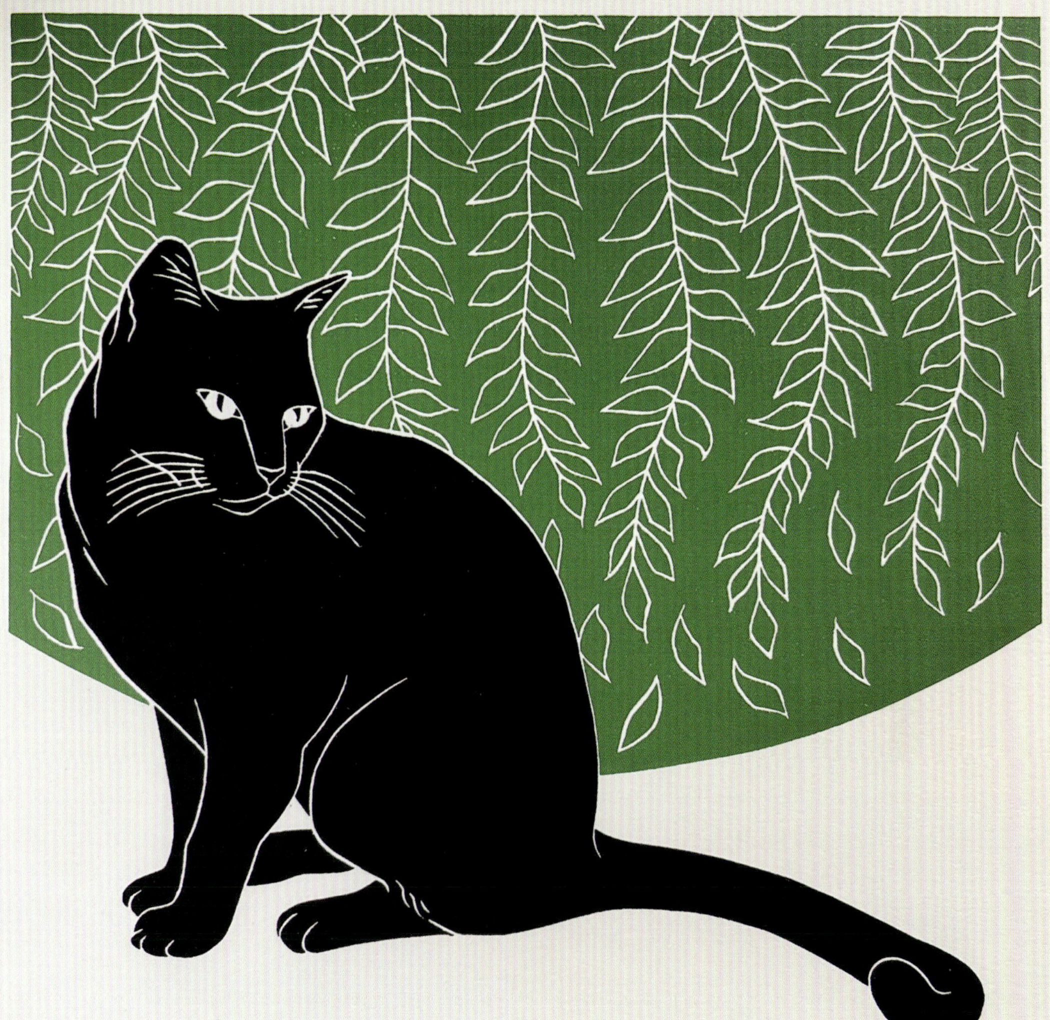
7/100
"Summer Breeze"
Mary Ann Testagrossa

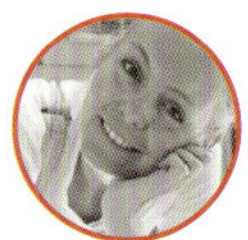

ESTHER VAN DAM (STUDIO TOKEK)

Illustrator & printmaker | *studiotokek.com*

Esther van Dam is an illustrator and printmaker based in the Netherlands.
Studio Tokek combines her passions for printing and fabrics.

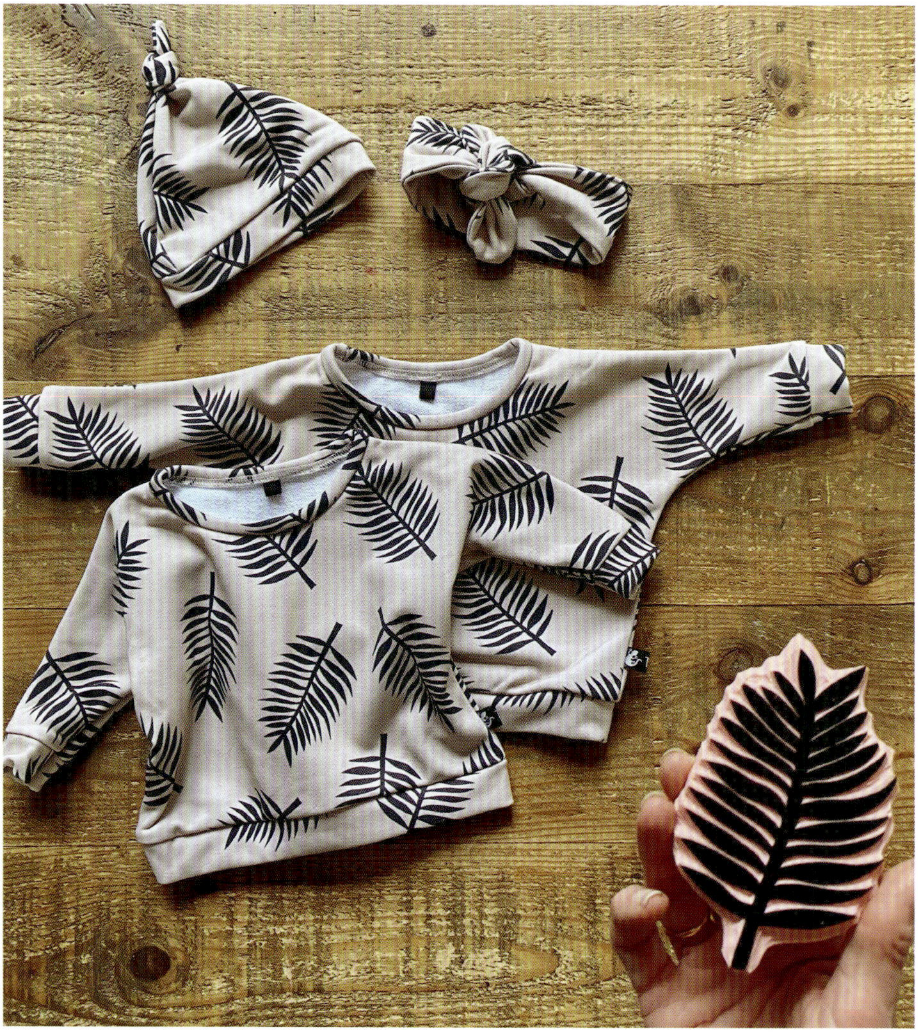

ALL ARTWORK © ESTHER VAN DAM (STUDIO TOKEK)

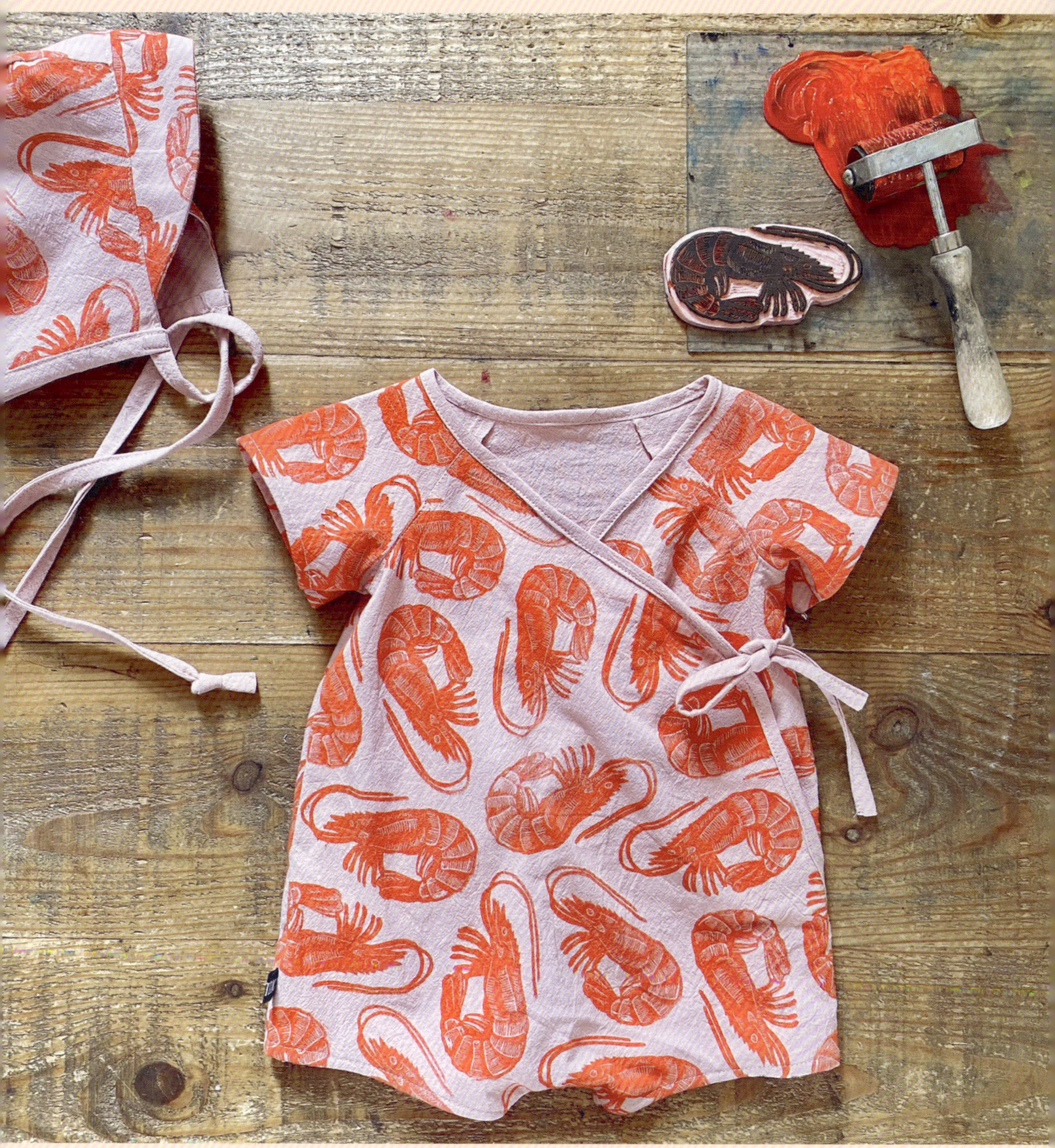

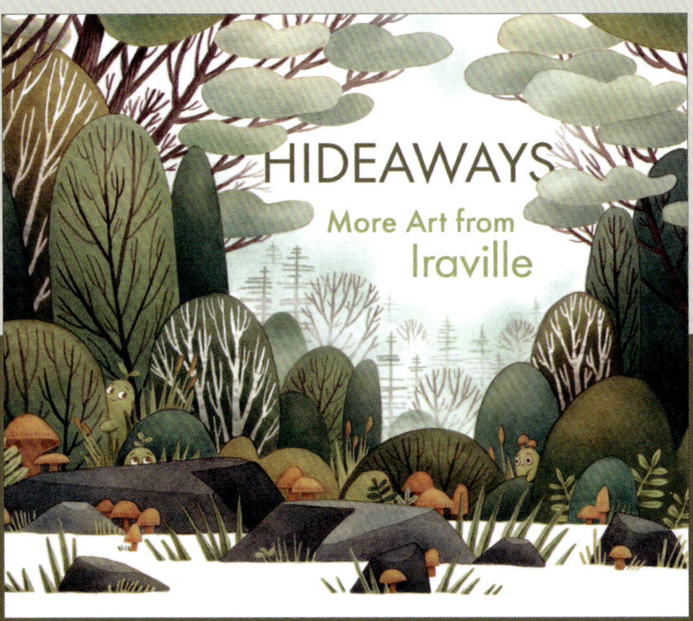

HIDEAWAYS

More Art from
Iraville

This beautiful second instalment from Munich-based illustrator Iraville is the perfect follow-up to *Cozy Days* with its serene watercolour artworks that are sure to inspire readers into the great outdoors. *Hideaways: More Art from Iraville* continues to explore the theme of escaping reality into a world of tranquillity with the help of multiple brand-new tutorials, including how to paint a watercolour image and create ink from natural materials. Ira also shares insights into her mixing methods, colour theory, and why perfectionism is overrated.

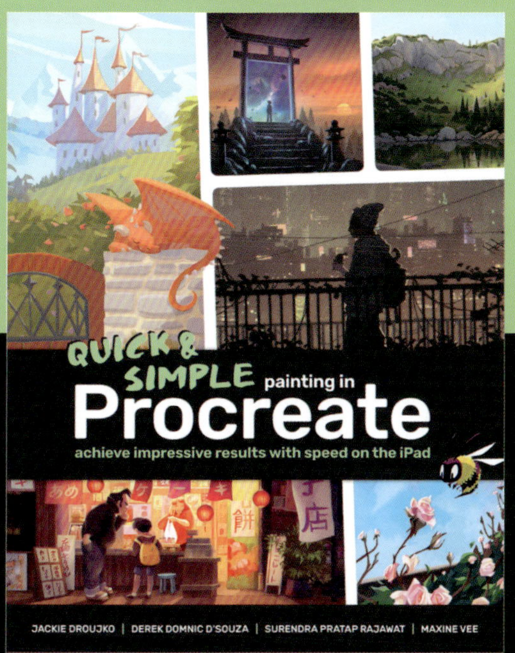

QUICK & SIMPLE painting in
Procreate
achieve impressive results with speed on the iPad

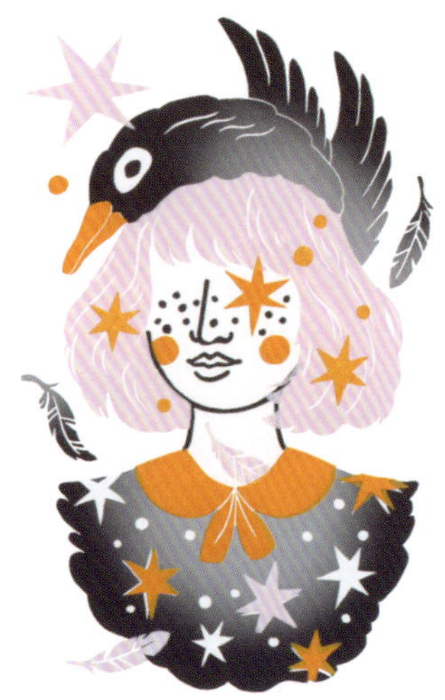

3dtotalPublishing

3dtotal Publishing is a trailblazing, creative publisher specializing in inspirational and educational resources for artists.

Our titles feature top industry professionals from around the globe who share their experience in skilfully written step-by-step tutorials and fascinating, detailed guides. Illustrated throughout with stunning artwork, these bestselling publications offer creative insight, expert advice, and essential motivation. Fans of digital art will enjoy our comprehensive volumes covering Adobe Photoshop, Procreate, and Blender, as well as our superb titles based around character design, including *Fundamentals of Character Design* and *Creating Characters for the Entertainment Industry*. The dedicated, high-quality blend of instruction and inspiration also extends to traditional art. Titles covering a range of techniques, genres, and abilities allow your creativity to flourish while building essential skills.

Well-established within the industry, we now offer over 100 titles and counting, many of which have been translated into multiple languages around the world. With something for every artist, we are proud to say that our books offer the 3dtotal package:

LEARN • CREATE • SHARE

Visit us at store.3dtotal.com

3dtotal Publishing is part of 3dtotal.com, a leading website for CG artists founded by Tom Greenway in 1999.